IN PRAISE OF WINCHESTER

IN PRAISE OF WINCHESTER

AN ANTHOLOGY
IN PROSE AND VERSE

COMPILED BY

A. AUDREY LOCKE

LONDON
CONSTABLE AND COMPANY LTD.
10 ORANGE ST. LEICESTER SQUARE W.C.

1912

FOREWORD

Winchester, though she has undergone many vicissitudes, has never before been ' anthologised.' This is my justification for gathering together material ' in praise of Winchester.' This, and my love for her.

No attempt has, of course, been made to give a complete suggestion of the history of Winchester by means of the chosen excerpts. That would involve, in the early centuries, at least, a history of England. I have simply caught at a few echoes. It may be objected that some of them are not harmonious echoes; that is to say, are not ' literature.' To this I would answer that the connotation of the term ' anthology,' although its natural limits cover only ' a collection of the flowers of verse,' has been so widely extended that it might even be used to describe a collection of political speeches.

In dealing with ' Winchester in fiction,' it will be seen that I have rejected the whole-hearted identification of Anthony Trollope's *Barchester* with Winchester. Here and there he has certainly introduced a memory of Winchester, as for instance in the description of what is obviously St. Swithun's Church, disguised as ' St. Cuthbert's,' in *The Warden*. However, a careful study of *The Warden, Barchester Towers*, and the *Last Chronicle of Barset* shows the topography to be rather that of Salisbury than Winchester. Moreover, we know from Trollope's *Autobiography* that *The Warden* was conceived when wandering round the close of Salisbury Cathedral   ' I visited Salisbury,

▼

and whilst wandering there one midsummer evening round the purlieus of the Cathedral I conceived the story of *The Warden*, from whence came that series of novels of which Barchester with its bishops, deans and archdeacon, was the central site.' John Hiram, of 'Hiram's Hospital,' is probably John Halle, wool merchant of Salisbury, who built a banqueting-hall therein about 1470. The Hospital itself is identifiable with Trinity Hospital, Salisbury, founded in 1420 for twelve poor men. Thus, though in some of its details the description of the Hospital may suggest that of St. Cross, Winchester, the suggestion is not clear enough to warrant any quotation of it in an anthology of Winchester.

I am conscious that in quoting details and anecdotes which concern some famous Wykehamists, I have neglected many well-known names, and have given only scant details where much might be told. I must plead in justification the contrast between the limits of a normal book and the infinite number of famous men among 'Wykeham's sons.'

Of Winchester herself little need be said here ; perhaps this gathering of extracts may serve not only to recall Winchester to those who already love and understand her, but also to awaken something of that love and understanding in those who have not yet learnt her secret.

She, like Oxford, throws her spell over her children, enchanting them with her memories and her moods, as she stays, quietly brooding among her river valleys and her downlands, gazing, Demeter-like, across the centuries.

A. A. L.

HAMPSTEAD, *July* 1912.

CONTENTS

BOOK I

PART I

A ROYAL CITY

' Winchester, that grand scene of ancient learning, piety, and munificence.'—
WILLIAM COBBETT, *Rural Rides.*

ECHOES OF HISTORY

PAGE

§ 1. **Memories.**—Venta—A city of memories—Serene old age—Our royal town—Past times—The stream of ages—A quiet city—The old white city—City tables—The tomb of empires—'Redolent with the atmosphere of ancient times,'   3

§ 2. **Pre-Norman Times.**—The Hudibras myth—Mythical builders—The city walls—The Emperor Claudius besieges Winchester—Roman Winchester—Fighting near the city—Venta Belgarum—The myth of King Arthur—King Arthur's Round Table—His court—Itchen vaunteth herself—King Arthur's Hall—Egbert—'A Mecca'—'The Hethene' destroy Winchester—'The fell Dane'—The Saxon metropolis—Ancient glory—A leader in learning—King Alfred's book—'The breaker of the Dane'—In Hyde Meadow—Guy of Warwick—The Danemark—Wynchester, the ryche towne—Ethelwulf—Edward the Elder—Edwy—Edgar—The ordeal of Queen Emma—The reconciliation of Edward the Confessor and Queen Emma,   .   .   .   9

§ 3. **Mediæval Ways.**—The Book of Winchester—Earl Waltheof beheaded—The death of Rufus—His burial—Henry I. made king—Winton Domesday—Allegiance to Empress Matilda—She besieges Winchester—The praises of the city—Second coronation of Richard I.—William Marshall the younger besieges Winchester—The King of France repairs the city walls—Fair Winchester—The days of our forefathers, ...   26

vii

CONTENTS

PART II

THE CATHEDRAL

'That most beautiful cathedral in Europe.'—WARD BEECHER.

BOOK II

THE COLLEGE

'Concinamus, O Sodales!'

SCHOOL DAYS AND SCHOOL WAYS

CONTENTS

NOTE

I HAVE much pleasure in acknowledging my indebtedness to several authors and publishers for their kindness in allowing me to use copyright matter in this volume. Among others, I have especially to thank the following: Mrs. William Allingham and Messrs. Longmans, Green, and Co. for passages from William Allingham's *Varieties in Prose*; Mr. F. Bumpus and Mr. T. Werner Laurie for a passage from *The Cathedrals of England and Wales*; the Hon. Evan Charteris for passages from Lord Elcho's *Affairs in Scotland* (David Douglas); Sir A. Conan Doyle for a passage from 'The Copper Beeches' in *The Adventures of Sherlock Holmes* (George Newnes); Mr. R. C. K. Ensor for two verses from his poem 'At School'; Mr. Arundell Esdaile for his poem 'The Breaker of the Dane'; Mr. Griffyth Fairfax and Messrs. Smith, Elder and Co. for Mr. Fairfax's poem 'Winchester'; Mr. W. H. Jacob for a passage from his paper on 'The Westgate of Winchester'; Mr. E. H. Lacon Watson for passages from *Christopher Deane* (John Murray), and *Verses* (A. D. Innes and Co.); Mr. C. D. Locock and the St. Catherine's Press for a passage from Mr. Locock's 'Ballade of Red Tape'; the Rev. W. Moore for passages from his poem *Venta* (David Nutt); Mr. Montagu J. Rendall, Headmaster of Winchester College, for his poems 'College Tow Row, 1907,' 'E.D.A.M.,' and 'Ad Amicos'; Lady Laura Ridding and Mr. Edward Arnold for passages from *George Ridding, Schoolmaster and Bishop*; Mr. R. W. Seton-Watson for three poems from *Scotland for Ever* (David Douglas); Mrs. Wood Stephens and Messrs. Macmillan and Co. for passages from Dean Wood Stephens's *Life of Dean Hook*, and *Memoir of Lord Hatherley*; Mrs. T. A. Trollope and Messrs. Macmillan and Co. for passages from T. A. Trollope's *What I Remember*.

Also I have to thank Messrs. George Allen and Co. for passages from *Memorials of Old Hampshire* (Bemrose and Son); Mr. Edward Arnold for passages from a poem by Mr. E. D. A. Morsehead in *Winchester College*, 1399-1899; Messrs. A. and C. Black for passages from *Wessex* by Clive Holland, and *Winchester* by the Rev. Telford Varley; Messrs. William Blackwood and Son for passages from Anthony Trollope's *Autobiography*; Messrs. Chatto and Windus for a passage from Mr. A. C. Ewald's *Life and Times of Prince Charles Stuart*; Messrs. Longmans, Green and Co. for passages from Dean Kitchin's *Winchester* (Historic Towns Series); Messrs. Macmillan and Co. for a passage from Mr. Thomas Hardy's *Tess of the D'Urbervilles*; Mr. Elkin Mathews for verses from 'Winchester' by Lionel Johnson in *Ireland and Other Poems*; Messrs. Kegan Paul, Trench, Trübner and Co. for passages from 'Evening Hills' in the Rev. W. Moore's *New Poems*; Messrs. Isaac Pitman and Sons for passages from Canon Benham's 'Winchester Cathedral' in *Our Old Minsters* (Isbister and Co.); Messrs. P. and G. Wells for full permission to quote from *The Wykehamist*, and for passages from A. R. Bramston and A. C. Leroy's *A City of Memories*, and for poems from J. L. Crommelin-Brown's *Poems and Parodies*, and A. P. Herbert's *Poor Poems and Rotten Rhymes*.

Further, I have to thank the Editors of the *Daily Graphic*, the *Daily News*, the *Illustrated London News*, and the *Victoria County History* for passages from articles in their publications.

I sincerely trust that in this list I have not, inadvertently, left any kindness unrecognised.

A. A. L.

BOOK I

PART I

A ROYAL CITY

ECHOES OF HISTORY

§ 1. MEMORIES

O *Venta! Caer Gwent!* great and glad
   Wast thou, ere Saxon yeoman,
Ere nobler *Normandy's* mailed bowman,
   Saw thee : *Apollo* had
      His temple bright
      Of song and light,
Here, when the world was *Roman*.

Venta

And wert thou *Camelot* ?   Wert thou
   That shrine of all things knightly ?
Through the dark shrouding mists, how brightly
   Those glories flash forth now !
      High chivalry,
      Fair courtesy,
Enriching *Winton* rightly.

Surely the magic of the *Celt*,
   White City, doth not fail thee
Whatever change and chance assail thee,
   Still is that spirit felt :
      That ancient grace
      Still haunts thy face ;
And long may it avail thee.

Where reigned *Apollo*, *Wykeham* trod,
   Child of a *Saxon* peasant :
Surely, *Apollo* still was present,
   The old world's goodliest god :
      Light's king, and songs,
      His reign prolongs,
Throned in a place so pleasant.

On this trenched hill, new come from sea,
   The robber *Danes* have clustered ;
On yonder hill, have *Roundheads* mustered,
   Oliver's Battery :
      Oh ! blade and ball,
      And crossbow, all
Down *Itchen* vale have blustered !

   .   .   .   .   .   .

                  Lionel Johnson.
        ' Winchester,' in *Ireland and other Poems*.
              Elkin Matthews, 1897.

A City of Memories

IT is no small thing to live in a city of memories where, not here and there, but at every turn, the past is brought before us. . . . *Non nobis nati*, not for ourselves are we born, and Winchester, of all the cities in England, owes its greatest debt of gratitude to the past.

            A. R. Bramston and A. C. Leroy.
                  A City of Memories.
         P. and G. Wells, Winchester, 1893.

' Serene old age '

To have been the capital of Wessex, to have welcomed in her early days the arrival of every prince and prelate of great name, for a while to have been the chief city of England, the home of the great Alfred, the refuge of letters, the mother of English public-school life—these are the titles on which the city rests her high renown, and these the memories amidst which she lives. Her ancient buildings, her many customs and usages of the past, her tranquil beauty and pleasant neighbourhood, give to the venerable city a right to the undying affection of all whose lot has fallen to them in such pleasant places. It is not in death, but in the beautiful tranquillity of serene old age, that Winchester reposes in her sweet green valley low down amidst the swelling hills that compass her about. No English city has a nobler record in the past, or a life more peaceful in our rushing, hasteful age.

Dean Kitchin's *Winchester* (Hist. Towns Series).
Longmans, Green and Co.

HERE as the white road winds from off the down, Our Royal
We greet thee first, erewhile our royal town ! Town
Roman and Celt of old long dwelt in thee,
Till Saxon Cerdic's warriors from the sea
Swept like a tempest o'er the land, and drave
The Britons to the distant western wave,
And this clear stream ran red with Celtic gore,
And yon hill shouted with the din of war.
Now ruby roofs o'erstud the emerald lands,
And grey with age the giant Minster stands,
And the fair chapel by the city wall,
And Waltheof's scarpéd hill, o'ertopping all.

Down this same road the holy prelate passed,
Ere Eastern morn had crowned the Lenten fast ;
Journeying from Waltham, o'er the hills, to found
His stately college, where the grassy ground
Scarce held her own amid the wildering maze
Of chalky Itchen's myriad water-ways.

Once more, when six long years of toil had flown,
And hammer spake no more to wood and stone,
Nor vaulted roof stood o'er the new-built shrine,
Then rode our Founder by this self-same way.

To bless his college on her natal day.
Yet once again he passed.   Ah ! sad and slow,
His scholars saw the dark procession go !
Winding their way beneath their new-built home,
Passing St. Swithin's Arch, they chanting come
To the great Minster's forest of wrought stone,
Where for all time the grave must keep her own.
There in the honoured shrine he ever lies,
Where all around the ghostly pillars rise,
And shines the painted clerestory aglow
With moonlight streaming to the floor below,
Then kindle all the glimmering stones, and shed
A dim mysterious glory round his head.

R. A. Johnson.
'The Birthday of Winchester College,'
in the *Wykehamist*, July 1893.

'Past times' NOWHERE in England do the stones speak more eloquently of past times than in Winchester, the city of kings and of priests ; the city where religion flourished, and ecclesiastics fought with greater warmth than in any other of England's fair cities. Philistines there have been in the shape of Puritan soldiers who destroyed carving and effigies ; way wardens who mended the roads with stones taken from the massive city gates ; modern builders who run up cheap red brick tenements on the site of seventeenth-century houses or of time-honoured city walls, and all these have between them left England's first capital with but a small proportion of its ancient glory.

And yet though the bishop's castle and the king's castle no longer tower over the surrounding houses, though the many convents and churches remain only in traditional sites—even with what is left we can, helped by history and imagination, build up the past again, still hear the discord between king and bishop, bishop and prior. . . .

A. R. Bramston and A. C. Leroy.
A City of Memories.
P. and G. Wells, Winchester, 1893.

WHO suffereth not low care still to enfold
His thought in narrow circle of to-day,
But liveth to all time, will love to stray,
WINTON, among thy stately piles of old,
And read the tale, in moving language told
By Druid and by Roman stone, and grey
Monument of the Saxon's nobler sway,
How fraught with wondrous change for thee hath rolled
The stream of ages. . . .   Christopher Wood.
                            Reminiscences of Winchester, c. 1860.

A HALO of antiquity and romance surrounds the quiet city of the   A Quiet City
Itchen. . . . Winchester has played a most important part in
the history of England. Centuries ago Rome's imperial legion-
aries drove the light-armed Britons before them through its
streets, and planted here one of their impregnable ' castra '
which dominated the surrounding country. A monk of Venta's
cathedral departed hence to assume the imperial purple,[1] and to
sway the sceptre which once held the world in awe. At the union
of the Heptarchy, Winchester became the capital of England,
holding that proud position henceforward for five hundred years,
and here the first ' King of all England ' was crowned. From
Winchester issued the Royal Edict which abolished all distinctions of nationalities in the kingdom, and here the people of
England were first called ' English.' The grey cathedral has
looked down on a long line of Saxon kings ending with Edward
the Confessor, who within its walls received their crowns from
the hands of the archbishops of the realm, and here lie the ashes
of many of these kings. And although during the reign of the
Norman and Plantagenet monarchs Winchester still held her
own as a place of the greatest importance—the castle-palace
being the habitual residence of the monarch of England—
her glory waned before the growing power of London, and
eventually she was entirely superseded by the latter city.
          From *Winchester College Five Hundredth Anniversary,* 1893.

------

[1] The monk Constans.

'The Old White City'

SEE, where below the Old White City lies,
Calm, not decrepit, for her thousand years :
Lightly they lie, as this morn's radiance,
On all her darkened brickwork ; and she wears
Green tints of summer, where the waters glance,
And round her oratories
And long grey masses of her central fane.
She is just dreaming, as on Apennine
Long Alba dreamed, and saw her race divine,
The kings and pontiffs, in her streets again.
On such a morn the silver clarions blew
Through all her ways, to her great Minster-gate,
For crowning of some young Plantagenet ;
Then when beneath the canopies of state
The trefoils on their golden cirque were set
Upon him ; and men knew
On what far lands that mighty crown had sway.
Yet midst its jewels, on that day of grace,
One little kingdom had not found a place,
Which still should last, when greater passed away.

> W. M. (*i.e.* William Moore.)
> From *Anothen*.[1]
> James Parker, Oxford, 1893.

City Tables

A CITY which 'hath given place of birth, education, baptism, marriage, michol-gemots, gemots, synods national and provincial, and sepulchre to more Kings, Queens, Princes, Dukes, Earls, Barons, Bishops, and Mitred Prelates, before the year of Our Lord 1239, than all the cities in England together could do.'

> From the 'City Tables.'

'The tomb of empires'

PAUSE, traveller, upon this tree-crowned hill,
And see where England's capital of old
Lies in yon vale, a royal city still.
Within its mouldering walls thou mayest behold
The tomb of empires : there the Druids hold

---

[1] 'Anothen' is the name of a spring on Twyford Down near Winchester.

Their gloomy reign of mystery, and fill
The land with terror ; Rome did there unfold
Her eagle banner, and ruled and taught her skill
In arts and arms ! and in that city long
Uther, with many a brave Armoric knight,
Held court and tourney, and waged ceaseless fight
With Saxons who next raised their empire strong,
Shaken but not o'erthrown, by Norman or Dane,
Whose graves alone yon Saxon walls retain.

                              C. W., *c.* 1869.

BEAUTIFULLY placed amidst the chalk hills of Hampshire, full of historic memories, and still in a measure redolent with the atmosphere of ancient times, Winchester stands to-day one of the most interesting of Wessex cities, as in Saxon times it was one of the most important in the whole of England.   Much has been written concerning Winchester and its history, but words after all prove but imperfect media by which to translate into actuality the beauty, interest, and sentiment which permeate an ancient town like this.

'Redolent with the atmosphere of ancient times'

                              Clive Holland.
                              Wessex.
                  A. and C. Black, 1906.

§ 2. PRE-NORMAN WINCHESTER

AFTER hym [Eboras] Lud-Hudybras,
So Eboras sone ycleped was,
Hade this londe everuch del,
Ant hyt yemede suythe wel ;
He made Caunterbury anon,
Ant other tounes moni on,
Wynchestre and Schaftesburge
Ther spac an ern a prophecie,

B.C. 892
The Hudibras Myth

> Thre dawes and thre nyht,
> The prophecie he tolde riht :
> Wet in Englond schulde byfalle,
> That ther weren hit herden alle.
>
> *Ancient English Metrical Romances* (ed. Ritson), iii. 23.

Mythical builders

IT (Winchester) is said to have been first fortified with walls by Guidorius, A.D. 179, which were demolished in the civil wars of the West Saxon princes.   The present walls are reported to have been erected by Moleutius Dunwallo, A.D. 341.   On the south and east sides, for some distance, they remain entire ;   and many fragments of them are continued to a considerable extent on the north and west, particularly to the westward, where are the ruins of a bastion called the Hermit's Tower, the external appearance of which denotes it to have been of considerable strength.   The circumference of the walls is near two miles, to which originally belonged six gates, only one of which now remains, except a postern, called King's Gate, which gives its name to the street adjoining ;   though Leland says that some ancient writers call it St. Michael's Gate, from St. Michael's Church, which stands near it.   On the west, and on part of the north and south sides, is a foss of prodigious breadth and depth, which added considerable strength to the fortification ;   but to the meadows, which were easily floated by the river, such a defence was thought unnecessary.

A Winchester Guide, 1780.

The City Walls

THE town of Winchester is by estimacion a mile *dim.* in cumpace withyn the walles.

The length of it lyeth from est to west ;   the bredth from north to south.

Ther be in the waulles vi gates, by est one ;   by west an other ;   the third by south ;   the 4. by north.

The 5. is caullid the Kinges Gate and is betwixt the south gate and Wolvesey the Bisshopes palace.

The 6. is bytwixt north gate and estgate, no great thing but
a postern gate namid Bourne Gate.

John Leland's *Itinerary*.

CLAUDIUS the emperor · nolde noght gut bileue ·
Gef he com mid is ost · in to this lond weue ·
Aruirag at vinchestre · mid is men was echon ·
With is poer the emperour · biseged him anon ·
Aruirag greithed him · & is folc aboute ·
& wende worth to giue him · bataile withoute.

Robert of Gloucester (Rolls Series), ii. 106.

c. A.D. 50.
The Emperor
Claudius
besieges
Winchester [1]

WINCHESTER, like all Roman or Romano-British towns, had its
square form of mural defences, with an entrance at each of the
cardinal points marked by a gate named thereafter. The West
Gate had, doubtless, its Roman precursor, but all traces of this
structure above ground have vanished; Saxon, Norman, and
Plantagenet erections and changes having swept them away.
A few years ago a beautiful *Aureus* of Honorius was found within
a few yards of the old gate, and it is remarkable that during the
long years that the modern *fossor* has been at work for all sorts
of foundations and improvements, not a single legionary tablet,
or inscription, nor even evidence of auxiliary cohorts, has ever
been found in this locality.

W. H. Jacob.

The West Gate of Winchester, Hants Field Club, iv. 51-59.

Roman
Winchester

AN erl ther was in this lond · octaui [2] was is name ·
Romeins that were here bileued · he dude ofte ssame ·
& slou vaste her & ther · & that mē ssolde vewe ise ·
The brutons hii hin crounede tho · hor king vor to be ·

c. A.D. 366.
Fighting near
Winchester

[1] See Geoffrey of Monmouth, from whose imaginative and legendary
history the details of this story are culled. Aviragus is probably identical
with Caractacus.

[2] Octavius is said to be a certain Magnentius, of British family, who
assassinated Constans, one of the sons of Constantine, and possessed
himself of Britain and Gaul.

Tho this word com to constantin · he thoghte wat was to done ·
Traen is moder vncle · hider he sende sone ·
With gret poer ynou · to winne this kinedom ·
At an hauene bi southe · this folc alonde com ·
The king was of hom iwar · agen hom he sette ·
Bi side winchestre in a feld · to gadere hii hom mette ·
Bataile hii smite ther · & to grounde slowe vaste ·
So that octaui king · aboue was atte laste ·
& traen & moche of is folc · ywounded ney to dethe.

Robert of Gloucester (Rolls Series), i. 139.

Venta Belgarum

IT was, we may say, a country town like Calleva Atrebatum, perhaps a little larger, if the mediæval walls represent the ancient area, perhaps a little more important, a little more in touch with Roman administrative life. But the picture is dim, at the best, and those who prefer clearness to truth have tried to add one bright definite feature. Winchester, as we are sometimes told, was the capital of that King Lucius who introduced Christianity into Britain in the second century; the present cathedral stands on the site of the first Christian church built in Britain, and Constantine added a priestly college of which the ruins are still visible. So far the tale, as old as the fifteenth-century monk of Winchester, Thomas Rudborne, and repeated as lately as the last edition of Milner's *History*. It is, of course, false. Lucius is mythical, as scholars of all denominations now agree: the Romano-British cathedral is a mere imagination: the supposed ruins of Constantine's college date in reality from the Decorated period of mediæval architecture. Vestiges of Romano-British Christianity might well occur at Winchester, as at Silchester, but none have hitherto been discovered.

F. Haverfield.
'Romano-British Hampshire,'
Victoria County History, Hants, i. 293.

The Myth of King Arthur

THE ancient castle of this city is celebrated, and has been celebrated for some centuries past, as having been founded by the renowned British king, Arthur, in the year 523. This, however, is a palpable error that has arisen from confounding the history of Caer Gwent, or Winchester, of Monmouthshire (an ancient city which has long been destroyed, and which appears to have been actually the residence of Arthur) with our city of the same name. The latter, at the time we are speaking of, namely, the reign of Arthur, was firmly and finally settled as the capital of the West Saxon kingdom under the victorious Cerdic.

Historical and Descriptive Guide to Winchester, 1829.

WHERE Venta's Norman castle still uprears
Its rafter'd hall, that o'er the grassy foss,
And scatter'd flinty fragments clad in moss,
On yonder steep in naked state appears ;
High-hung remains, the pride of warlike years,
Old Arthur's board ; on the capacious round
Some British pen has sketched the names renown'd
In marks obscure, of his immortal peers.
Though joined by magic skill, with many a rhyme,
The Druid frame, unhonour'd falls a prey
To the slow vengeance of the wizard Time,
And fade the British characters away ;
Yet Spenser's page, that chants in verse sublime
Those chiefs, shall live, unconscious of decay.

Thomas Warton.
On King Arthur's Round Table at Winchester.

HERE may Tradition's fairy tale unfold
The courtly pageants of each baron bold,
The skilful labour of some minstrel hoar,
Snatch'd from the wreck of legendary lore,
When fam'd St. Tristram deck'd good Arthur's Court,
And knights romantic shone in vary'd sport ;
When the glad youth rush'd forth to break the lance,
To chase the wolf, or join the antic dance,

And the fair damsels' all-subduing eyes
Of tilts and tournaments bestow'd the prize :
Or the brave equals round th' encircled board
With blood-red wine and British viands stor'd,
In native melody their prowess sang,
While the arch'd roof with pealing plaudits rang.

John Wooll.
The King's House, etc., 1793.

Itchen vaunteth herself

AND for great Arthur's seat, her Winchester prefers,
Whose old round-table yet she vaunteth to be hers ;
And swore, th' inglorious time should not bereave her right ;
But what it would obscure, she would reduce to light.
For, from that wondrous pond, whence she derives her head,
And places by the way, by which she 's honoured,
(Old Winchester, that stands near in her middle way,
And Hampton, at her fall into the Solent sea).
She thinks in all the isle not any such as she,
And for a demigod she would related be.

From Drayton's *Polyolbion*, Song II.

TUESDAY, *October* 24, 1738.

King Arthur's Hall

NEAR the King's House stands an ancient large building which
is called King Arthur's Hall. It is a good room, the length is
better than one hundred and eight feet, the height I take it to be
about thirty feet, there are five arches, each arch distant from one
another eighteen feet. There is nailed up against the wall at
the end of the hall a top of what they call King Arthur's Round
Table, and the places marked where his knights sat. This I do
not very strictly believe, but that there was a King Arthur and
that he had many knights is most certain. The use that this
room is now put to is a Court of Justice, which is made use of
when the judges come their circuits to Winchester.

A Journey through Hampshire in 1738, in the handwriting of
the second Earl of Oxford, apparently addressed to his
wife (*Hist. MSS. Com.*, Duke of Portland's MSS.).

THO com kyng Egbryth,   **Egbert**
Ant, wyth batayle ant fyht,
Made al Englond yhol
Falle to ys oune dol ;
Ant sethe he reignede her
Ahte ant tuenti folle yer :
At Wynchestre lyggeth ys bon,
Buried in a marble-ston.

'Chronicle of England' (written *tempus* Edward II.) in *Ancient*
English Metrical Romances (ed. Ritson), vol. iii.

SURELY Winchester, which preserves the bones of him who first **A Mecca**
strove for and successfully realised the conception of national
unity, should be the Mecca for all true devotees of Great or
Greater Britain.
       Rev. Telford Varley.
        Winchester.
      A. and C. Black, 1910.

Ac at ssirebourne he [Æthelbald, 857-60] was ybured · & is **'The**
 brother adelbright · [Æthelbert, 860-6]   **Hethene'**
This kinedom adde after him · as lawe was & right ·   **destroy**
Bi is daye the worre com · of the hethene men wel prout · **Winchester**
In hampte ssire & destruede · wincestre al out ·
& that folc of hamtessire · hore red tho nome ·
& of barcessire & foghte · & the ssrewen ouercome.

     Robert of Gloucester (Rolls Series), i. 384.

HERE the fell Dane, by eager havoc led,   **'The fell**
Swift desolation o'er the city spread :   **Dane'**
His Raven standard from the turret wav'd
Of the sole edifice his plunder sav'd,
And, mocking still the fame of British might,
Defy'd the royal Ethelbert in fight.

       John Wooll.
    The King's House, a poem, 1793.

IN no place, perhaps, has this *Genius Loci* of monastic life more safely maintained its habitation than in the Saxon metropolis of England, the venerable and ancient Winchester ; it is impossible to visit it, in spite of the unsparing violences of the Reformation, without feeling that you are still in the visionary presence of abbots and priors, with all their collegiate brotherhoods about you. It looks the undoubted abode of monastic communities ; the stillness of the cell is felt, and hangs about every quarter of it ; its High Street and place of frequence is solemnised by a holy cross of lofty and venerable architecture ; you tread upon the foundation and fragments of ancient buildings in every open field and garden of the city ; the few people you meet abroad ; the quietness throughout the town, disturbed by no movements of trade or pleasure, preserve to every street an atmosphere of devotion ; the stillness of a daily Sabbath is upon them ; the narrowness and obscurity of many of them give an impression not unlike the vague notion we have of the solitary dimness of cloistral residence. The low valley in which the city is placed, its rich meadows and its glassy streams of delicious water, speak of ecclesiastical abundance and enjoyment, and the very trout that are everywhere poised motionless in the river, or shooting their way, sportful or scared, through the green weed, seem to have a reference to Catholic days, and the obligations to peculiar food which the religious discipline of the place and the times required.

Charles Townsend.
Winchester and a Few Other Compositions, 1842.

WHITE city of old time, whose turrets hoary,
With moss o'ergrown, mourn sad and silently
Over thy fallen grandeur ; doom'd to be,
Like all that is earth-born, so transitory,
Still the grey shadow of thy ancient glory,
Hovering around thy ruins, throws o'er thee
A time-wrought mantle of mild radiancy,
Imaging forth thy sadly pleasing story.

Oft 'neath thy walls, the lone hour to beguile,
I 've wandered musing by the crystal stream,
Perchance whose soft sweet murmurings erewhile
Lull'd Alfred's listening soul in many a dream
Of vision'd greatness, bidding his lov'd isle,
Nursed by his care, with countless blessings teem.

> Quoted in Prouten's *Hist. and Descrip. Guide
> to Winchester*, c. 1850.

WINCHESTER, again, was not only the strongest city, the royal residence, the seat of the principal bishopric, and the usual meeting-place of the Witan, but also the leader in learning.   In Wolvesey Palace was a school of learning and art.   It was here that King Alfred began, and for many years even wrote with his own hand the *English Chronicle*, the first great history-book of the English, the mother of a magnificent line of literature. Meanwhile the city was growing in splendour, as it was understood then.   The group of the three great minsters—the Old Minster, now the cathedral ; the New Minster, founded by Alfred, almost adjoining it on the north ; and the Nun's Minster, a little eastwards, near the Town Hall—must have been one of the most striking groups then to be seen, not only in England, but in all Europe.

A leader in learning

> G. E. Jeans.
> *Memorials of Old Hampshire.*
> Bemrose and Son, 1906.

AND of the bishops also
The clerks kept record.
Chronicles, it is called, a big book.
The English went about collecting it.
Now it is thus authenticated ;
So that at Winchester, in the cathedral,
There is the true history of the kings,
And their lives and their memorials.
King Alfred had it in his possession,

King Alfred's Book

And had it bound with a chain.
Who wished to read, might well see it,
But not remove it from its place.

*L'estoire des Engles solum la translacion Maistre
Geffrei Gaimar* (Rolls Series), ii. 76.

LIES he here, the breaker of the Dane ?
This was his New Minster once, where mere
Ruined gate and little low-towered plain
Grey church of the Servitors remain :
  King and Founder, lies he here ?

Long is fallen that house of his desire,
God's eternal House ; the columns' range
Springs no more about the vaulted choir ;
Waste and lost is all by axe and fire,
  Spoiled by Time and Fate and Change.

Nothing royal here : rough turf alone
Clothes the slope—and, past the straggling hedge,
Raw red streets of brick and slate are grown ;
Only at our feet this doubtful stone,
  Nameless, at the town's mean edge,

Marks his half-remembered dust.   But he,
Had we faith to follow, now as then,
Still might lead us, and, from sea to sea,
This our England that he brought to be
  Still be nurse of Englishmen.

Yet, though terror of the Dane no more
Vex us, passage of a thousand years
Finds us standing as we stood before,
Waiting still upon our island shore
  Vision of our formless fears

Gazing still across the sea for Fate.
Is not his, the teacher's, help our need,
While our enemies within the gate,
Gathering thick behind us, causeless hate,
　　Fear, and ignorance, and greed,

Sick mistrust, the politician's art,
Sloth, and ever unfulfilled delay,
Jealousy, that draws our ranks apart,
Wavering purpose, and unquiet heart,
　　Plot to ruin and betray ?

We can face them, scatter them like foam
Blown to landward, mighty though they seemed,
Then upon this rock-base of our home
Build Man's holier eternal Rome,
　　Truer than the Saxon dreamed.

Arundell Esdaile.

'On the so-called Tomb of King Alfred, by the Church of
St. Bartholomew, Hyde, Winchester,' 1912.

Oct. 30, 1825.

How . . . am I to describe what I felt, when I yesterday saw **In Hyde**
in HYDE MEADOW, A COUNTY BRIDEWELL standing on the **Meadow**
very spot, where stood the abbey which was founded and endowed
by Alfred, which contained the bones of that maker of the
English name, and also those of the learned monk, ST. GRIMBALD,
whom ALFRED brought to England *to begin the teaching at
Oxford* !

William Cobbett.
Rural Rides.

THE Danish Gyant Colebrand in Hyde-meads,　　**Guy of**
By Guy the Earle of Warwick was struck dead.　　**Warwick.**

John Taylor, the Water-poet.
A Memoriall of Monarchs.

A.D. 927.
The Dane-
mark[1]

SAXONS ! the Dane is at the gate !
  Lo, Athelstan, your monarch, calls.—
They rush to impose impending fate,
  And drive the spoilers from the walls.
Old Winton's battlements are strong,
And stout hearts may defend them long.

For many a day, in battle dread,
  The Northman poured his blood in vain,
Till, sickening of the strife, he said :
  ' Let one brave Saxon with one Dane
His prowess prove—the victor's sword
Shall to his king the palm award.'

There was a warrior, Colbrand hight,
  Among the Danes, of lion limb,
And of a more than human height :
  To be their champion chose they him ;
Deeming no Saxon in the land
Could such a mighty foe withstand.

Fain was the king the strife to end
  With victory at a single blow,
But he no warrior durst to send
  Against the giant Danish foe :
And while no champion did appear,
The Danes ceased not to scoff and jeer.

---

[1] See *Liber de Hyda* (Rolls Series). The city had been besieged two years by the Danes; finally a single combat was to decide the victory. Colbrand, the Danish giant, engaged with Guy, Earl of Warwick, the Saxon champion. Guy, assisted by a friendly crow, who fluttered about Colbrand, was victorious. The combat took place near Hyde Abbey, the site still being called Danemark; Athelstan watched it from a turret in the city wall, known until the nineteenth century, when it was destroyed, as Athelstan's chair.

Much grieved the king that brave Sir Guy
  Had journeyed to the Holy Land,
For well might he that Dane defy ;
  None could his vigorous arm withstand.
Sad went the king that night to bed,
But by a dream was comforted.

He heard a voice of angel say :
  ' Rise, king, and seek the eastern gate ; [1]
There shalt thou meet a palmer grey,
  To him entrust thy country's fate.'
Up rose the king, and long ere dawn,
Unto the eastern gate was gone.

Who yonder in the glimmering light,
  In palmer's weeds, draws slowly nigh ?
The king is mad with wild delight ;
  He welcomes home his faithful Guy.
Soon enter they the city gates,
And the glad king the war relates.

    .   .   .   .   .   .

Then said the king : ' To front this Dane
  Take thou the sword of Constantine,
And the good spear of Charlemagne,
  Shall in this holy fight be thine ;
May heaven direct both spear and sword
To rid us of this savage horde ! '

On Athelstan's best steed the knight
  Rode forth to meet his foeman grim,
And anxious crowds to view the fight
  Of gallant Saxons followed him,
And priest, and sire, and lady fair,
Breathed for him many an ardent prayer.

[1] The metrical *Romance of Guy of Warwick* (Early English Text Society), from which most of the facts given in this indifferent poem are gathered, indicates the north gate ; ' And go vnto the northe gate.'

Upon a steed that panted sore
   Came the huge Colbrand to the field ;
A ponderous battle-axe he bore,
   That, save himself, no man could wield.
Sneering, he cried, ' And art thou he
That fears not to encounter me ? '

' My sword shall answer,' Guy replied.
   The trumpets blew—he struck amain
His spurs into his courser's side.—
   God speed thee, lance of Charlemagne !—
Dire was the shock, but vain the stroke,
The spear in thousand splinters broke

On Colbrand's shield—with treble might,
   The furious Dane his axe then raised,
Deeming that blow would end the fight.
   Guy's helm the weapon lightly grazed,
But laid the king's proud courser dead,
A bleeding trunk, with severed head.

The Danes loud shouted—Colbrand threw
   Aside his axe, and seized a mace
Of spiked iron, and Guy drew
   His sword, with that and shield to face
His giant foe.—May power divine
Assist the sword of Constantine !

Then not a breath was heard around
   As the mace fell with thunder stroke ;
Though Guy escaped it with light bound,
   His shield it all to fragments broke.
Loud yelled their joy the Danish host,
And all the Saxon's hope was lost.

Yet Guy, eluding every blow,
  Still with his sword the giant stung,
Till, foaming with fierce ire, the foe
  High in the air his weapon swung
With might and main.—With sudden dread
The Saxons deemed their champion dead.

Guy leaped aside, unscathed, the Dane
  With the rash force of his fell aim,
Let fall his mace ; and to regain
  His ponderous arm, stooped low.—Up came
Sir Guy, with light step, and his brand
Cut off the giant Dane's right hand.

And now the Saxons raised a cry
  Of triumph, while in blank despair
The Danes were mute.   Then cried Sir Guy
  To Colbrand : ' I thy life will spare
If thou wilt yield thee to my sword,
And the Danes own our English lord.'

No answer made the wrathful foe,
  But with his left hand seized the mace,
And strove to deal another blow,
  But strove in vain : scarce could he pace
With reeling step the soil, his strength
Fast ebbing with his blood ; at length

Guy, more in pity than in ire,
  Pierced to the heart the hapless Dane—
The baffled enemy retire,
  And Athelstan in peace may reign.
Then to his royal lord's abode
The brave Sir Guy in triumph rode.

                        Christopher Wood.
      Reminiscences of Winchester, c. 1860.

The Ryche Towne

AND blythe ys Kyng Adelston
And hys barons euerychone,
There they toke Syr Gye
And lad hym forthe, sekurlye,
To Wynchestur, the ryche towne.

The Romance of Guy of Warwick (Early Engl. Text Soc.)

Ethelwulf

AT the hyde of Wynchestre
Were his bones don in cheste.

From 'Chronicle of England,' in *Ancient Metrical Romances* (ed. Ritson), vol. iii.

Edward the Elder

EDWARD reignede her
Vour ant tuenti yer ;
At Wynchestre liggeth ys bon,
Buried in a marbre ston.

Ibid.

Edwy

HE reignede foure yer,
To Wynchestre mē him ber.

Ibid.

Edgar

HERE the hot king,[1] whose unrequited lust
O'er his once valu'd friend in vengeance burst,
And paid his faith once stain'd with forfeit life,
Who stabb'd the husband, and then won the wife,
First claim'd the fair Elfrida as his own,
And, propp'd by crafty monks, his vicious throne.

John Wooll.
The King's House, a poem, 1793.

---

[1] The story here referred to is the romance concerning Elfrida, told by William of Malmesbury (*Gesta Regum*, Rolls Series, 165). See Freeman, *Historical Essays*, i. 15. Earl Ethelwald being sent to see the beautiful Elfrida on behalf of Edgar, fell in love with her himself and married her. Edgar afterwards discovering his treachery, slew him in a wood near Winchester, and married Elfrida himself.

The author of the poem states that Edgar was crowned in Winchester Castle. The more general belief is that he was not crowned until late in his reign, and then at Bath (see various chroniclers).

HIRE riche clothes were of ydo · bote that heo was bi weued ·
Hire bodi with a mantel · a wimpel aboute hire heued ·
Hire legges bare binethe the kne · that mē mighte ech stape ise ·
A wey vuele bicom it quene · so bar uor to be ·
Mē broghte vorth this fury ssares · and leide is al arewe ·
In the bar erthe isuope · godes grace to ssewe ·
The bissopes blessede the ssares · and the quene al so ·
And ladde ire uorth in either alf · this judgement to do ·
The quene thoghte al on god · an to heuene caste ire eye ·
And ne lokede nothing donward · & as hii alle yseie ·
Heo stap upe this furi yre · euerich stape al clene ·
Nuste heo hire sulf hou it was · ne bleincte noght ene ·
Ther was ioye & blisse ynou · & moni a wepinde eye ·
Verst uor fere & suthe vor Ioye · tho hii this iseye ·
The bissopes that hire ladde · vor ioye wepe al so ·
& herede god & sein swithin · tho this miracle was ydo ·
And ladde ire outward of the chirche · The quene bigan to crie ·
Vor the loue of ihesu crist · ne doth noght the vileinie ·
To do my penaunce withoute · ac in alle manere ·
As it mē it iloked was · In holi chirche here ·
Ma dame quath this bissopes · thou it ast ido iwys ·
So helpe me god quath the quene · I nuste noght er this ·

Robert of Gloucester (Rolls Series), ii. 501.

THO hii broghte hire to the king · the king ligginge hii founde ·
Wepinde & ope heued · to sprad al to the grounde ·
Hit was longe ar he mighte speke · vor deol that he made ·
Atte laste he rose vp · as the bissopes him bade ·
& vel to is moder vet · aduun anon akne ·
Moder he sede ich abbe misdo · agen god & the
That i nam noght wurthi to be thi sone · ac par seinte charite ·
Vor pite that of the Magdalein · god adde uor gif it me ·
Sone quath the moder tho · as al this men iseth ·
God ath vaire issewed · that we gultelese beth ·

Atte biginninge theruore . agen the bissop ich rede .
Amendement do that is . gultles of the dede .
& suthe thou might agen me . vor ich mot nede be milde .
As kunde of moder wole . & blod agen my childe
Tho the bissop was icome . wepinde wel sore .
The king vel doun to is vet . & criede him milce & ore .
The bissop wepinde al so . uorgef it him anon .
So that thoru the kinges bone . the bissopes ech on .
Ech after other asoilede . the king of this trespas .
Mid gerden in is naken rug . and that gret pite was .
Thre strokes the moder ek . wepinde wel sore .
Gef him him to asoily . & ne mighte uor reuthe more .
Tho custe the king is moder . & the bissop suthe al so .
& herede gerne seint swithin . that such miracle adde ido .

Robert of Gloucester (Rolls Series), ii. 503.

§ 3. MEDIÆVAL WAYS

The Book of Winchester . . . THE only name which Domesday Book gives itself in its own pages is that of ' the book of Winchester ' (fo. 332*b*). It was at Winchester that Domesday Book was kept ; at Winchester that it must have been compiled, and at Winchester that the last original returns were preserved, far into the next century, in the Treasury of the Norman kings.

From Mr. Round's article on the Domesday Survey,
Victoria County History, Hants, i. 399.

IN the Hampshire [Domesday] Survey we have to lament the total omission of Winchester ; but this, perhaps, as in the case of London, is a tribute to the greatness of its position.

Ibid. i. 432.

Earl Waltheof beheaded, 1076 ESTWARDE on the Toppe of an Hille in the way to London is a chapelle of S. Giles, that sumtyme, as apperith, hathe bene a far

bigger thyng, wher Waldavus, Erle of Northumbreland, a Noble
Saxon or Dane was behedid by the commaundement of King
Wylliam Conquerour.

John Leland's *Itinerary*.

BUT as the King was hunting in Hampshire,   **The Death of**
Sir Walter Tirrill shooting at a deere,   **Rufus**
The Arrow glauncing 'gainst a Tree by chance,
Th' vnhappy King kild, by the haplesse Glaunce.
A Colliers Cart to Winchester did bring
The Corps, where unbemoaned they laid the King.

John Taylor, the Water-poet.
A Memoriall of Monarchs.

To Winchestre he was ilad . al mid is grene wounde .   **His Burial**
That euere as mē him ledde . the blod orn to grounde .
Amorwe anon he was ibured . In the munstre ywis .
Right biuore the heye weued . as is bodi yut is .
At is buriinge was moni a mon . ac wepinde vewe .
He adde endinge as he wurthe was .
& such it is to be ssrewe ·

Robert of Gloucester (Rolls Series), ii. 619.

YMAD was King of Engelond . at Winchestre in the place .   **Henry I.**
At is brother buriinge . thoru oure louerdes grace .   **made King**

Ibid., p. 620.

HENRY the King, wishing to know what King Edward had in   **Winton**
Winchester in his lordship, ordered it to be inquired of and **Domesday**
approved under oath of burghers.

From the Winton Domesday (see *Victoria County
History, Hants*).

ONE fleeting ray of prosp'rous fortune shed   **Allegiance to**
Here its bright radiance o'er Matilda's head,   **Empress**
When rescued from a curst usurper's pow'r   **Matilda**
Th' unsettled crown, for one short passing hour,

Deck'd its fair mistress' legal brow in vain,[1]
And strove its native honours to regain,
Till the same spot, where each fond hope was fed,
Saw her deserted, famish'd, vanquish'd, fled.[2]

John Wooll.
The King's House, a poem, 1793.

L'EMPERERIZ asist Vincestre.

Ove lui fu li Mareschas

Qui tuz diz fu ver lui loi[a]ls,

E des autres baruns asés

Out entor la vile amasez

Qui la cité quidoent prendre ;

Mais dedenz avoit por defendre

Bons cheval[i]ers e gent hardie

Qui por faire chevalerie

S'en issoient chascun jor fors

Por tornïer a cels defors ;

Mais Phelippe de Columbiers

I estoit toz diz as prem[i]ers ;

Yembles d'anné[e]s ert e proz,

Ke de deus parz les venquit tuz.

Li reis [3] inelement e tost

Assembla grant gent e grant ost

Pur venir Vincestre rescorre

E por sa bone gent sucure.

Quant la 'mpereriz l'oï dire

Qu'a si grant ost e a tel ire

Veneit li reis por lu[i] sosprendre

Ou por lu[i] ocirre ou por prendre,

---

[1] Empress Matilda held a conference with the Legate on a plain near Winchester Castle, when Stephen was a prisoner at Bristol in 1141, and resuming the crown on certain conditions, gained the promise of allegiance from her subjects (see *Chronicle of Reigns of Stephen*, etc. (Rolls Series), iii. 74-5).

[2] Referring to her defeat and flight from the city in the same year.

[3] As a matter of fact, King Stephen was still a prisoner at Bristol, and the army was gathered by his queen, Maud.

E si li fu dit, c'est la sume,
Qu'el n'aveit pas le dissime home
En sun host k'il aveit el suen,
Ne li sembla ne bel ne buen,
N'ele n'ont si haut conseillier
Qui lors la s[e]üst conseill[i]er
Fors li Mareschas, tote voie,
La fist tantost metre a la voie
Tot dreit a Lotegaresale.
Mut fu cele jurné[e] male,
Quer li reis o trestot son ost
Enchausa vistement & tost,
Et cil souvent li trestornoent
Qui o la dame s'en aloent ;
E saciez k'en ces trestornées
Vit l'om maintes seles turnées,
Mainz cheval[i]ers abatre & prendre.
Ne[l] purrent suffrir ne atendre
Cil qui o l'empereriz érent :
Al meiz ku'il purent s'en alérent ;
Poingnant si que regne n'i tindrent,
[J]esque soz Varesvalle vindrent ;
Mès forment les desavancha
L'empereriz qui cheva[l]cha,
Cumme femme fait, en seant :
Ne sembla pas boen ne seant
Al Marechal, anceis li dist :
' Dame, si m'aït Jesucrist,
L'om ne puet pas en seant poindre :
Les jambes vos covient desjo[i]ndre
E metre par en son l'arçum.'
Let le fist, volsist ele ou non,
Quer lor enemis le[s] grevoient
Qui de trop pres les herd[i]oient.

L'Histoire de Guillaume le Maréchal, lines 166-224
[ed. Paul Meyer, 1901].

ABRIDGED TRANSLATION

[THE Empress was besieging Winchester. With her were the
Marshall and numerous barons who thought they could take
the town. However, there were several valiant knights defend-
ing it, and they made sorties every day against the besiegers.
To oppose them the young and brave Philip de Colombiers was
always one of the first, and he drove them back. The King
hastened to assemble a formidable army to succour Winchester.
When the Empress heard that the King was marching against
her with a force ten times more numerous than hers she was
in great trouble. None could advise her except John the
Marshall, who at once suggested she should go on to Ludgershall.
It was a hard day : the King and his host pursued them closely,
and those who accompanied the lady often faced them, and, in
these encounters, there were many saddles twisted, many knights
unhorsed and captured. The partisans of the Empress being
weak in numbers retreated as well as they could. By dint of hard
spurring they came near to Wherwell. However, the Empress
kept them back, riding side-saddle as is the wont of women. The
Marshall realising this must not be bade her put her leg over the
pommel and ride astride. Unwilling though she was, she obeyed
him, since the enemy were pressing them close.]

The praises of the city in 1192

HAEC est in partibus illis Judaeorum Hierosolyma, in hac sola
perpetua pace fruuntur, haec est schola bene vivere et valere
volentium. Hic fiunt homines, hic satis est panis et vini pro
nihilo. Sunt in ea tantae monachi misericordiae et mansuetu-
dinis, clerus consilii et libertatis, cives civilitatis et fidei, feminae
pulchritudinis et pudicitiae, quod parum me retinet quin ego
vadam illuc cum talibus Christianis fieri Christianus. Ad istam
te dirigo civitatem, urbem urbium, matrem omnium, et omnibus
meliorem. Unum est vitium et illud solum, cui de consuetudine
nimis indulget. Salva pace literatorum dixerim et Judaeorum,
Wentani mentiuntur ut vigiles, sed in fabulis faciendis. Nus-

quam enim sub coelo de tam facili tot rumores falsi fabricantur,
ut ibi ; alias, per omnia sunt veraces.

[Winchester is for the Jews the Jerusalem of those parts ;
here and here only they enjoy continual peace ; here is the school
of all who desire to live well and to prosper. Here men are
men ; here is bread and wine in plenty and for nothing. Here
the monks are so full of pity and kindness, the clerks so wise and
free, the citizens so civil and faithful, the women so beautiful
and so pure, that I declare I am half tempted to become a
Christian when I am with such Christians as these. I advise you
to go thither, to the city of cities, the mother of all, the best of all.
They have one failing, and one only, and that is after all but a
matter of custom.

Wintonians tell lies, like watchmen, but only in inventing tales.
Nowhere under Heaven are false reports so easily concocted ; in
other ways they are truthful enough.]

Chronicle of Reigns of Stephen, etc. (Rolls Series), iii. 438.

THEN King Richard, being clothed in his royal robes, with the
crown upon his head, holding in his right hand a royal sceptre,
which terminated in a cross, and in his left hand a golden wand,
with the figure of a dove at the top of it, came forth from his
apartment in the priory, being conducted on the right hand by
his chancellor, the Bishop of Ely, and on the left by the Bishop
of London. . . . The silken canopy was held upon four lances
over the king by four earls. . . . The king being thus conducted
into the cathedral and up to the high altar, there fell upon his
knees, and devoutly received the archbishop's solemn benediction.
He was then led to the throne, which was prepared for him on
the south side of the choir. . . . When Mass was finished, the
king was led back again to his apartments, with the solemnities
that have been described above. He then laid aside his ponderous robes and crown, and put on other robes and a crown that

Second Coronation of Richard I., 1194

were much lighter, and so proceeded to dinner which was served in the monks' refectory.

Milner, *History of Winchester.*

William
Marshall the
younger,
besieges
Winchester,
March 1217

Isi fut fet com ge vos di,
& l'endemain se departi
Li gienvles Mar. del pére.
Il & li quens de Salesbére
Qui ren aceet bien se tindrent
O lor genz a Wincestre vindrent :
Le chastel de Wincestre assistrent.

  . . . . .

E li dui qui Wincestre assistrent
A La Hide lor ostels pristrent ;
E [si] vos di por verité
Que il assistrent la cité,
Le premier jor petit i firent,
Mès l'endemain il l'essallirent.
Tant me feit li escriz entendre
Que l'endemain, sanz plus atendre,
Enveia li péres por l'ost
Que dessi qu'a lui venist tost.

  . . . . .

Tant tost cum [li] chastelein virent
Que cil de l'ost d'els se partirent,
Sachiez que molt ço lor fu bel.
Lors eissirent de lor chastel.
En la vile, si la robérent
E ar[s]trent, car cor[o]cié érent,
Por ce que recetez aveient
Lor enemis & lor nuiseient.
Ne porent pas tot lor afaire
En poi d'ore fornir e faire,
Kar l'ost si sodement revint
Q'onques as chastele[i]ns ne tint

De fere ce que a lui quistrent.
Arriére en lor chastels se mistrent,
Mes itels fu li meseürs
Que la vile defors les murs
As chasteleins plus consentirent,
Dont trop leidement se sentirent.
Li cuens de Salesbire assist
Le menor chastel, si le prist,
E li plus gienvles Mar.
Herdiement, comm[e] vassals,
Le greingnor des chastels asist.
Tant maniéres de gent i mist
E tant d'ommes e nuit e jor
Que par puissance, par valor,
Uit jors tot pleins si les destreinst
Qu'onques ne s'i lacha ne feinst,
C'onques lai[e]nz ne reposérent
N'onques descovrir ne s'osérent.

E itant vos [voil] je bien dire
Que quant li cuens de Salesbire
Ont pris l'un [des] chastels a force,
Vers l'autre se haste & esforce
Por entrer al gienvle Mar.
En aïe e en grant estal.
E sachiez que tant se penérent
Li dui buen ami qui la alérent,
E tant trestrent & tant lanciérent
Qui si durement s'avanciérent
Que li encloz qui dedanz érent
S'esmaiérent molt & dotérent.
Endementiers issi avint
Que li e[i]nznez Mar. vint
O grant ost & o grant compaigne,
Que la riviére e la champaigne

C

En fu pleine & la vile entor.
Lors virent bien cil de la tor
Quil n'i porent gueres durer
Car fort lor ert a endurer

.   .   .   .   .

C'est nuls nez, en ço n'a que dire,
Kar n'i a me[n]chonge ne gile,
Tels fu li gaaignz en la vile
Que li povr[e] qui voldrent prendre
Ne al gaaign voldrent entendre
Furent tuit en richece mis
De l'aveir a lor enemis.

L'Histoire de Guillaume le Maréchal.

ABRIDGED TRANSLATION

[The following day the young Marshall and the Earl of Salisbury went to Winchester and besieged the castle. . . . The young Marshall (William) and the Earl of Salisbury took up their quarters at Hyde Abbey, and besieged the city of Winchester. The first day they did little, but the second day they gave assault. That day the elder Marshall (William, Earl of Pembroke) sent them word to rejoin him without delay. . . . However, the garrisons of the castles (of Winchester) seeing that the English host had gone, made a sortie, sacked the town and set it on fire because the inhabitants had given shelter to their enemies. They could not, however, do all they would, because the host returned so suddenly that they were obliged to re-enter their castles. Unluckily, however, the inhabitants of the suburbs agreed with the garrison of the castle, which cost them dear. The Earl of Salisbury besieged and took the smaller of the two castles. The young Marshall besieged the larger, and during eight days pressed it so closely that the defenders dared neither take rest nor lay down their arms.

The Earl of Salisbury having taken the smaller castle hastened to the aid of the young Marshall, and both made such efforts that the garrison soon began to be discouraged. Further, the elder Marshall came with so great a host that country and town were filled by it. The castle defenders saw very well they could not resist much longer. . . . Winchester in the meantime surrendered, and so great a haul was made that the poor who wished to do so became rich through the booty of their enemies.]

AINZ s'en vint tot dreit a Wincestre
Dunt grant ennuis el cuer li germe
En poi de jors e en brief terme
Refist la tor & les murs hauz
Richement de p[i]ere e de chauz,
E totes les trebucheüres
Des murs & les desquasseüres
Fist ratorner fortes e beles,
Cum s'els fus[s]ent totes noveles.
Quant il se parti del chastel,
Qu'il out fait fort e boen e bel,
Lessa le conte de Nevers
Qui ert orguilos & porvers
O molt trés riche garnison,
Mes pu[i]s fist mainte mesprison
Que l'en li torna a [grant] honte,
Mes n'en vuil or ci tenir conte.

L'Histoire de Guillaume le Maréchal.

The King of France repairs the City Walls, April 1217

ABRIDGED TRANSLATION

[Louis of France went straight to Winchester, and in a little while he had repaired the tower and the high walls with stone and lime, and stopped up the breaches. He left the Comte de Nevers, a proud and cruel man, in the city, with a strong garrison. The Count afterwards committed many excesses, to his great shame, but I do not wish to speak of them here.]

**Fair
Winchester**

UNDER the Saxon Heptarchy this city, though pillaged more than once, recovered itself, became the palace of the Saxon kings, embellished with magnificent churches, was the see of a bishop, and had from King Ethelstan the privilege of six mints.   In the Norman times it increased considerably, and the archives or public records were kept here.   It continued in this flourishing state, except that it suffered by one or two accidental fires, and by the licentious soldiery during the civil wars between Stephen and Matilda.   Whence our Neckam,[1] who lived then, says of it :

> 'Guintoniam titulis claram gazisque repletam
> Noverunt veterum tempora prisca patrum,
> Sed jam sacra fames auri, jam caecus habendi
> Urbibus egregiis parcere nescit amor.'

> 'For wealth and state, for honour and renown,
> In antient times fair Winchester was known.
> In these degenerate days for gold our rage,
> The richest cities only can assuage.'

Edward III. relieved its distress by fixing here a market for cloth and wool, commonly called the *Staple*. What was the appearance of the city in those early times is not easy to say, since as Neckam goes on :

> '[Quam] flammis totiens gens aliena dedit.
> Hinc facies urbis totiens mutata, dolorem
> Praetendit, casus nuncia vera sui.'

> 'But hostile fire so oft has changed her face,
> Her ruins represent her piteous case.'

At present (*c.* 1586) it is well peopled, and watered by several cuts from the river.

Camden, *Britannia* (ed. Gough), i. 118.

**The days of
our fore-
fathers**

In the days of our forefathers, the gallant days of old,
When Cressy's wondrous tale in Europe's ears was told ;
When the brave and gentle prince, with his heroic peers,
Met France and all her knighthood in the vineyards of Poictiers ;

[1] See Alexander Neckam, *De Laudibus Divinae Sapientiae*, ed. Wright (Rolls Series), p. 459.

When captive kings on Edward's state right humbly did attend,
When England's chivalry began the gartered knee to bend ;
Then in the foremost place, among the noblest of the land,
Stood Wykeham, the great bishop, upon the king's right hand.

But when gracious Edward slept, and Richard wore the crown,
Forth came good William Wykeham, and meekly knelt him
    down.
Then out spake young King Richard: 'What boon can Wykeham
    ask,
Which can surpass his worth, or our bounty overtask ?
For art thou not our Chancellor ? and where in all the realm
Is a wiser man or better, to guide the labouring helm ?
And thou know'st the holy lore, and the mason's cunning skill.'

' I ask not wealth or honour,' the bishop lowly said,
' Too much of both thy grandsire's hand heaped on a poor monk's
    head :
This world is a weary load, it presses down my soul ;
Fain would I pay my vows, and to Heaven restore the whole
Grant me that two fair colleges, beneath thy charter sure,
At Oxford and at Winchester, for ever may endure,
Which Wykeham's hands shall raise upon the grassy sod,
In the name of Blessed Mary, and for the love of God.'

The King he sealed the charters, and Wykeham traced the plan,
And God who gave him wisdom, prospered the lowly man,
So two fair colleges arose, one in calm Oxford's glade,
And one where Itchen sparkles beneath the palm-tree shade.
There seventy true-born English boys he nourished year by year
In the nurture of good learning, and in God's holy fear ;
And gave them steadfast laws, and bade them never move,
Without sweet sign of fellowship, and gentle links of love.

They grew beside his pastoral throne, and kept his counsels sage,
And the good man rejoiced to bear such fruit in his old age :
He heard the pealing notes of praise, which morn and evening rung
Forth from their vaulted chapel, by their clear voices sung ;
His eye beheld them two by two their comely order keep,
Along the Minster's sacred aisles and up the beech-crowned steep ;
And when he went to his reward, they shed the pious tear,
And sang the hallowed requiem over his saintly bier.

Then came the dark and evil times, when English blood was shed
All over fertile England, for the White Rose or the Red ;
But still in Wykeham's Chapel the notes of praise were heard,
And still in Wykeham's College they taught the sacred Word ;
And in the grey of morning, on every saint's day still,
That black-gowned troop of brothers was winding up the hill :
There in the hollow trench, which the Danish pirate made,
Or through the broad encampment, the peaceful scholars played.

.   .   .   .

And after that when love grew cold and Christendom was rent,
And sinful churches laid them down in sackcloth to repent ;
When impious men bore sway, and wasted church and shrine,
And cloister and old abbey the works of men divine ;
Though upon all things sacred their robber-hands they laid,
They did not tear from Wykeham's gates the Blessed Mother-Maid :
But still in Wykeham's cloisters fair wisdom did increase,
And then his sons began to learn the golden songs of Greece.

And all through great Eliza's reign, those days of pomp and pride,
They kept the law of Wykeham, and did not swerve aside :
Still in their vaulted Chapel, and in the Minster fair,
And in their lamplit chambers, they said the frequent prayer :

And when the Scottish plague-spot ran withering through the
    land,
The sons of Wykeham knelt beneath meek Andrewes' fostering
    hand,
And none of all the faithless, who swore the unhallowed vow,
Drank of the crystal waters beneath the plane-tree bough.

Dread was the hour, but short as dread, when from the guarded
    down
Fierce Cromwell's rebel soldiery kept watch o'er Wykeham's
    town ;
Beneath their pointed cannon all Itchen's valley lay,
St. Catherine's breezy side, and the woodlands far away,
The huge Cathedral sleeping in venerable gloom,
The modest College tower, and the bedesman's Norman home.
They spoiled the graves of valiant men, warrior and saint and
    sage,
But at the grave of Wykeham, good angels quenched their rage.

Good angels still were there, when the base-hearted son
Of Charles, the royal martyr, his course of shame did run ;
Then in those cloisters holy, Ken strengthened with deeper
    prayer
His own and his dear scholars' souls to what pure souls should
    dare ;
Bold to rebuke enthroned sin with calm undazzled faith,
Whether amid the pomp of courts, or on the bed of death ;
Firm against kingly terrors in his free country's cause,
Faithful to God's anointed against a world's applause.

Since then, what wars and tumults, what change has Europe seen !
But never since in Itchen's Vale has war or tumult been ;
God's mercies have been with us, His favour still has blest
The memories sweet and glorious deeds of the good men at rest ;

The many prayers, the daily praise, the nurture in the Word,
Have not in vain ascended up before the gracious Lord.
Nations and thrones and reverend laws have melted like a dream ;
Yet Wykeham's works are green and fresh beside the crystal
    stream.

Four hundred years and fifty their rolling course have sped,
Since the first serge-clad scholar to Wykeham's feet was led ;
And still his seventy faithful boys, in these presumptuous days,
Learn the old truths, speak the old words, tread in the ancient
    ways :
Still for their daily orisons resounds the matin chime ;
Still linked in bands of brotherhood St. Catherine's steep they
    climb :
Still to their Sabbath worship they troop by Wykeham's tomb,
Still in the summer twilight sing their sweet song of home.

Verses by Roundell Palmer (first Earl Selbourne).

§ 4. TUDORS AND STUARTS

' What shall we do for a gay young Spaniard ?
What shall we do for a gay young Spaniard ?
Wooing a wife from England.'

[Winchester Pageant.]

The Spanish Marriage   ON the 23rd (July) he (Philip of Spain) left Hampton for Winchester, accompanied by many marquises, dukes, earls, and other lords and gentlemen, besides those from Spain, having with him upwards of a thousand horse. He dismounted at the cathedral, where he was received by six bishops, and next day he went to visit the Queen, who came to meet him at the large hall. On the 25th the espousal was celebrated with great pomp and rejoicing in the said church, with marvellous signs of great joy and satisfaction on the part of all the spectators ; and during this ceremony the marriage articles were confirmed and sworn to by the Prince, and the marriage was to be consummated that night.

There were present at the espousal the ambassadors from the Emperor, from the Kings of the Romans and Bohemia, from your Serenity, from Savoy, Florence, and Ferrara, and many agents of sovereign princes. The proclamation was entitled thus : Philip and Mary, by the grace of God, King and Queen of England, France, Naples, Jerusalem, Ireland, Defender of the Faith, Prince of Spain, Archduke of Austria, etc.

Cal. S. P. Venetian, vol. v. No. 923.

A WHILOM Mayor of Winchester was fortunate enough to have attained that position when Queen Elizabeth was visiting the city.[1] The Mayor was more celebrated for his virtues than for his grammar. ' Mr. Mayor,' said the Queen, ' yours is a very ancient city.' ' It has a-been, your Majesty, it has a-been,' replied the local dignitary. Good Queen Bess

Local Tradition.

' *Of the favorers and mislikers of the present estate of religion.*'

AND because the citie of Winchestre is moste noted in hamp- shiere either for good example or evill (all that bear aucthoritie there except one or two beinge addicte to thold supersticion and earnest fautores thereof), It should be well donne to associate for the commission in the sayde citye the Busshopp of Winton, Sir Henrye Seamour, William Uvedall, henrye Wallopp, John ffoster, and George Acworthy, the busshopps chauncelour, and for hedd officers there . . . non be appoynted unto nor continue to exercise anie of the . . . offices or callinges but they whose religion is approved, nor none likewise placed or displaced by one or two, but by common consent [of] the benche at some generall session, which will easelie drawe the common p[eople] to one good conformitye when they in aucthoritie goe all one waye, or do the not crosse or hinder the well doinges of another. 'Favorers of thold supersticion'

The Bishop of Winchester to the Privy Council,
13th November 1564.
Camden Miscellany (Camden Society), ix. 54-5.

---

[1] Elizabeth visited Winchester in 1560, 1569, 1574, and 1586, and pos- sibly also in 1591. See *The Wykehamist*, July 1912, pp. 30-1.

WESTERN CIRCUIT (AUTUMN), 1596

(i) *Rewards for Presents at Winchester sent to the Judges on circuit.*

Inprimis of Mr. Maior of Winton & his brethren,
  one mutton, one veale   .   .   . nil.

Of Mr. Norton, one bucke, the rewarde   . v^s

Of my Lo. Bishopp of Winton, one bucke   . v^s

Of Mr. Tichborne, two capons, iiij rabetts, and iiij
  pewetts, the rewarde   .   .   . xij^d

Of Mr. Fashion, one freshe samon   .   . xij^d

Of Mr. Kirby, one freshe samon and vj puetts, the
  rewarde   .   .   .   .   . xij^d

Of Sir Thomas Weste, one freshe samon and one
  samon-peale   .   .   .   . xii^d

Of Mr. Gifforde, one buck and six coople of
  conyes, the rewarde   .   .   . v^s

Of Mr. Sheriff,[1] half a buck & one freshe samon nil.

From the Colledge of Winton, one mutton, the
  rewarde   .   .   .   .   . vi^d

Of the Lord Marques of Winchester, one bucke,
  the rewarde   .   .   .   . v^s

Suma for p'sents at Winchester   .   . xxiiii^s vj^d

(ii) *Private Charges of Judges.*

Provision bought at Winchester :

Inp'mis three quarters of lambe   .   . iij^s ij^d

It. a rostinge-pigge   .   .   .   . xviii^d

It. for capers and olives   .   .   . vi^d

It. a strayner   .   .   .   .   . vi^d

It. two capons   .   .   .   . xxii^d

It. a quarter of veale   .   .   . ij^s iiij^d

It. for suett   .   .   .   .   . iiij^d

It. a neates foote & tripes   .   .   . vi^d

It. for two pulletts and viij chickings   . iij^s x^d

---

[1] Robert Oxenbridge, Esq., of Hurstborne.

It. for bread & flower, viz. iiij bushels & three
    pecks   .   .   .   .   xxvj[s] vj[d]

It. five barrells & one firkyn of beere, at v[s] the
    barrell   .   .   .   .   xxvij[s] vj[d]

It. wood & coles   .   .   .   xj[s]

It. butter, tenne pounds   .   .   iij[s] iiij[d]

It. for egges   .   .   .   .   xij[d]

It. for iiij chickings   .   .   .   xx[d]

It. salt & candles   .   .   .   xx[d]

It. peases   .   .   .   .   ii[s] vj[d]

It. a paire of calves feete   .   .   ij[d]

It. for bacon   .   .   .   .   vj[d]

It. yo[r] LL. chambers   .   .   .   xx[s]

It. to the butler   .   .   .   ij[s] vi[d]

It. to the helpes in the kitchen   .   iij[s] vj[d]

It. to the turnespit   .   .   .   xij[d]

It. to the porter   .   .   .   ii[s]

It. to M[r] White's man that waited   .   xij[d]

It. the grocer's bill   .   .   .   vj[s]

It. for wyne   .   .   .   .   vij[s]

Suma totalis of joynt chardges at Wynchester   .   vij[l] xvij[s] x[d]

Medietatis inde   .   .   .   .   iij[l] xviij[s] xi[d]

> Accounts of Thomas Walmysley, one of the Judges of the
> Court of Common Pleas, on his riding the Western
> Circuit with Edward Fenner, one of the Judges of the
> Queen's Bench (*Camden Miscellany*, vol. iv.).

September 17, 1603.

WE are now removing shortlie to Winchester, where we shall **Unwelcome visitors**
staie till we have also infected that place, as we have donne all
others where we have come. It is intended to give audience
there to the Spanishe Amb[r], who is gonne before wth other
Amb[rs] to lodge at Southampton.

> Sir Thomas Edmonds to the Earl of Shrewsbury from Woodstock.
> Nichols' *Progresses of James I.*, i. 271.

September , 1603.

Fear of the
Plague

. . . Our Treaty is not begonn, for y^t Sp. Emb. hath yet not had his audience by reason y^t ye Plague fell in his howse. On Sonday he comes to receave it at Wynchester, where the K. meanes to ly as long as ye Plague can escape us,[1] which drives us and down so rownd as I think we shall come to York. God bless the King ; for once a week one or other dyes in our Tentes.

Sir Robert Cecil to the Earl of Shrewsbury from Woodstock.
Nichols' *Progresses of James I.*, i. 272.

James I. at
Winchester

The King arrived at Winchester on the 20th of September [1603] ; and with the Queen (who went there two days before him) was received by the Mayor and Corporation with great solemnity ; and their Majesties were graciously pleased to accept two large silver cups, accompanied by the following speech from Sir John Moore, Recorder of that City :—

' If my tongue, the natural messenger off the heart and mynde, could soe lively expresse, most high & mighty Prince, & our most deere & dread Soveraigne, the exceeding joy and gladness of this your Highness ancient Citty of Winchester as they are sensably conceived within us all ; then needed I not, though the meanest off your Majestie's subjects, fearr to undergo the office of my place, & be the mouth of this politique body, a body consisting of many bodies, & yet relying onely upon one body, your sacred person, by whose happy entrance into this famous island, decreed & ordeyned by the God of Heaven, we finde & acknowledge ourselves possessours off our present felicity. . . . And let me presume, my dread Sovereigne, heare before your Majestie's feete, in the name & behalfe off all these grave Majestrates and Citizens off your Highnesse's auncient & in times past most famous City of Winchester, being sometimes the seate of your Majestie's Progenitors, the place off their Parliaments & sepulchers, the place of the Minte and Staple, whose now

[1] James remained at Winchester from September 20 to October 4, and was there again in November.

decayed walls and ruynous buildings presenting to your Majestie's view a desolation, are again re-edified with the joy & comfort of your Majestie's presence and access to this place; lett me, I say, presume to yield & give up unto your Highness all that we enjoy & possess under your Majestie & by your gracious permission, hoping that your Highness, off your clemency & goodness, will again restore unto us all our ancient liberties heretofore granted by your Highness' progenitors ratifyed & confirmed. . . . We your Citizens off your Highness ancient City of Winchester, in all obedient & dutyfull manner, & in all humbleness presume to present this cupp, most humbly beseeching your Royall Majestie to accept the faythfull hearts and good wills off your Highness poore Citizens off this City. . . .'

> Nichols' *Progresses of James I.*, i. 274-6, quoting
> Harl. MS. 852, p. 8.

In the month of November [1603] the City of Winchester became **The trial of Sir Walter Ralegh** the scene of much public business of great notoriety; and it was probably owing to the attachment of the High Sheriff (Sir Benjamin Tichborne) to the King's person and government, and the great interest which he was found to possess in the County, that when the rifeness of the Plague in London rendered it impossible to hold the Court of Justice there, his Majesty removed them to Winchester. He had previously sent orders to the Wardens, Fellows, and Students of the College to quit their respective apartments and offices, for a certain time, in order to make room for the judges and other Public officers who were appointed to lodge there; and he had provided the Episcopal Palace of Wolvesey for holding certain Courts therein.

By the middle of the month Winchester was crowded, not only with the Crown Officers, but also with the Peers of the Realm, and their several attendants; for now matters of the utmost importance were to be discussed, which equally required the attendance of the latter as of the former. This was no other than the trial of the pretended Conspirators, for what was called

Sir Walter Raleigh's Conspiracy; in which certain Noblemen, who, of course, were to be tried by their Peers were implicated, no less than persons of almost every other quality and description.

Nichols' *Progresses of James I.*

The scene of the trial

WHILST these transactions were carrying on, the eyes of the whole kingdom were directed towards Winchester, where the conflux of great personages, and the expenditure that this must have occasioned, exhibited some faint image of its former consequence.

Milner, *History of Winchester.*

The accused

IT is sayd that Sr W. Raleighe's arraynmět held from eight in the morninge till seven at night. That he caryed hym self both so temperate in all his answeres, and answered so wisely & readily to all objections, as it wrought both admiration in ye hearers for his good p^ts, and pitye towardes his ꝑson.

Michael Hickes to the Earl of Shrewsbury.
Nichols' *Progresses of James I.*

Winchester 'beares up her head'

WINCHESTER is a very famous & ancient citty, it was the Royall seat of the West Saxon Kings; it had 6 houses in it for coining & minting mony in the raigne of King Athelstane; & long since that all the publike Records & Evidences of the whole kingdom of England were kept there. This Citie hath been twice fired by sudden mis-fortunes; and in King Stephens raigne it was sack'd and spoil'd by rude soldiers that belong'd to the King, & Mawd the Empresse factions; but after it was much enrich'd by the royall favour of King Edward the 3, who caused a mart or staple of Wooll & Cloth to be kept there, but since (as times hath altred) this worthy city hath suffred many changes, yet still with Fame and Reputation she beares up her head.

John Taylor, the Water-poet.
A Catalogue of Tavernes in ten Shires, 1636.

THY reign, O Charles ! my Muse reluctant sings
And treats of rights of people, and of Kings ;

.   .   .   .

While by degrees the din extends afar
Of civic slaughter, and intestine war,
Thy walls, O Venta, feel th' internal rage,
The savage fury of this blinded age ;
Rous'd by the sparks of Freedom's sacred flame,
To aid in arms a British senate's fame,
Thy Castle's champion, Waller, calls to arms,
And eager quits retirement's wonted charms,
By zealous fury 'gainst his Monarch steel'd,
Erects his patriot standard in the field,

.   .   .   .

In vain the long-try'd Castle's sturdy rock
Oppos'd the chance of war, and brav'd the shock
Of foes, contending to direct the helm,
And wield the sceptre of the shaken realm ;
First round the walls the Royal leader mann'd
Each stubborn fortress with his trusty band,
High o'er the tow'r th' inviting standard wav'd,
And each attack of rebel fury brav'd,
But brav'd in vain ; the savage waste of war
Levell'd its turrets, left its ramparts bare,
And its first master gave the last destructive stroke.

John Wooll.
The King's House at Winchester, 1793.

WINCHESTER, *6th October* 1645.

I CAME to Winchester on the Lord's day the 28th of September.
. . . After some dispute with the Governor, we entered the
Town.   I summoned the Castle ; was denied ; whereupon we
fell to prepare batteries, which we could not perfect (some of
our guns being out of order) until Friday following.   Our battery
was six guns ; which being finished, after firing one round, I sent

in a second summons for a treaty; which they refused.   Whereupon we went on with our work, and made a breach in the wall
near the Black Tower; which after about 200 shot, we thought
stormable; and purposed on Monday morning to attempt it.
On Sunday night about ten of the clock, the Governor beat a
parley, desiring to treat.   I agreed unto it; and sent Colonel
Hammond and Major Harrison in to him, who agreed upon these
enclosed Articles.

Sir, this is the addition of another mercy.   You see God is
not weary in doing you good. . . .   His goodness in this is much
to be acknowledged: for the Castle was well manned with Six-
hundred-and-eighty horse and foot, there being near Two-
hundred gentlemen, officers, and their servants; well victualled,
with fifteen hundred-weight of cheese, very great store of wheat
and beer; near twenty barrels of powder, seven pieces of cannon;
the works were exceeding good and strong.   It's very likely it
would have cost much blood to have gained it by storm.   We
have not lost twelve men. . . .

Carlyle, *Oliver Cromwell's Letters*.

The Restora-
tion

AT Winchester, the mayor and aldermen, in their scarlet gowns,
met at the market cross, and went down to the cathedral, where
they heard a very loyal and eloquent sermon from Mr. Complin,
minister of Avington, near Winchester.   Marching thence into
the High Street the mayor with the rest of the corporation
ascended a scaffold, covered with a red cloth, and there solemnly
proclaimed King Charles.   The which ended, the musquetteers
gave a gallant volley; then, silence being commanded, the
remaining part of the cathedral singing-men, whereof Mr. Burt,
a gentleman of eighty years of age, was one, with the master of
the choirister and other musical gentlemen, sung a solemn
anthem, in a room built on purpose somewhat above the mayor's
scaffold, the words, 'O Lord, make thy servant Charles our
gracious King, to rejoice in thy strength,' etc.

Quoted in *The Winchester Guide*, 1796.

September 16, 1683.

THIS [an accidental fire at Newmarket] made the king more
earnest to render Winchester the seat of his autumnal field-
diversions for the future, designing a palace there, where the
ancient castle stood ; infinitely preferable to Newmarket for
prospects, air, pleasure and provisions. The surveyor has already
begun the foundation for a palace, estimated to cost £35,000,
and his Majesty is purchasing ground about it to make a park, etc.

Charles Il.'s Palace

Evelyn's *Diary*.

FROM the troubles of the state, and the noise of the Town,
  From being as busy as great,
From the tedious Pomp that attends on a Throne,
  To Quiet and Us you retreat.

Charles II.'s visit

Here you spend those soft hours in Princely delight
  Which alone do the recompense bring
For the business and cares which wait on the Great,
  For being so wise, so gracious a king.

Thus while the World was innocent and new,
  Gods, kind and bountiful, like you,
Tir'd with the long Fatigue of Majesty,
  Oft forsook their Thrones on high.

And to some humble Cell vouchsaf'd to go,
  And by their sweet Retreat below,
Bless'd both themselves and Mortals too.

Chorus

Welcome, great Sir, with all the joy
  That 's to your sacred presence due ;
With all the Mirth which we enjoy,
  That mirth which we derive from you.

D

Blest by your presence everything
   Does with new Vigour now appear.
Another fresh and blooming spring
   Seems to recall the aged Year.
The happy Hours, which hasten hither,
   Creep hence unwillingly and slow.
Time doubting stands, and knows not whether
   Nature to obey or You,
Yet might it your acceptance find,
   Each minute should for ever stay :
But see ! the Crowds which press behind
   Force the foremost Hours away.
Ceres for you would have reserv'd her store,
But for such greatness thought the sight too poor :
And not unjustly fear'd she might become,
By being too officious, troublesome.
And the God of our Art bids us come to salute you,
And begs you would kindly accept of our Duty :
But refus'd to assist us with his Divine Fires,
How should they want a God whom Your Presence inspires.

Chorus

Therefore we freely come to praise
You, the Author of our Joys ;
To own our happiness, and grow
Much more happy by doing so.
For Angels themselves, who are perfect in joys,
No more happiness know than this,
To see and adore, to love and to praise
The fountain of their bliss.

Thomas Fletcher.[1]
A Song to His Majesty at Winton, 1684.

---

[1] See below, p. 53, note.

On that same site, where once the castle stood,   **The new**
With many a Gothic arch and turret proud,   **creation**
How chang'd the scene, that meets the exile's eye !
How proud the new creation seems to rise !
Thy hand, O Wren ! portrays the vast design,
And its stupendous beauties all are thine.

Yet, ah ! in vain th' ingenious Master plies
His happiest skill, and each glad labour tries ;
In vain the eager sculptor boasts his art,
And proud mechanicks, ardent, take a part
To swell the triumphs of the royal dome,
Above the patterns of immortal Rome,
Death, unrelenting, breaks th' illusive spell,
And drags the Monarch to an humbler cell.

John Wooll.
The King's House, etc., 1793.

The monarch occupied with his splendid visions of fountains,   **Charles II.**
statues, and all the pomps of architectural decoration, seemed to **and Thomas**
forget—the lesson is, alas ! too seldom remembered—how soon **Ken**
the short-lived projectors of ' the gorgeous palaces ' may be
gathered to the dust on which they stand. Two magnificent
structures, crowning the valley of the Itchen, yet remain—the
Cathedral and the College ; and within a few years here stood the
wreck of this royal work ; the first venerable pile, from age to age,
call succeeding generations to the contemplation of far more
enduring scenes—the other is associated from age to age with
ideas of early piety and learning—the site and fragments of the
last remain to mock at human vanity, and the presumptuous
hopes of earth. Looking forward to length of days the thoughtless monarch now more frequently visited Winchester for oblivion
of public cares and often with different harlot-duchesses. It will
be anticipated that I am about to relate the well-known anecdote
of a beautiful courtesan, in humbler station, but no less a favoured

companion of his libertine hours.   Of the truth of this story there can be no doubt, for it is related by Hawkins, and we know that Hawkins recorded nothing of the life of Ken except what he received from the mouth of Ken himself, in his last days.   The kindness which the King had ever shown to this virtuous man forms one of the best traits in his character.   His own lodgings were mostly at the Deanery during his stay at Winchester.   A lodging at the adjoining prebendal residence of Ken was demanded for the King's favourite of the hour.   '*Not for his kingdom !*' was the virtuous reply.

The 'bowing' Dean (Dr. Meggot), horrified at the outrage on the principles of 'passive obedience,' was far more compliant. There is a small attached room,[1] built of brick at the end of the large drawing-room in the Deanery, from tradition called 'Nell Gwyn,' where it is supposed she lodged whilst the King was at the Deanery.

When many applications [for bishopric of Bath and Wells] the services of the Dean, Canon of Windsor, etc., were put forth, the King remarked, 'Odds fish ! who shall have Bath and Wells but the little fellow who would not give " poor Nelly " a lodging ? '

Of this unexpected elevation, in the dedication of his hymns to Hooper, Ken wrote :—

> 'Among the herdsmen, I, a common swain,
>   Liv'd pleas'd with my low cottage on the plain ;
>   Till up, like Amos, on a sudden caught,
>   I to the pastoral chair was trembling brought.'
>
> W. L. Bowles.
Life of Ken, ii. 54, etc.

'Like some
calm ghost'

To show our joy were but to bid you go ;
Such farewells are to parting Tyrants due,
To base, dull men, and all who are unlike to you.
Yet can we grieve, and wish you always here ?

[1] This brick appendage was taken down by Dean Reynell.

Mere envy that, and no less madness were,
Than to wish our Friends, who with th' Immortal reign
Themselves Immortal, here on Earth again.
Yet you vouchsafe to bless us with your stay,
And slowly hence even to Glory fly :
But smiling thro' these peaceful Shades you glide,
Like some calm Ghost where all his Treasure 's hid.

. . . .

When future times shall Wickham's offspring count,
Who did by steps the Seat of Honour mount,
Then, then shall you, and only you, be found,
Who reach'd a Mitre from so low a ground.
When others often pitch'd and stop'd for ease,
At one bold flight you gain'd the mighty Space ;
Thus all e'en the Uninteress'd admire
The glorious height you 've reached, and wish you high'r.

> From a poem by Thomas Fletcher,[1] written in 1685, ' To
> Thomas Ken, Lord Bishop of Bath and Wells, staying at
> Winton after his promotion.'

. . . OH ! if that day arrive,
And we, old friend, though bowed with age, survive,
How happy, whilst our days on earth shall last,
To pray and think of seasons that are past,

'In one
hallowed
pile'

[1] Fletcher wrote this and most of his other poems when a boy at Winchester College. In dedicating his *Poems on Several Occasions*, of which the above is one, to ' The Revd. William Harris, D.D., School-master of the College near Winton,' he writes : ' Many of these verses were written while I was under your care, and being the Product of Hours which I stole from the ordinary Business of your School, and employed otherwise than You directed; I am obliged to seize this only Opportunity which is left me, of making You restitution.' Further in his preface he tells the reader : ' I am afraid the Reader need not be informed that these are youthful Poems. I have now spent very little more than a third part of my threescore years and ten, and I was much younger when many of these poems were written.'

Till on our various ways the night shall close
And in one hallowed pile,[1] at last, our bones repose.

From W. L. Bowles' 'Morley's Farewell to the Cottage of
Izaak Walton,' among his Poems.

Izaak Walton HE ended his days on the fifteenth day of December 1683, in the great frost, at Winchester, in the house of Dr. William Hawkins, a prebendary of the church there, where he lies buried.

The Compleat Angler, ed. 1797. Preface.

September 16, 1685.

James II. at Winchester SETTING out early we arrived at Winchester to wait on the King, who was lodged at the Dean's (Dr. Meggott). . . . His Majesty was discoursing with the Bishop (of Bath and Wells) concerning miracles . . . the Bishop added a great miracle happening in Winchester to his certain knowledge, of a poor, miserably sick, and decrepit child (as I remember long kept unbaptized), who immediately on his baptism recovered. . . . I went out to see the new palace the late King had begun and brought almost to the covering. It is placed on the side of the hill where formerly stood the old castle. It is a stately fabric, of three sides and a corridor, all built of brick, and cornished, windows and columns at the west and entrance of freestone. It was intended for a hunting-house when his Majesty should come to these parts, and has an incomparable prospect. I believe there had already been £20,000 and more expended ; but his now Majesty did not seem to encourage the finishing it, at least for a while.

Evelyn's Diary.

§ 5. LATER DAYS

Thursday, October 11, 1770.

'A genteel congrega- tion' ABOUT eleven I preached at Winchester to a genteel and yet serious congregation.

John Wesley's Journal.

---

[1] Both Bishop Morley and Izaak Walton are buried in Winchester Cathedral : Walton ob. 1683, aged ninety ; Morley ob. 1684, aged eighty-seven.

Wednesday, October 6, 1780.

At eleven I preached in Winchester, where there are four thousand French
prisoners five hundred French prisoners. I was glad to find they have plenty of wholesome food ; and are treated, in all respects, with great humanity.

John Wesley's Journal.

The King and Queen set out from Windsor at one in the afternoon George III.
and Queen
Caroline at
Winchester
Sept. 28-30
1778 and arrived at Winchester camp at half after five. The light infantry lined the avenue from the camp [on Morn Hill] to Mr. Penton's house [in Eastgate Street] where their Majesties were lodged. Soon after their arrival, the mayor and corporation awaited upon his Majesty with the following elegant address :—

'*Most Gracious Sovereign,*

' The mayor, bailiffs, and commonalty of the city of Winchester, at all times eager to testify their loyalty to your Majesty, and their attachment to your illustrious family, most humbly approach your Majesty, to express their unfeigned joy at seeing, within the walls of this ancient city, a sovereign under whose government they experience so many and so extensive blessings,' etc. , . .

They were afterwards introduced to the Queen and addressed her Majesty.[1] . . .

The dean and prebends of Winchester also waited upon his Majesty, with the warden and fellows of the college and the two masters of the school.

The next day, at nine in the morning, their Majesties went from Mr. Penton's house to review the troops. The concourse of people assembled on this occasion was very great, which together with the fineness of the weather, made the whole a most pleasing scene. . . . On the 30th their Majesties were pleased to take a view of the cathedral, its antiquities, architecture, etc., and after-

[1] In the course of this speech they ' testify ' to the ' excess of their joy in being admitted to the presence of a princess possessed of every accomplishment which can adorn her sex, and graced with every virtue that can give lustre to her exalted position.'

wards to visit the college, where their Majesties were addressed in a Latin speech by Mr. Chamberlayne, son of William Chamberlayne, Esq., Solicitor of the Treasury, the senior scholar on the foundation, and fellow elect of New College, Oxford; and in English by the Earl of Shaftesbury. As soon as they returned they set off immediately for Salisbury. They ordered sums of money to be left for the poor, at the disposal of the mayor; for the three senior boys on the foundation, for the debtors in the prisons, and for other charitable purposes.

Gent. Mag., xlviii. 493-4.

March 1784.

Winchester Assizes

AT Winchester one and twenty prisoners were capitally convicted. There were 103 felons, the greatest number ever known.

Gent. Mag., liv. 224.

[For ten towns there were *eighty-eight* capital convictions in the Spring Assizes of 1784. Probably this was the result of the publication of Madan's *Thoughts on Executive Justice*.]

The City in 1829

OF the many inquiring visitors who annually bend their steps to this ancient and interesting city, not a few, it is fair to presume, are under the influence of that peculiar feeling, which derives its greatest enjoyment from the recollection of past occurrences and from the connexion of monuments of art with the history of former ages. ' Far from me and from my friends (said Dr. Johnson) be such frigid philosophy, as may conduct us indifferent and unmoved over any ground, which has been dignified by wisdom, bravery, or virtue.' And although the majority of these hoary relics with which Winchester once abounded, are either unblushingly consigned to destruction, as a source of individual profit, or immediately lapsing to decay, through the apathy of modern proprietors; yet monuments enough remain, with the ' smell of antiquity ' upon them amply to recompense the contemplative tourist for any portion of time he may choose to spend in their examination. For not to mention those which must ever remain inviolate, so long as existing institutions in church and state are upheld by the people—such as our immense and richly decorated cathedral, or our celebrated college, with its many beautiful appendages—he will find, in the noble ruins of Wolvesey Castle—in the Western and King's Gates—in the Guildhall and City Cross as in the ancient chapel of St. Stephen— in the kingly and episcopal Palaces—in the hospitals of St. John and St. Cross—in the old Roman defences upon Catherine Hill, and in the republican post immediately facing it, called ' Oliver's Battery,' many pleasing sources of retrospective instruction.

Historical and Descriptive Guide to Winchester, 1829.

I SUPPOSE that Winchester would be considered rather a war-like city now ; it is a garrison town, it is the centre of a splendid militia, and stout yeomen (descendants of the ' hynen stalworthe ' of old) annually display their skilled horsemanship about its streets, it boasts an excellent rifle corps, and is proud to be represented by a member of military style. Well, the citizens may claim this warlike character as an acquisition of their own ; for unless it has, so to say, skipped over a generation, and they are now reproducing the citizens of the fifth or sixth centuries, whose highest pleasure was to ' quaff strong ale out of the skulls of their slaughtered enemies,' the citizen of Winchester in old days was not a very war-loving person. In a great invasion of Wessex in 1006 the Danes passed close by the gates of Winchester displaying in triumph to its inhabitants the spoils of the inland shires. The citizens made no attempt to cut them off, but submitted in silence to their insults. Backward, however, as they were to meet the enemy in the field, they were forward enough to cut him off by treachery ; and Winchester won an evil celebrity by having begun the general massacre of the Danes, and commenced the shocking Hocktide sports. And again, when William the Conqueror sent a demand for submission to the city, no resistance was attempted. Eadgyth, the ' old lady,' Harold's

A Warlike City

mother, who held the city, took counsel with the chief men, who, remembering that discretion is the chief part of valour, prudently added large gifts to an immediate offer of surrender. During Stephen's reign the 'poor, prudent, faint-hearted citizens' had a rough time of it ; and we can well understand the joy of the chronicler when he exclaims, 'Oh, how blessed was the day, when the illustrious youth Henry was received and conducted by the King himself in a solemn procession of mitred prelates and armed heroes through the streets of Winchester, amidst the joyous acclamations of an infinite multitude of people ! '

'Winchester in Olden Times,' in *The Wykehamist*, June 1, 1876.

A Winchester   . . . SOME of the town [Bedwin] treated your Lordship as the
Surgeon   surgeon did Mr. Bridges at Winchester, who had bruised only his toe, and with fair practice it might have been soon cured, but the surgeon applied contrary salves on purpose to make it appear a great and difficult cure, and let it go so far that he could not retrieve it, and though he did not design it at first yet he destroyed the gentleman, who lost his life by it.

1714, December 3.   C. Beecher to Lord Bruce, *Hist. MSS. Com.*
(Marquess of Ailesbury's MSS.), p. 220.

A poetical   IT was during my last year at Winchester that I made my first
prologue   attempt at authorship.   Old Robbins, the grey-headed book-seller of College Street, who had been the college bookseller for many years, had recently taken a younger partner of the name of Wheeler, and this gentleman established a monthly magazine called the *Hampshire and West of England Magazine*, to which I contributed. . . . The Rev. E. Poulter, one of the prebendaries of Winchester, who had a somewhat wider than local reputation as a wit in those days, was the anonymous contributor of a poetical prologue of such unconscionable proportions that poor Wheeler was sadly puzzled what to do with it.   It was impossible to refuse or neglect a reverend prebendary's contribution, besides that the

verses, often doggerel, had some good fun in them. So they were all printed by instalments in successive numbers, despite the title of prologue which their author gives them.

T. A. Trollope.
What I Remember, i. 148.
R. Bentley and Son, 1887.

WE have no Grub Street in our learned city ;   'No nursery of fools'
Winchester is no nursery of fools,
But seat of chapter, college, clergy, schools ;
To which, if universities we add,
Our firm, how small soe'er the help thence had,
Will still remain some good, indiff'rent some, some bad ;
Western our circuit, Winchester our sessions,
From whence we make *diversions* and digressions,
Of which the last at least, this wand'ring 's one,
With more, were better ended than begun.

From ' Poetical Prologue ' to *Wheeler's Hampshire Magazine*, 1828.

FROM your Castalia's to our Itchin's rill,   To the Muses
From your Parnassus to our Cath'rine Hill,
On which you most may take delight to rove,
Surmounted with its Academic grove,
Thither to lead the scholars of the College,
Inspire them with your genius, taste, and knowledge ;
Or to St. Cross's Pegaseian fount,
Or Oliver's, for your Pierian mount ;
Or to the distant *Horse-shoe* hills, if true,
The *Hippocrene* of Hampshire there we view.
On which of these 'tis your delight to wander,
On banks of Itchin, or your own Meander—
May you on us, the suitors of the town,
Your vot'ries, if not fav'rites, look down !

For should it your wise mightinesses suit,
As your own Orpheus tam'd the Grecian brute,
You may enlighten our dark civic cit,
And bless Boetian plains with Attic wit.

From 'Poetical Prologue' to *Wheeler's Hampshire Magazine*, 1828.

The coming of the Prince of Wales [Edward VII.]

THE venerable city of Winchester is working itself up into very unwonted excitement. Coming into it to-day straight out of the hurly-burly of London, and strolling down its quaint old streets through the Cathedral Close, and out into the College grounds, I thought it looked exceedingly pleasant, and for all its babbling excitement wonderfully restful and placid. . . . The mayor has posted the town with bills referring to the arrival of the Prince of Wales, specifying the route he will take from the station to the College, and intimating that the mayor will deem it a great favour if householders along the route will decorate their fronts, and thus give a loyal welcome to the illustrious guest. The citizens seem to be responding heartily. The shops are trying to look busy, and the hotels are full. But for all its strenuous activity there is an air of slumbering peace about the old place with its 'meads' and its gardens and its grand old cathedral and venerable trees, that it looks as though hardly anything could very greatly disturb.

Daily News, July 25, 1893.

George V. and Queen Mary at Winchester

'It is a great pleasure to us to visit your famous city and ancient capital of this country, and I am glad to remember its close associations with so many of my ancestors. Few cities can claim to have played so notable a part in the early history of this realm, and your citizens may feel just pride in the memories of the past brought constantly before them by the many old buildings which are still happily preserved to adorn your beautiful city.'

The King's reply to the Mayoral Address.
July 15, 1912.

TOPOGRAPHY

§ 1. GREY CITY OF ETERNAL TOWERS

WINCHESTER

To R. D. B.

O MOTHER of our golden hours,
Grey city of eternal towers,
Begirt with legendary walls,
Lit with a fitful light that falls
Aslant through mist and veiling rain ;
As first we saw you, once again
The memory of you rises clear,
Distant indeed, but not less dear,
And through the waste of space and time, in visions always near.

Mother of longings and desires,
Dim city of immortal spires,
And leafless, silver trees, and woods
Where the long winter silence broods,
Upon whose stillness breaks alone
The languorous, slow monotone
Of some deep-voiced, regretful bell,
Swinging reluctantly to tell
His ancient message, and to breathe his old melodious spell.

Mother of memories and dreams,
Pale city of slow-flowing streams
That down a narrow channel wind,
More white than pearl, and emerald-lined,

61

Where vivid mosses turn and sway
Their restless arms to meet the day.
City of dreams that drowsily
Glide southward in a reverie,
And float their idle secrets down in whispers to the sea.

Mother of marvel and delight,
Rich city of enchanted night,
Prisoned behind whose darkened bars
Quiver a phantom host of stars,
While spectral shadows dimly sweep
Your sombre cloisters, dear to sleep,
And through the slender tracery
A winter moon looks lovingly,
As though she longed to stoop and leave her palace of the sky.

Mother of melodies and songs,
To whom the meed of verse belongs,
Whose beauty woke the heart and smote
From Collins' lyre a tender note,
And won a dearer spirit yet
Whose star will never fade or set,
Lionel, who left not all his days
Songs for the singing of your praise,
But ever at your altar laid his proud immortal bays.

Poems by Griffith Fairfax.
Smith, Elder and Co., 1908.

'Pillowed on
meadow and
hill'

PALE with ten centuries burden,
    Pillowed on meadow and hill,
Stands, England's past as her guerdon,
    England's prime Citadel still.
Hard by where clear streamlets embower
    Chapel and Chamber and Court,
Graced with youth's magical dower,
    Heirs of futurity sport.

The soft moon smiles on the city
    And kisses its minster grey :
The spirits troop from the churchyard,
    Shunning the glamour of day.
Saxon and Dane and Norman,
    King, lord, and prelate proud ;
Chaste dame, and fair pale damsel,
    Through the crumbling gateways crowd.
And the mist with the dawn uprising,
    The ghostly pageant enshroud !

        Song by C. H. H. in *The Wykehamist*, July, 1893.

WITH respect . . . to the site of Winchester . . . it is one of the best adapted spots in the kingdom for the residence of the human species ; as, in fact, it is one of the first that was inhabited upon the peopling of our island.

One of the first to be peopled

        Milner, *History of Winchester*, 1798.

EAST and west the hills (though then unspoilt by buildings) rose above the town ; then, as now, the Itchen divided the low flat water meadows with many a silver thread ; and then, as now, St. Catherine's Hill—a spur from the long down—looked like an isolated sentry keeping guard outside the ancient capital lest any foe should come up the valley from Southampton Water ; only, instead of being crowned with a clump of trees, it was then consecrated by a small chapel (the foundations of which can still be discerned on the uneven grass), but which, disendowed by Cardinal Wolsey, was in the seventeenth century allowed to fall into decay.

Fourteenth-century Winchester

        A. R. Bramston and A. C. Leroy.
            A City of Memories.
          P. and G. Wells, 1893.

ME lyketh ever, the lengerè the bet,
By Wyngester, that joly citè.
The ton is god and wel y-set,
The folk is comely on to see ;

'That joly cite'

The aier is god both inne and oute,
The citè stent under an hille ;
The riverès renneth all aboute,
The ton is ruelèd upon skille.

Benedicamus Domino,

Alleluia,

Alleluia.

De Walden MSS.   Fifteenth-century verses.

'A body with-
out a soul'

ON Thursday the 21st of August [1623] I took Winchester in my
way homewards, where I saw an ancient city, like a body without
a soul; and I know not the reason of it, but for ought which I perceived, there were almost as many parishes as people.   I lodged
at the sign of the Cock, being recommended to the host of the
house by a token from Salisbury ; but mine host died the night
before I came, and I, being weary, had more mind to go to bed
than to follow him so long a journey, to do my message or deliver
any commendations.   But the whole city seemed almost as
dead as mine host, and it may be they were all at harvest work.
But I am sure I walked from one end of it to the other, and saw
not thirty people of all sorts.   So that I think if a man should go
to Winchester for a goose, he might lose his labour, for a trader
cannot live there by vending such commodities.

John Taylor, the Water-poet.
*A New Discovery by Sea with a Wherry from
London to Salisbury*, 1623.

'In a
pleasant
bottom'
(*c.* 1662)

WINCHESTER, about thirty miles from Abingdon, the chief and
only city in Hampshire, is the next eminent place in the road
to Southampton, whose situation is in a pleasant bottom by a
sweet river running among the hills.   It is strongly immured
with deep trenches, the wall that ingirts it containing two
English miles or more.   It has a castle, but now almost demolished.   It has also seven gates and seven churches, besides
that stately ancient fabrick, the Cathedral, under whose vault
do rest the bones of divers kings, some of whose bodies lie in

chests of stone upon the high altar.   Those sepulchres since the King's restoration have been beautified and adorned with colour, the oversight of these and other reparations in the church being left to the care of my worthy friend, Dr. Dayrell, one of the prebends, who has here built for himself and his succeeding prebends a very fair house ; he has also belonging to it a very fine garden, on one side of which there is such a wall of flint as for height the like is not to be seen.   At the west end of the choir— to which there is a fair ascent—did stand in brass the effigies of King James and Charles the First, but before our return—we then going a voyage to Newfoundland a few weeks after the beheading of the King—they were pulled down, but since have been set up again.   Here is erected by the present Bishop Morley near the church a good alms-house for such clergymen widows as stood in need of his charity.   This city has been formerly adorned with nine churches whose ruins are now scarce discernible ; but at the west end of the Cathedral there still remains some part of a heathen temple ; 'tis a great thick piece of wall built of lime and flint, now more like a natural work than any artificial workman-ship, 'tis so strong cemented.   And as touching the walls of the city, being built with the same materials, when any part has fallen, it lies like rocks several yards in length without separating, so skilful were they in former times in this sort of building. . . .

Here is now kept one of the most famous schools in England, from whence do yearly go some hopeful scholars to New College in Oxon.

Half a mile without Winchester in the way towards Hampton whither we are now going, doth stand St. Cross's church and hospital being endowed with good revenues.

Hist. MSS. Com. (Duke of Portland MSS.), ii. 286.

As to the town itself, the Buildings are not magnificent, but there appears such an Air of Antiquity in them, as makes them venerable.   The Streets are broad and clean enough, and the Situation healthy and pleasant, being in a Valley between two

'An Air of Antiquity'

very steep Hills, which defend it from cold Airs and boisterous Winds.   The River *Itching* runs on the Borders of it.

Magna Britannia (ed. 1720), ii. 857.

Looking
from 'Hills'

At Juvenis, cui sunt meliores pectore sensus,
Cui cordi rerum species, et daedalus ordo,
Et tumultum capit, et sublimi vertice solus,
Quae late patuere, oculos fert singula circum.
Colle ex opposito, flaventi campus aristâ
Aureus, adversoque refulgent jugera sole :
At procul obscuri fluctus, et rura remotis
Indiciis, et disjunctae juga caerula Vectae :
Sub pedibus, perfusa uligine pascua dulci,
Et tenues rivi, et sparsis frondentia Tempe
Arboribus, saxoque rudi venerabile templum
Apparet, mediâ riguae convallis in umbrâ.
Turritum, a dextrâ, patulis caput extulit ulmis
Wiccamici domus alma chori, notissima Musis :
Nec procul ampla aedes, et eodem laeta patrono,
Ingens delubrum, centum sublime fenestris,
Erigitur, magnâque micant fastigia mole.
Hinc atque hinc extat vetus Urbs, olim inclyta bello,
Et muri disjecti, et propugnacula lapsa ;
Infectique Lares, laevisque palatia ducta
Auspiciis.   Nequeunt expleri corda tuendo,
Et tacitam permulcet imago plurima mentem.

Mons Catharinae, by Thomas Warton.

The Second
Earl of
Oxford at
Winchester

After these views [of the city and its sights] we returned to our inn, very hungry, very wet, and very cold, for it was a drizzling rain all day.   We had a very good dinner and a fish which is much prized and valued called a surmullet, but I did not like it; we had most excellent whitings.   I wish this poor narration may give you the thousandth part of the pleasure my dinner did me, and then it will be very well.   Thus ended Tuesday, October 24, 1738.

Wednesday, October 24, 1738.—We set out in the morning which was fine, and the remainder of the day proved so, and went to pay a visit and dine with my Lady Peterborough at her house at Mount Bevis according to her most kind invitation. We were extremely well entertained in all respects, but the most agreeable part was her conversation and cheerful behaviour, and genteel civility.   We walked over the garden which was still new to me and most delightful, but the cross tide would not come up. I was very sorry that we could stay no longer, but the days were short and the ways not very good towards Winchester, but we were very thankful for the time and pleasure we had.   I thank God we got safe to Winchester just as it grew dark.

If you remember there was about two miles from Mount Bevis towards Winchester a sort of a pavilion upon the brow of a hill which you took for Mr. Holman's, but it is Colonel Fleming's that married a Crowley. . . . While I was at Winchester I did not hear one word of my old acquaintances, nor set eyes on them the day I walked over Winchester, and was in the school too, but the morning before I went to Mount Bevis, came some strange young gentlemen quite strangers to me, with their humble service and desired I would beg them a play.   I sent them my service and that I begged their excuse for I could not possibly do it.   Now just as I was going into my chariot on Thursday to go for Salisbury I sent Rawlings with my service to Master Brudnells Master Tryons, desired to know how they did, and also to Master Bathurst that I wondered I had not seen him, being two days in Winchester.   He said he was very sorry for it, but he heard I was gone out of town.   Now my design was that as he had sent the young gentlemen to me, they should understand that if he had come himself I would have granted their request.   Rawlings went to the school, they all flocked about him, were in hopes he came for a play, but blank was the word.

A Journey through Hampshire, in the handwriting of the
second Earl of Oxford, apparently addressed to his wife.
Hist. MSS. Com. (Duke of Portland's MSS.).

STRAWBERRY HILL, *September* 18, 1755.

Horace Walpole disappointed

. . . I WAS disappointed in Winchester : it is a paltry town and small : King Charles the Second's house is the worst thing I ever saw of Sir Christopher Wren, a mixture of a town-hall and an hospital ; not to mention the bad choice of the situation in such a country ; it is all *ups* that should be *downs*.   I talk to you as supposing that you never have been at Winchester, though I suspect you have, for the entrance of the cathedral is the very idea of that of Mabland.

Horace Walpole to Richard Bentley.
Letters (Clarendon Press ed.), iii. 341.

Dr. Johnson at Winchester

THE same year [1778 according to Boswell, 1777 according to Charlotte Burney] Dr. Johnson not only wrote to Dr. Joseph Warton in favour of Dr. Burney's youngest son [Richard], who was to be placed in the college of Winchester, but accompanied him when he went thither.

Boswell's *Life of Johnson*.

[Dr. Johnson had before visited Winchester in 1765 on his way to Devonshire with Reynolds (Leslie and Taylor, *Life of Reynolds*, i. 214), and writing to Dr. Warton in 1765 he says : ' Mrs. Warton uses me hardly in supposing that I could forget so much kindness as she showed me at Winchester.   I remember, likewise, our conversation about St. Cross ' (Wooll's *Warton*, p. 309).   In September 1770 he wrote to Dr. Warton : ' Make my compliments to Mrs. Warton.   I sometimes think of wandering for a few days to Winchester, but am apt to delay ' (Boswell's *Life of Johnson*). Concerning the letter which Johnson wrote on behalf of Dick Burney, Mrs. Piozzi tells us how she had ' teized him many weeks to write a recommendatory letter of a little boy to his school-master ; and after he had faithfully promised to do this prodigi-ous feat before we met again—" Do not forget dear Dick, sir," said I, as he went out of the coach ; he turned back, stood two minutes on the carriage step—" When I have written my letter for Dick, I may hang myself, mayn't I?" and turned away in a very ill humour indeed' (*Anecdotes of Dr. Johnson*, ed. 1786). Further, Charlotte Burney tells us that Mrs. Thrale had 'interisted herself so much in regard to getting little Dick to Winchester school (where he went on Tuesday last) that she has seemed to think of nothing else, and has not only made him a present of a piece of fine holland to set him up in shirts with but has likewise furnished him with an intire set of school books' (F. Burney, *Early Diary*, ed. Ellis).]

IN May 1817 she was persuaded to remove to Winchester for the sake of medical advice from Mr. Lydford. . . . Jane and her sister Cassandra took lodgings in College Street. . . . It was shortly after settling in these lodgings that she wrote to a nephew the following characteristic letter :—

Jane Austen in College Street

> 'MR. DAVID'S, COLLEGE ST., WINTON.
> *Tuesday, May 27th.*

' . . . Mr. Lydford says he will cure me, and if he fails, I shall draw up a memorial and lay it before the Dean and Chapter, and have no doubt of redress from that pious, learned, and disinterested body. Our lodgings are very comfortable. We have a neat little drawing-room with a bow window overlooking Dr. Gabell's garden.' [1]

> *A Memoir of Jane Austen*, by J. E. Austen-Leigh.
> Richard Bentley, 1870.

EVENING ON HILLS

HERE where the legendary height
Is plumed with beech and pine
And the dim shadows lengthen, and the streams
Wane to the southward in the waning light
And the skies grow from dreamy to divine,

Keats at Winchester

---

[1] The little low house with its characteristic bow window is a well-known feature of College Street. After Jane Austen's day it was long sacred to La Croix ('Octo') and his ices and pastries.

Here for five hundred years
Have lived their little life Youth's hopes and fears,
   Here, in the land of Dreams.

.   .   .   .

And one, who was not of us, here had past,
Diana's kiss yet newly on his brow,
And the great song, he knew not for the last,
Still on his lips ; he saw the autumn glow
On the low sallows, on the ' hilly bourn,'
And sang full-voiced—alas ! he could not know
What shade, more dark than Autumn's shortening day,
Was closing round him, not to pass away :
It crept between him and his love forlorn,
And hung a viewless veil 'twixt him and home,
   And tracked him o'er the foam,
Till, under southern skies, mid vernal breath,
   It gathered and was Death,
And gave him peace, and one more memory to Rome !
Surely his nightingale it was that sang
Last May, when all the thicket rang
With the old echoes of the Daulian height,
   Till, at the noon of night,
Sleep taught sweet silence to the singing-bird
   And scarce the reed-grass stirred.

                     E. D. A. Morsehead.
               Winchester College, 1393-1893.
                  Edward Arnold, 1893.

                WINCHESTER, *August* 15, 1819.

'An exceed-ing pleasant town' WE removed to Winchester for the convenience of a library, and find it an exceeding pleasant town, enriched with a beautiful cathedral, and surrounded by a fresh-looking country. We are in tolerably good and cheap lodgings.

                John Keats to Benjamin Bailey.
                 Letters of John Keats.
                Macmillan and Co., 1891.

WINCHESTER, *August* 28, 1819.

. . . IT is more than a fortnight since I left Shanklin chiefly for the purpose of being near a tolerable library, which, after all, is not to be found in this place. However, we like it very much : it is the pleasantest town I ever was in, and has the most recommendations of any. There is a fine Cathedral which to me is always a source of amusement, part of it built fourteen hundred years ago ; and the more modern by a magnificent Man, you may have read of in our history, called William of Wickham. The whole town is beautifully wooded. From the hill at the eastern extremity you see a prospect of Streets, and old Buildings mixed up with Trees. Then there are the most beautiful streams about I ever saw—full of Trout. There is the Foundation of St. Croix about half a mile in the fields—a charity greatly abused. We have a Collegiate School, a Roman Catholic School ; a chapel ditto and a Nunnery ! And what improves it all is, the fashionable inhabitants are all gone to Southampton. We are quiet—except a fiddle that now and then goes like a gimlet through my Ears—our Landlady's son not being quite a Proficient. I have still been hard at work, having completed a Tragedy I think I spoke of to you. . . . For all I can guess I shall remain here till the middle of October. . . . My greatest regret is that I have not been well enough to bathe though I . . . live now close to delicious bathing. . . .

> John Keats to Fanny Keats.
> *Letters of John Keats.*
> Macmillan and Co., 1891.

'The pleasantest town I was ever in'

WINCHESTER, *September* 5, 1819.

. . . SINCE I have been here at Winchester I have been improving in health—it is not so confined—and there is on one side of the City a dry chalky down, where the air is worth Sixpence a pint. . . . Brown likes the tragedy very much. . . . I hope you will then not think my labour misspent. Since I finished it, I have

'Sixpence a pint'

finished *Lamia*, and am now occupied in revising *St. Agnes's Eve*, and studying Italian. . . .

John Keats to John Taylor.
Letters of John Keats.
Macmillan and Co., 1891.

Saturday, September 18, 1819.

'Not one loom'

THIS Winchester is a place tolerably well suited to me.   There is a fine cathedral, a college, a Roman Catholic chapel, a Methodist do., and Independent do. ; and there is not one loom, or anything like manufacturing beyond bread and butter, in the whole city. There are a number of rich Catholics in the place.   It is a respectable, ancient, aristocratic place, and moreover it contains a nunnery.

John Keats to George and Georgiana Keats.
Letters of John Keats.
Macmillan and Co., 1891.

Monday, September 20, 1819.

The Eve of St. Mark

THIS day is a grand day for Winchester.   They elect the mayor. It was indeed high time the place should have some sort of excitement.   There was nothing going on—all asleep.   Not an old maid's sedan returning from a card-party ; and if any old women have got tipsy at christenings, they have not exposed themselves in the street.   The first night, though, of our arrival here there was a slight uproar took place at about ten of the clock.   We heard distinctly a noise patting down the street, as of a walking-cane of the good old dowager breed ; and a little minute after we heard a less voice observe, 'What a noise the ferril made—it must be loose.'   Brown wanted to call the constables, but I observed it was only a little breeze, and would soon pass over. . . . He ! He ! There is none of your Lady Bellaston ringing and rapping here ; no thundering Jupiter-footmen, no opera-treble tattoos, but a modest lifting up of the knocker by a set of little wee old fingers that peep through the grey mittens and a dying fall thereof.   The great beauty of poetry is that it makes everything in every place interesting.

The palatine Venice and the abbotine Winchester are equally interesting. Some time since I began a poem called ' The Eve of St. Mark,' quite in the spirit of quietude. I think I will give you the sensation of walking about an old country town in a coolish evening. I know not whether I shall ever finish it ; I will give it as far as I have gone. Ut tibi placeat :—

The Eve of St. Mark

Upon a Sabbath-day it fell ;
Twice holy was the Sabbath-bell,
That call'd the folk to evening prayer ;
The city streets were clean and fair
From wholesome drench of April rains ;
And, when on western window panes,
The chilly sunset faintly told
Of unmatured green vallies cold,
Of the green thorny bloomless hedge,
Of rivers new with spring-tide sedge,
Of primroses by shelter'd rills,
And daisies on the aguish hills,
Twice holy was the Sabbath-bell :
The silent streets were crowded well
With staid and pious companies,
Warm from their fireside orat'ries ;
And moving, with demurest air,
To even-song, and vesper prayer.
Each arched porch, and entry low,
Was fill'd with patient folk and slow,
With whispers hush, and shuffling feet,
While play'd the organ loud and sweet.

Bertha was a maiden fair,
Dwelling in the old Minster-square ;
From her fireside she could see,
Sidelong, its rich antiquity,

Far as the Bishop's garden-wall,
Where sycamores and elm-trees tall,
Full-leav'd the forest had outstript,
By no sharp north-wind ever nipt,
So shelter'd by the mighty pile.
Bertha arose, and read awhile,
With forehead 'gainst the window-pane.
Again she try'd, and then again,
Until the dusk eve left her dark
Upon the legend of St. Mark.
From plaited lawn-frill, fine and thin,
She lifted up her soft warm chin,
With aching neck and swimming eyes,
And dazed with saintly imageries.
All was gloom, and silent all,
Save now and then the still footfall
Of one returning homewards late,
Past the echoing minster-gate.
The clamorous daws, that all the day
Above tree-tops and towers play,
Pair by pair had gone to rest,
Each in ancient belfry-nest,
Where asleep they fall betimes,
To music and the drowsy chimes.

          John Keats to George and Georgiana Keats.
                 Letters of John Keats.
              Macmillan and Co., 1891.

A daily walk

I TAKE a walk every day for an hour before dinner, and this is generally my walk : I go out the back gate, across one street into the cathedral yard, which is always interesting ; there I pass under the trees along a paved path, pass the beautiful front of the cathedral, turn to the left under a stone doorway—then I am on the other side of the building—which, leaving behind me, I pass on through two college-like squares, seemingly built for the dwelling-place of deans and prebendaries, garnished with grass and shaded with trees ; then I pass through one of the old city gates, and then you are in one college street, through which I pass, and at the end thereof crossing some meadows, and at last a country alley of gardens, I arrive, that is my worship arrives, at the foundation of St. Cross, which is a very interesting old place, both for its Gothic tower and alms square and for the appropriation of its rich rents to a relation of the Bishop of Winchester. Then I pass across St. Cross meadows till you come to the most beautifully clear river—now this is only one mile of my walk. I will spare you the other two till after supper, when they would do you more good. You must avoid going the first mile best after dinner.

John Keats to George and Georgiana Keats.
Letters of John Keats.
Macmillan and Co., 1891.

WINCHESTER, *September* 22, 1819.

THE side streets here are excessively maiden-lady-like : the door-steps always fresh from the flannel. The knockers have a staid, serious, nay almost awful quietness about them. I never saw so quiet a collection of Lions' and Rams' heads. The doors are for the most part black, with a little brass handle just above the keyhole, so that in Winchester a man may very quietly shut himself out of his own house. How beautiful the season is now. How fine the air. A temperate sharpness about it. Really, without joking, chaste weather—Dian skies—I never liked stubble-fields so much as now—Aye, better than the chilly green of the Spring. Somehow, a stubble-field looks warm—in the same way that some pictures look warm. This struck me so much in my Sunday's walk that I composed upon it (e.g. *The Ode to Autumn*).

'Maiden-lady-like'

John Keats to Reynolds.
Letters of John Keats.
Macmillan and Co., 1891.

I CAME to this place in hopes of meeting with a Library, but was disappointed. The High Street is as quiet as a Lamb. The

'As quiet as a Lamb'

knockers are dieted to three raps per diem.   The walks about are
interesting from the many old buildings and archways.   The
view of the High Street through the Gate of the City in the
beautiful September evening light has amused me frequently.
The bad singing of the Cathedral I do not care to smoke—being
by myself I am not very coy in my taste.   At St. Cross there is
an interesting picture of Albert Dürer's—who living in such warlike times perhaps was forced to paint in his Gauntlets—so we
must make all allowances.

John Keats to Haydon, October 3, 1819.

Letters of John Keats.

Published by Macmillan and Co., 1891.

**'Winchester
stubble-
fields'**

LOOKING down from this old West Gate a-top of the High Street,
'tis pleasant to see at the street's end a green hill rising bold and
steep.   Many a cheerful country walk stretches out from this
ancient city ; through the meadows, with clear streams full of
gliding fish and waving weeds, across little bridges, by willows
and mills ; over breezy chalk-downs, wide-viewing, with farms
and hamlets in their vales ; by shady roads and field-paths
through the corn and clover.   Here wandered once on a time,
solitary and somewhat sad, a certain young poet—now for ever
young.   In these fields, one Sunday, among the corn-stacks
and orchards, he felt and sung the rich sadness of autumn.
' How beautiful the season is now,' he wrote to his friend Reynolds, 22nd September 1819, ' how fine the air—a temperate
sharpness about it.   Really, without joking, chaste weather—
Dian skies.   I never liked stubble-fields so much as now—ay,
better than the chilly green of Spring.   Somehow a stubble-
field looks warm in the same way that some pictures look warm.
This struck me so much in my Sunday's walk that I composed
upon it.'

' Seasons of mists and mellow fruitfulness ! . . .

Where are the songs of spring ?   Ay, where are they ?
  Think not of them, thou hast thy music too,
While barrèd clouds bloom the soft-dying day,
  And touch the stubble-plains with rosy hue.

Then in a wailful choir the small gnats mourn,
  Among the river sallows, borne aloft
Or sinking as the light wind lives or dies ;
  And full-grown lambs loud bleat from hilly bourne ;
Hedge-crickets sing ; and now with treble soft
  The redbreast whistles from a garden croft,
And gathering swallows twitter in the skies.'

Young Keats's gaze that Sunday evening was upon the Winchester stubble-fields like a spiritual setting sun, and left them lying enchanted in its fadeless light.

William Allingham.
Varieties in Prose, ed. by his widow, 1893.
Longmans, Green and Co.

October 31, 1825.

WE went to King's Worthy, that is about two miles on the road from Winchester to London, and then, turning short on our left, came up upon the downs to the north of Winchester Race-course. Here, looking back at the city and at the fine valley above and below it, and at the many smaller valleys that run down from the high ridges into that great and fertile valley, I could not help admiring the taste of the ancient kings who made this city a chief place of their residence. There are not many finer spots in England. Here are hill, dell, water, meadows, woods, cornfields, downs, and all of them very fine and very beautifully disposed.

The taste of Ancient Kings

William Cobbett, *Rural Rides*, 1830.

THE city of Winchester is situated principally on the eastern bank of the river Itchen. The High Street, which is about half a mile in length, extends from the bridge to West Gate, and from it diverge on both sides a number of less important streets. The portion of the town eastward of the river, and the southern suburb of the city, as confined within its ancient ramparts, have long been known as the Soke, and is a liberty belonging to the Bishop of Winchester, who appoints constables and other manorial officers. The houses have in general an unpretending appearance, and are mostly of modern erection, nearly the whole

The City in 1850

of the antique buildings having gradually disappeared during the present century. Eighty years ago the town was neither paved nor lighted, whilst a gutter ran down the middle of the High Street, then extremely narrow in some parts and inconvenient and dangerous from the overhanging of many of the houses. In the wide part, now the fair ground, stood a number of dilapidated houses, amongst which were the County and City Bridewells.

Prouten's *Winchester Guide, c.* 1850.

This wonderful treasury

I HAVE been to Winchester again in order to show certain young friends this wonderful treasury of things ancient and lovely. They were rewarded for their trouble. As for myself, I am always rewarded for any amount of trouble in going to Winchester.

Sir Walter Besant.

High charges and low bows

TRAVELLERS from London to the ancient and once royal city of Winchester get a very fine view, as they draw near it, of a wide stretch of downs on both sides of the railway, but that on the left much the widest. The great sweeping undulations of smooth green turf, with here and there a wood dotted over them, have been the scene of many a conflict in olden days, and many legends and traditions belong to particular sites.

.   .   .   .

One conspicuous object has disappeared which I well remember on the most isolated of these downs : the semaphore [Greek= ' signal-carrier ']. The roof of the house, which stood on the apex of the hill, was furnished with signals, and there was a continuous line of them all the way to London. They were established in 1795, in the period of the great French war, to convey intelligence from Southampton and Portsmouth to London. The electric telegraph has superseded them, and most, if not all, of these ' houses set on a hill ' have been pulled down.

.   .   .   .

As the train slackens speed we catch one glimpse, and only one, of the low central tower of the Cathedral. Very little of the city is visible from the station, for it lies in a hollow, and the shoulder of the hill which flanks the Station Road on the city side hides it.

.   .   .   .

On alighting, we may go down the broad but short Station Road to the site of the old city wall, turn to the right along Jewry Street, and so come into the middle of the ' High.' But instead of this we will keep along a footpath beside the line over the rising ground I have before mentioned. This brings us to the top of the ' High,' and we turn down it to the left. It is a continuous but not steep descent for the whole length of the city. And Winchester High Street is the most picturesque that I know, at home or abroad. As soon as the West Gate is passed the picturesque character of the street becomes manifest. The buildings are not stately ; but the gables and varied heights, the low arcades, the great projecting clock, the graceful ' Butter-Cross,' all present an enchanting appearance ; the more so because some of the best shopkeepers have preserved the quaint fronts which were good enough for their forefathers, and have not been bitten by the desire for plate-glass. One of the old-fashioned shops formerly belonged to one who is said to have been the most prosperous tradesman in Winchester. ' However have you been able to make so much money ? ' said a friend to him. ' By always charging very high and bowing very low,' was the unhesitating answer.

' Winchester Cathedral,' by Canon Benham, in
Our English Minsters.
Isbister and Co., 1897.

UPPER WINCHESTER, near the station, is becoming thoroughly villafied, as cockney-suburban in appearance as Haverstock Hill. But the entrance to a town from the railway station is almost always ugly. How pleasantly Winchester must have greeted the coach-traveller, whirling up the green valley, seeing the great Cathedral grow larger through its elms,[1] then turning a corner of

Coach versus Railway

[1] *i.e.* limes.

the Close, a corner of the High Street, into the courtyard of the 'George.'

William Allingham.
Varieties in Prose, ed. by his widow, 1893.
Longmans, Green and Co.

Famous for a bishop!

THE city of Winchester is famed for a cathedral, a bishop—but he was unfortunately killed some years ago while riding—a public school, a considerable assortment of the military, and the deliberate passage of the trains on the London and South-Western line.

R. L. S. and L. O., *The Wrong Box*, iv.

§ 2. FAMILIAR LANDMARKS

APUD HORTUM JUCUNDISSIMUM WINTONIAE

A Winchester Garden

Ac nec deliciae, licet suäves,
Tales te poterit diù tenere,
Quin mirabere, quae micant utrinque
Tecta ingentia, maximumque templum,[1]
Antiquumque larem decus camenis [2]
Hac dum prospicias, jugi sacrati [3]
Sub clivo ancipiti, domus superbae [4]
Olim, fragmina vasta, dirutasque
Arces ; ah memor, hospes, esto, ut ipsae,
Quas nunc egregio vides decoras
Cultu, et magnificas, utrinque moles
Mox traxisse queant parem ruinam
Et musco jaceant situque plenae ;
Quamvis utraque Wiccamus beatus
Diti fecerit auxeritque sumtû,
Te, Phoebi domus alma ; teque templum,
Centum surgere jusserit columnis.

Thomas Warton.

---

[1] The Cathedral.　　　　[2] St. Mary's College.
[3] St. Giles' Hill.　　　　[4] Ruins of Wolvesey Palace.

FROM the spring, whose ceaseless bubble
   Freshly sings in summer heat ;
Through the leas in mazy double,
   Washing every shy retreat ;
Where gold-lidded king-cup flowers
   On my bosom loose their tears,
Gathered from cool evening showers,
   Slip my waters through a thousand years.

.   .   .   .   .   .

When my shadow-blotted water,
   Heaving, caught the dying sun,
And the sail would droop and falter,
   And the silent boat slipt on ;
On between the brimming rushes,
   Black against the lucent stream ;
With the silence-smitten thrushes
   In black elm-boughs, it was sweet to dream.

Sweet to watch the bursten hatches,
   Sunny foam and silver spray :
More than sweet to him that watches,
   Loving, ere he turns away,
But a sweeter band of union,
   Sons of Wykeham us enthralls ;
With your sleep I held communion,
   Lapping low beneath your ancient walls.

Now confused, now fresh and single,
   Came the voices of my stream,
When my wave would mingle, mingle
   With the murmuring of your dream,—
Syllables of pleasant burden,
   Never loud, though ever heard,
' Lovely calm, and all her guerdon,'—
   That was ever my abiding word.

The Itchen

F

Rose this tower, crowned with graces,
  To a noble kingdom grew,
Sending streams through sapless places,
  As I drench the meadows through,
All around, the downs—the scornful,
  Tawny, shrubless, parched with heat :
All around, the fierce or mournful
  World of troubles hems thy cool retreat.

.   .   .   .   .   .

In *The Wykehamist*, July 1, 1893.

I TELL you, scholar, when I sat last on this primrose-bank, and looked down these meadows, I thought of them as *Charles* the Emperor did of the city of *Florence* : ' That they were too pleasant to be looked on, but only on holy days ' ; as I then sat on this very grass, I turned my present thoughts into verse : 'twas a wish which I 'll repeat to you.

THE ANGLER'S WISH

I in these flowery meads would be :
These crystal streams should solace me ;
To whose harmonious bubbling noise,
I with my angle would rejoice,
Sit here and see the turtle-dove,
Court his chaste mate to acts of love ;

Or on that bank, feel the west wind
Breathe health and plenty, please my mind,
To see sweet dew-drops kiss these flowers :
Here hear my Kenna sing a song,
There see a blackbird feed her young,

Or a leverock build her nest ;
Here give my weary spirits rest,
And raise my low-pitch'd thoughts above
Earth, or what poor mortals love :

Thus free from law-suits and the noise
Of princes' courts, I would rejoice,

Or with my *Bryan*, and a book,
Loiter long days near *Shawford* brook ;
There sit by him and eat my meat,
There see the sun both rise and set :
There bid good morning to next day,
There meditate my time away :
And angle on, and beg to have
A quiet passage to a welcome grave.

Izaak Walton.
The Compleat Angler, Part i. chap. v.

. . . .

SAY, father *Itchen*, genial river, say,
What stripling bards on Catherine's summit stray ;
Where the deep Danish foss, and shatter'd heap
Of turf-rais'd ramparts, crown'd th' encircled steep ;
For many an infant muse in years unripe,
Of thy rude reeds first fram'd his artless pipe.
Thou in the vale hast spied thine Otway roam
To yon old mansion's hospitable dome ; [1]
Where kind Religion lavish'd heretofore
On the poor pilgrim all her social store ;
Where still Religion's charity bestows
Help to the wayworn traveller as he goes.

Father Itchen

. . . .

And he, sweet master of the pastoral oat,[2]
Old *Vaga's* bard ! first fram'd his woodland note ;
Here oft invoking Milton's laurel'd shade
On thy lov'd banks his infant off'ring paid ;
Or sung in numbers wild, and simple strains,
The blushing fruit of Ariconian [3] plains.

[1] St. Cross.　　　[2] Phillips.　　　[3] Herefordshire.

And he, whose Latian lines, by Maro's muse [1]
Attun'd, more widely Milton's name diffuse.
'Twas thine, bless'd stream! when first thy *Pope* had stray'd
With infant steps 'mid Twyford's glimmering glade,
To catch the fancied theme, or moral tale
Sung on thy banks, and echoed through thy vale ;

There *Young* first found the various-sounding lyre
That breathed on different themes an equal fire ;
Whether with poignant wit he lash'd the age
Or painted the dire fiends Revenge and Rage ;
Or at deep midnight silent walk'd and slow,
Indulg'd in grief, and pour'd forth strains of woe.

'The Prospect from the King's House, Winchester,'
under 'Poetry,' *The Hampshire Repository*, 1798.

Sonnet to the River Itchen, near Winton

A Sonnet

ITCHEN, when I behold thy banks again,
Thy crumbling margin, and thy silver breast,
On which the self-same tints still seem'd to rest,
Why feels my heart the shiv'ring sense of pain ?
Is it—that many a summer's day has past
Since, in life's morn, I caroll'd on thy side ?
Is it—that oft, since then, my heart has sigh'd
As Youth and Hope's delusive gleams flew past ?
Is it—that those, who circled on thy shore,
Companions of my youth, now meet no more ?
Whate'er the cause, upon thy banks I bend,
Sorrowing, yet feel such solace at my heart,
As at the meeting of some long lost friend,
From whom, in happier hours, we wept to part.

The Rev. W. L. Bowles.

[The author notes as follows: 'The lines were composed on an
evening journey from Oxford to Southampton, the first
time I had seen the Itchen since I left school.']

1 Dobson.

. . . THERE are also, in divers rivers, especially that relate to, or be near to the sea, as *Winchester*, or the *Thames* about *Windsor*, a little Trout called a Samlet or Skegger Trout ; in both which places I have caught twenty or forty at a standing, that will bite as fast and freely as Minnows ; these be by some taken to be young Salmons, but in those waters they never grow to be bigger than a Herring.

Izaak Walton.
The Compleat Angler, Part I. chap. iv.

Samlet in the Itchen

Tuesday, October 24, 1738.

FROM the church [Winchester Cathedral] we walked up the town and went to take a view of the King's House upon the hill. It stands very high in a very fine country, and overlooks all Winchester and St. Cross. Here did anciently stand a castle, upon part of the site of the old castle now stands this building. This house was proposed for a hunting seat for the King, being in a fine sporting country and not far from the famous New Forest. The plan or design was made by Sir Christopher Wren, and I believe is better than ever he executed, because in this he was left to himself by the King. It was just covered in before the King died. There were five marble pillars with their capitals all wrought and put up in cases, which lay there till the late King's time, when the late Duke of Bolton begged them of the King, and they were granted to him, and he carried them away above three hundred waggon loads of marble to his house at Hackwood, and there they remain still boxed up, never put up, or even seen by mortal eye. The front of the house is to the east, and the middle part of the house fronts directly upon the west end of the Cathedral : the project was to have a street of two hundred feet in breadth, and to have been noblemen's and gentlemen's houses of each side ; this would have been fine. The front in the middle was composed of four Corinthian pillars and two pilasters. The middle part without the two wings was two hundred feet, the whole front with the wings was three hundred and thirty ; the wings

The King House

were joined to the body of the house by a fine colonnade.   There was designed three cupolas, one upon each wing, and that in the middle, the third, to be so high that from thence you might see the men of war riding at Spithead.

This was to please the King who loved the fleet of England, and also his successor the Duke of York, who was Lord High Admiral, and loved and understood the fleet of England.   But his taste was not for building houses, for I do not know anything he built but a popish chapel which he had better have let alone.   Pardon this digression.   There was to be two chapels, one for the King and one for the Queen ; these were to go up two stories.

The middle story rooms were to be twenty feet high ; the lower story and the upper story were to be fourteen feet in height.   Queen Anne and Prince George went to see the house, and there was a staircase made for them to go up to the second floor, but the Queen liked Windsor much better, so in this sad condition lies the shell of this fine house.

A Journey through Hampshire in 1738, in the handwriting of the second Earl of Oxford, apparently addressed to his wife (*Hist. MSS. Com.*, Duke of Portland's MSS.).

Miss Burney visits ' The King's House '   AUG. 2, 1791.—We arrived early at Winchester ; but the town was so full, as the judges were expected the next morning, that we could only get one bedchamber, in which Mrs. Ord, her maid, and myself reposed. . . . We strolled about the upper part of the city leaving the Cathedral for the next morning.   We saw a large, uniform, handsome palace, which is called ' The King's House,' and which was begun by Charles II.   We did not, therefore, expect the elegant architecture of his father's days.   One part, they told us, was particularly designed for Nell Gwynn. It was never finished, and neglect has taken place of time in rendering it a most ruined structure, though as it bears no marks of antiquity it has rather the appearance of owing its destruction to a fire than to the natural decay of age.   It is so spacious, however, and stands so magnificently to overlook the city, that I wish it to be completed for an hospital or infirmary. I have written Mrs. Schwellenberg an account of its appearance and state, which I am sure will be read by Her Majesty.

Diary and Letters of Madame D'Arblay, London, 1842-46.

THE upper street is not attractive till we come to the fine West Gate, which marks the line of the ancient wall on this side. Before passing through it we glance at the County Hall on our right. The history connected with it is not altogether pleasing. Charles II. had it in his mind to build a great palace here which should rival that of his brother (and master), Louis XIV., at Versailles. There were to be fine roads and broad terraces, reaching down from the palace to the west front of the Cathedral, in such wise as to make the latter a mere appendage to the royal residence. What a grievous burden the French palace was, and what a frightful tragedy to the King's family it played no small part in producing, history knows too well. England was perhaps spared a like tragedy by the profligate King's death. The part which he built is now turned into the barracks. But in the ancient hall adjacent hangs the celebrated Round Table at which, so legend tells, the knights of King Arthur sat. On the site of this hall William Rufus held godless festival, and in it Judge Jeffreys sentenced Alice Lisle to death.

The County Hall

'Winchester Cathedral,' by Canon Benham, in
Our English Minsters.
Isbister and Co., 1897.

You impute to King William, Sir, the want of taste in Hampton Court—you therefore allow there was want of taste. Was I to blame when observing that want of taste? I imputed it to the architect. You will perhaps urge the same plea for the palace at Winchester. Forgive me if I say that to prove Sir Christopher had a taste for erecting palaces equal to what he had for churches, some building ought to be specified in which he has executed it. A prince may name some general style of building to his architect, but does not draw the design; and

Horace Walpole and the King's House

even if his choice is vicious, if the architect has taste he will
exert it, even in an injudicious style. The truth is the fault
was in the age, and to that I have already imputed it, not to
your grandfather.

Horace Walpole to Christopher Wren, August 9, 1764.

**Winchester
Castle**

VENTA! thy castled steep's romantic fanes
On yon lone brow scarce rear their rude remains ;
Where erst 'mid high-arch'd halls, in princely state,
Girt with his peers immortal Alfred sate ;
To join in Chivalry's fantastic rites
Each hardy tourney call'd the steel-clad knights,
And many a minstrel sang the fabled lore
To chear the war-worn chiefs with martial tales of yore.

   .   .   .   .   .   .

No more the moated castle's frame sublime
Braves the wild waste of all-devouring time ;
Fall'n are the massy spires of Norman state,
Around is spread the scatter'd wreck of fate.
'Mid these rude scenes, and desolated tow'rs,
High ruined piles, and dim sequestered bow'rs,
At Charles's call another palace rears
Her gorgeous dome, the pride of after years ;
By Wren's fam'd hand, whose plan sublime but chaste,
Attemper'd matchless skill with faultless taste,
The stately mansion rose ; where mimic art
Might lavish grace to naked scenes impart,
With magic charms of livelier beauties please,
And deck the court of indolence and ease.
Now to our wond'ring, disappointed eyes,
Rude and unwrought th' unfinished turrets rise,
Reft is each Tuscan column's crested crown ;
And time has spurn'd the well-wrought arches down ;
The trophied portals rang'd in radiant row,
No more with sculptur'd pannels proudly glow ;

But o'er the naked steep, and shatter'd dome,
Wide wasting ruin throws a gradual gloom.
    In these lone walls, this vacant sad retreat,
Once a gay Monarch's happy, chosen seat,
Where vaulted roofs, and long-drawn chambers shed
A death-like silence, and an awful dread ;
With voice unknown, the pensive captive train
Wept o'er their wounds, and bore the galling chain ;
Oft as they look'd tow'rds Gallia's distant shore,
Much did the anxious thought of home, but more
Of helpless wives, fond parents, children dear,
Rush on their minds, and rouse the tender tear ;
Yet sometimes pleasing hopes of future peace
Would soothe each sigh, and bid each sorrow cease ;
Would to their wishes tell the flatt'ring tale
When they should cease their fate, as now, to wail ;
No more in cells should waste the tedious day,
But to their native climes resume their welcome way.

.   .   .   .

On ' The King's House, Winchester,' under ' Poetry,'
The Hampshire Repository, 1798.

HERE is the bridge that spans it [the Itchen]. It is the site of **The Soke Bridge**
one of the many picturesque legends of St. Swithun, that of the
old woman's broken eggs, which he restored to her. But it
also marks the former limit of the navigability of the Itchen.
This river used to be popularly called, and may be so still for
aught I know, ' the barge river.' . . .

' Winchester Cathedral,' by Canon Benham, in
Our English Minsters.
Isbister and Co., 1897.

Tuesday, October 24.

WINCHESTER.—I think I left you at the College, if I mistake **Wolvesey Palace in 1738**
not, at the end of my last. We went then a little lower down
to see the Bishop's palace. It was rebuilt by Bishop Morley
soon after the Restoration. It is a good house, very good rooms

below, a very good large dining-room above, and a very handsome gallery.   Bishop Trelawney much repaired it, and lived there a great part of his time.   Trimnel liked it, but his time was short. There is an old chapel, there are very great ruins of the palace Cardinal Wolsey built, and even the new palace is called Wolsey House to this day.   Bishop Trelawney had put upon the pillars that were of each side the gate two wolves, being his own crest. This Bishop [Hoadly] took them down, said it was too bare-faced to have wolves before an episcopal palace.   He, good man, being Dr. Smooth, chooses rather to be a wolf in sheep's clothing.

A little below the Bishop's house is the quay.   The river is navigable to Winchester, boats of thirty and forty tons come up to the quay from Southampton.   There is a very fine useful library here, the benefaction of Bishop Morley.   We could not get to see it because that the person that had the key was gone out, and not to return in some days ; so being for public use and benefit designed by the good Bishop, this worthy person locks it up for his own private use, but more I suspect to hinder anybody else the use of it.   I mention this with more concern because one of the noblest books that we have in the English Language was compiled by the sole help of this library: the book I mean is Mr. Bingham's *Ecclesiastical History*.

A Journey through Hampshire in 1738, in handwriting of the second Earl of Oxford, apparently addressed to his wife (*Hist. MSS. Com.*, Duke of Portland's MSS.).

Wolvesey's Ruined Pile

COME roam with me 'neath Wolvesey's ruined pile,
'Mid ivied stone and grass-grown courts awhile,
And think of all that was in days gone by,
When great De Blois reared up those turrets high,
That bid defiance to proud Scotland's King
And Glo'ster's earl.   What sacred memories cling
Around the walls that sheltered fugitives,
And sheltering paid the cost !   Thy glory lives,
O Wolvesey, shrined in words of the land !
Defaced and scarred by Cromwell's ruthless hand,

Yet reared again from ruined majesty,
Once more thou sawest the pomp and pageantry
Of princely state troop through thy corridors,
And feltest sainted footsteps tread thy floors.
But now—thy holy denizens have fled ;
Lo ! desecrating carpenters instead
Defile thy hallowed haunts with hammerings.

. . . .

Shall it be ever thus ?   No !   Once again
Shall rise the Palace worthy of the Fane,
Which now derisive, peeping through the trees,
Soars high above such base indignities.
Once more return ye Bishops in your might,
Live in your palace, pity its sad plight.
Ghosts of the Great, arise !   De Blois appear,
With Langton, Fox, and Morley, hover near ;
Chase from your home, the impious revel rout
With Bell, Book, Candle, Crosier, poke them out,—
Rats, bandsmen, reptiles, carpenters and owls,
Indifferent artists, cameras and fowls,
Hutches and hammers, poultry, paint-pots, too,
Away, away, with all the motley crew !
Hence, shows of flowers !   Hence flaunting fancy fairs,
Find more congenial precincts for your wares !
Hence, past the walls that scorned 'fore foe to bend,
Now fall'n to trait'rous and insidious friend !
Sweep out the scuttling pack and slam the gate !
If not restore, at least respect, poor Wolvesey's piteous state !

In *The Wykehamist*, March 1887.

WE descend the High Street as far as the Butter Cross and **The Butter** examine it at leisure.   Its surroundings are almost as picturesque **Cross** as itself.   Look at that ' Piazza,' formerly better called ' the Penthouse,' the houses overhanging the street, the odd gables and barge-boards and rough ridge-tiles, and say what Continental city has a more perfect setting for a piece of beautiful architecture. . . .

'Winchester Cathedral,' by Canon Benham, in
Our English Minsters.
Isbister and Co., 1897.

'The Gothic market-cross'

By an archway, where the little church of St. Lawrence lurks behind the houses, we pass into the High Street of the White City (taking the old British name to have been *Caer* Gwent), and see its Gothic market-cross in a corner, beside the shop of a serious bookseller who is always to be found in ecclesiastical precincts.

William Allingham.
Varieties in Prose.
Longmans, Green and Co., 1893.

'A grey landmark of forgotten time'

Was it blind bigot zeal that half enclosed
This holy Cross, grey witness of the past,
Beneath those envious houses, whose bent brows
With puritanic grimness frown on it,
Hiding its beauty from the mid-day sun ?
When the stern mansions totter to their base
Rebuild them not, Wintonians ! let a spark
Possess you of that noble fire that once
Foiled antiquarian Dummer [1] of his prize
And kept inviolate your royal city.
Widen the public way, that so the Cross
May boldly rear its light and graceful form
Full in the general gaze . . .
. . . When in the deep night
The city lies in slumber, 'tis the hour
To hold communion with the past, to live,
Grey landmark of forgotten time, with thee

[1] The Cross was secretly sold under an order of the Commissioners of Pavements in 1770 to Mr. Dummer of Cranbury Park, and scaffolds were raised to take it down and remove it to Cranbury, when the townspeople rose in defence, and, driving away the workmen employed to take it down, preserved it for Winchester.

As thou wert in thy youth—then in the mart
Of work-day traffic, 'mid the busy crowd
Thou stood'st, a sacred monitor to man ;

.   .   .   .

. . . Weary wayfarers
And pilgrims on thy steps would rest, and breathe
A passing prayer ; then wend, with courage new,
Their toilsome way.—A holy spot wert thou
In the mid-city, where at every hour
World-busy men communion held with Heaven.

Ages have rolled, and thou, time-honoured Cross,
No longer aw'st the multitude—blind zeal
Hath overthrown three statues of thy saints ;
Yet one, St. Lawrence, holding the noble palm
Of martyrdom, in Gothic niche enshrined
Thou bearest, emblem of faith and constancy:
But pilgrims call upon his name no more.
Now on thy steps, old Cross, blithe children play
Their merry gambols ; aged sires there rest
Their weary limbs, and in the joyous scene
Find antidotes for grief ; there pauses oft
The antiquary full of curious lore,
Musing on every stone ; the tourist there
Will stop, guide-book in hand, admiring much
Each airy arch and taper pinnacle.
There the rich townsman, in the mellow fall
Of age, from the world's harsher duties free,
And vexed with none but magisterial cares,
Pacing his much-loved city, will indulge
Short converse with the aged grateful poor,
And a gay laugh with prattling infancy :
Then view with pride his City's antique Cross,
And meditate upon the flow of time.

                                        Christopher Wood.
                    Reminiscences of Winchester, c. 1860.

From St. Giles's Hill

FROM St. Giles's Hill one looks down on the famous old city. Its Cathedral among lofty trees, Wykeham's College with the lads at cricket, the water-meadows leading to St. Cross, the swelling green downs with one grove, a ' peculiar coronet,' on St. Catherine's Hill, show fair in the May sunlight.   Methinks a flagstaff would stand well at one angle of the low Cathedral tower.   Brisk and clear runs the shallow river below, by small grey and red houses and their gardens, mill-sluices, the quaint little flint-built church of St. Peter's Chesil, and a vine-clad remnant of the city wall.

William Allingham.
Varieties in Prose.
Longmans, Green and Co., 1893.

' That white cliff '

THE curious stranger will not fail, whilst sojourning in Winchester, to ascend the top of that white cliff which overhangs the city, and once formed part of it, called St. Giles's Hill, where he will have the whole city under his feet, and command a bird's eye view of its streets, churches, palaces, and ruins, intermingled with gardens, fields, groves, and streams.

Historical and Descriptive Guide to Winchester, 1829

' PEACE ' ATTACKS ' WRONG ' (*i.e.* the King's purveyors)

' Seint Gyles doune '

' BOTHE my gees and my grys . and my gras he taketh,
Ich dar nouht for his felaweshepe . in faith,' Pees seide,
' Bere sikerlich eny selver . to seint Gyles doune ;
He waiteth ful wel . whanne ich seluer take,
What wey ich wende . wel ʒerne he aspieth,
To robbe me and to ryfle me . yt ich ryde softe.'

Piers the Plowman, C. Passus v., 49-53.

' Winchestre Faire '

THENNE can Couetyse . ich can not hym discryue,
So hongerliche and so holwe. . . .

.   .   .   .

' Ich haue be coueitous,' quath thys caitiyf, ' ich byknow hit here.
For som tyme ich served . Symme at the style,
And was his prentys yplyght . hus profyt to waite.

Furst ich lerned to lye · a lesyng other tweye ;
Wickedliche to weye · was my furst lesson.
To Wy and to Winchestre · ich wente to the faire
With many maner marchandises · as my maister heghte ;
Ne hadde the grace of gyle · gon among my ware,
Hit hadde ben vnsold thys seuen ʒer · so me god helpe !
Ich drow me among drapers · my donet to lerne,
To drawe the lisure a-longe · the lenger it semed ;
Among the riche rayes · ich rendered a lesson,
To brochen hen with a batte-nelde · and bond hem togederes ;
Ich putte hem in pressours · and pynned hem therynne,
Tyl ten ʒerdes other twelue · tilled out threttyne.

Piers the Plowman, C. Passus vii., 196-97, 206-220.

ʒUT thauh thei wenden on way · as to Wynchestre fayre,
The marchaunt with hus marchaundise · may nat go so swithe
As the messager may · ne with so mochel ese ·
For that on bereth bote a boxe · a breuet ther-ynne,
Ther the marchaunt ledeth a male · with meny kynne thynges,
And dredeth to be ded there-fore · and he in derke mete
With robbours and reuers · that riche men dispoilen ;
Ther the messager is ay murye · hus mouthe ful of songes,
And leyueth for hus letteres · that no wight wol hym greue.

Wynchestre Fayre

Piers the Plowman, C. Passus xiv., 52-60.

THE mayor is scorned ; no suppliant that day
Humbly implores his worship to look gay :
His keys are wrested from him, and his gown
Stripped from his back, no longer awes the town.

The Humbled Mayor

Quoted in A Guide to Winchester,
W. Savage, 1869.

[*N.B.*—During the sixteen days of the St. Giles's fair in the time of Henry ii., the mayor of the city gave up the keys of the four gates, and with them his authority, to a temporary magistrate appointed by the bishop.]

St.
Catherine's

MANY of the Winchester recollections most indelibly fixed in my memory are connected with 'hills.' It seems impossible that sixty years can have passed since I stood on the bank of the circumvallation facing towards Winchester, and gazed down at the white morning mist that entirely concealed the city and valley. How many mornings in the late autumn have I stood and watched the moving, but scarcely moving, masses of billowy white cloud! And what strange similitudes and contrasts suggested themselves to my mind as I recently looked down from the heights of Monte Gennaro on the Roman Campagna similarly cloud hidden! The phenomenon exhibited itself on an infinitely larger scale in the latter case, but it did not suggest to me such thick-coming fancies and fantastic imaginings as the water-mead-born mists of the Itchen!

T. A. Trollope.
What I Remember, i. 106-8.
R. Bentley and Son, 1887.

Winchester
from 'Hills'

WHEN in the morning air
A Sabbath stillness reigns,
And all below is bright and fair
With sunlight over hills and plains,
Come from the walled town,
And climb the slope of some soft down
That looks on Itchen's valley green,
Where the thousand rills are seen
That wind, a many-sparkling train,
With their bright queen to the main,
By many a bower, and many a grove,
Which Venusia's bard might love—
Mount ye till on every side
The thin-clad hills spread far and wide
To where the green melts into blue,
And earth and heaven recede from view:
There pause awhile, and look ye down
On the old grey Saxon town.

How nobly from the churchyard grove
Rise the Cathedral walls above
The regal city !   Many an age
Hath stamped on them a deathless page.
Listen to the deep-toned bell
That from the massive tower doth swell

.   .   .   .   .

And with a solemn grandeur fills
The amphitheatre of hills,
Where Winton lies embosomed deep,
And Itchen loves its shade to keep
In her clear mirror, till the grey
Horizon steals it slow away.

.   .   .   .   .   .

Christopher Wood.
Reminiscences of Winchester, c. 1860.

AERII Catharina jugi quà vertice summo
Danorum veteres fossas, immania castra,
Et circumducti servat vestigia valli,
Wiccamicae mos est pubi celebrare palaestras
Multiplices, passimque levi contendere lusu,
Festa dies quoties rediit, concessaque rite
Otia purpureoque rubentes lumine soles
Invitant tetricæ curas lenire Minervae,
Librorumque moras et iniqua remittere pensa.

Thomas Warton.

**Mons
Catharinae**

THOU grassy steep, that rear'st thy fir-crown'd head,
The tow'ring monarch of the peaceful mead,
While yet I view thy summit known so well,
Receive a son of Wickham's last farewell !

Yes ! I have loved upon thy dizzy brow
To gaze upon thy fair domain below,

**' Thou grassy
steep '**

Thy meadows water'd by a thousand rills,
Yon barren amphitheatre of hills,
Till my glad eye exulting wide to roam,
Sought far beyond them all my island home ;

.　　　.　　　.　　　.　　　.　　　.　　　.

And I have lov'd on thee reclin'd, to stray
O'er the rude legends of thy early day,
Then to my view gigantic forms would rise,
The painted Briton with his azure eyes ;
Again Caswallon, from his scythed car,
Would hurl destruction through the ranks of war,
Whirl his huge mace, nor fear again to feel
The dint of Roman arm, the edge of Roman steel.
But hark ! along the heights where now no more
The humble chapel rears its sacred door,
To fancy's ear, in measured cadence dim,
Steals on the whispering breeze the vesper hymn ;
Ave Maria ! thus the vestal throng
Their Virgin Mother's evening chaunt prolong,
While, as the mellow'd numbers float around,
The hills responsive echo back the sound.

.　　　.　　　.　　　.　　　.　　　.　　　.

'To Catherine Hill, on leaving Winchester College,'
The Hampshire Repository, 1828.

'On the
brink of that
huge foss'

BUT if perchance youth's gayer mood,
The spirit bounding in the blood,
Spurred them to exercise, they found
Green stretches for their revel ground
On the near Down ; their eager feet
Spurned the crisp moss with bound as fleet
As any now ; the rarer joy
Lent vigour to the student boy.
His brow was fanned by such a breeze
As ruffles now St. Catherine's trees,

Where mazes of the Labyrinth twine
Beneath the murmur-haunted pine,
Echoing the music that has been ;
For then the martyr-maid was Queen
Of that high hill.   Full often there
Would pilgrims climb the chalky stair,
And voices at the chantry door
Would lead them to the hallowed floor.
Near to that crest, yet unprofane,
Around the wide camp of the Dane,
Gay sons of Wykeham scoured the sod,
Sporting where once the warrior trod.
And one might linger on the brink
Of that huge foss awhile, to drink
The freshness of the southern gale.

.   .   .   .   .

Hark ! how the tolling vesper bells
Break on the stillness of the fells
From Winton's towers.   He turns again ;
The carpet of the emerald plain
Sweeps up to red monastic walls,
Grey fanes, and steeples, convent halls,
Majestic, bravest, best array
Of Piety's meridian day
In England's stateliest city ; there
The homes of Charity and Prayer
Are crowded in sweet union, save
Where Itchen's cool dividing wave
Feeds garden greeneries.   And now,
As from the sounding towers below
Thick calls of evening come, his eye
Rests on the gleaming symmetry
Of those long lines which Wykeham gave
To bear the heaven-aspiring nave ;

On storied chapel windows yet
Fresh from his chisel, jewels set
In branching stone ; on that fair tower
High pinnacled in elmy bower,
Youngest among the clashing spires,
Whose vesper bells shall sound when theirs
For ever cease.

W. Moore.
Venta and other Poems.
D. Nutt, 1882.

St. Cross IT is beautifully situated on the river bank, and embowered on the south among shady stately trees, so calm and peaceful, that a good man might choose to die in it.

M. E. C. Walcott.
Memorials of Winchester, 1866.

' Amid sunny hills ' IN the well-watered valley of the Itchen, amid sunny hills and flowery meads, the position of St. Cross offers no exception to the proverbial sagacity with which our forefathers chose the sites of their religious houses and charitable foundations. Distant only a mile from the Cathedral City, and within a few yards of the high road to Southampton, the lofty church of De Blois rises majestically from the midst of the domestic buildings which are picturesquely grouped about it ; and, fringed by luxuriant elms and magnificent walnut-trees, presents an aspect as charming as it is imposing.

Thus situated it is a conspicuous object to the traveller approaching Winchester from various directions, and from a considerable distance. And on a nearer approach, the lower buildings, which cluster round the church, add their full share to the general effect. This is more especially the case from the Southampton direction, whence the noble gateway of Beaufort, the refectory with its striking porch, and the long range of tall, quaint chimneys combine, with the church and the foliage, and the occasional peeps of the river between the trees, and St. Katharine's Hill in the background, to form a complete picture.

Let us enter the well-kept quadrangle, or, as it is more usually termed, the court, from the direction just indicated. Leaving the high road by the little wicket gate, crossing the green close, leaving the old walnut-trees on the right hand, across the corner of the park, we pass through the iron gate into the Hospital premises. We are at once impressed by the calm repose of the antiquated place, which certainly possesses an indescribable air of its own ; and, with its tall box edgings, and old-fashioned flowers, and luxuriant fig-trees, vines, and creepers, is very unlike an ordinary college quadrangle. . . .

A Guide to the Hospital of St. Cross, by the Rev. L. M. Humbert
(thirteen years Master of St. Cross).

W. Savage, 1869.

LOOK at yon archway, which the hand of time
Has touched but to adorn—the well-head there
Which from King Stephen's brother, good De Blois,
Took rise, flows yet.—The houseless wanderer,
Footsore and famished, no sleek menial finds
To spurn him from that gate : the brother there
Welcomes each outcast of the churlish world,
And for his hunger carves the wheaten loaf,
And fills the goblet to his thirsting lip ;
Then speeds him on his way with friendly speech,
Kind words, whose every tone is charity ;
And with a lighter heart and nimbler step
The poor man journeys on.   The swallow knows
And cherishes the dome ; for he fears not
Each spring to build his clayey tenement
Even in the hospitable porch.—Heaven wraps
These quiet walls in a sweet atmosphere
Of peace and love.   Pass we beneath the Lodge.
See where, with silver cross upon his breast,
The porter stands. . . .

St. Cross :
an ideal of
Charity

Christopher Wood.
Reminiscences of Winchester, c. 1860.

'Pious roofs'

HAIL! pious roofs, by grateful Henry raised,
Where toil-worn age may rest, and Christ be praised!
The tidal sweep of time on kindred halls
Has scarcely left a remnant of their walls,
Save where that faithful friend to ruined things,
The mantling ivy, timely succour brings,
And by her strong, tough arms and hands sustains
The crumbling vestiges of what remains.
But thine, *St. Cross*, a kinder fate have found;
No ruins here deform thy hallowed ground;
Nor e'er has echo from thy towers been driven
Since first they rose and heard the song of heaven.

Quoted in Canon Humbert's *Hospital of St. Cross*, 1868.

Henry de
Blois

ONE charitable deed is father still
To many more: . . . and thus through time
The streams of wisdom and of charity
Are ever fed, still widening as they flow;
E'en as yon Itchen, whose translucent wave
In narrow bed these venerable walls
Now sweetly laves; then, widening through the vale,
Far down a broad and ample water rolls
Into the friendly Solent.   May *De Blois*
Be cherished here till Itchen cease to flow!

Christopher Wood.
Reminiscences of Winchester, c. 1860.

Emerson at
St. Cross

JUST before entering Winchester, we stopped at the Church
of Saint Cross, and, after looking through the quaint antiquity,
we demanded a piece of bread and a draught of beer, which the
founder, Henry de Blois, in 1136, commanded should be given
to every one who should ask it at the gate.   We had both
from the old couple who take care of the church.   Some twenty
people every day, they said, make the same demand.   This
hospitality of seven hundred years' standing did not hinder
C. from pronouncing a malediction on the priest who receives

£2000 a year, that were meant for the poor, and spends a pittance on this small beer and crumbs.

Emerson, *English Traits*, 1856.
Concerning a Journey to England in 1833 and 1847.

APART from the picturesque beauty and architectural importance of the buildings, the ancient character of the Institution, one of the few now left to us of its kind, with its common brotherhood, its religious garb, and its old form of hospitality, affords a link with ages gone by, which the Conservative character of our nation makes us cherish gratefully. Unfortunately, however, Conservatism has not always been discriminating as to what is worth preserving, and the Masters of St. Cross have, with the dole and the silver cross, tenaciously kept up other institutions of far more objectionable character. Thus, the Hospital archives record of one in the last century, that ' he died three weeks after he had whitewashed the church.' Mark, this is by no means to be regarded as a judgment on him ; on the contrary, as memorial records are always framed upon the principle of *de mortuis nil nisi bonum*, it is rather to be construed as if he had added one more jewel to his crown and so was ripe for departure. And when I last saw St. Cross in the Exhibition year of 1851, that new era of light in art, the walls of the church had just received their periodical coating, at the especial command, as I was told, of the Master. Under the whitewash *régime*, then, the condition of Holy Cross Church had become rather discouraging, when the present enlightened Master first assumed the silver cross. The nave was a desert, the choir and sanctuary were blocked up with pews, dirt (save the whitewash) damp and decay reigned everywhere, and things probably would have been even worse, but for the archæological and historical interest attaching to the place, which brought it much under the notice of outsiders. Moreover, the most beautiful feature of the building, the east end, was disfigured by the zeal of a good Warden (*he* was no Conservative), who had

St. Cross in
the Fifties

blocked up the wonderful Norman windows with a Perpendicular reredos.

Quoted in *The Hospital of St. Cross*, by the Rev. L. M. Humbert, 1868, App. 1.

'Restorations' in Winchester

THE western porches of the Cathedral have been *done-up*, and look as pretty as a wedding-cake ; the college chapel has been done-up ; old St. Cross is partly done-up—well or ill I say not, but done-up they are ; and whoever likes clean white stone-work, like a door-step on Sunday morning, and fresh paint, and the brightest coloured glass that an eminent London firm can manufacture, and no trace left that can be obliterated of Time's finger, in tint or line, must be pleased with what he finds going on in nearly every old place in England.

Yet what boots grieving ? The use and significance of a structure gone, how should the thing escape ruin of one kind or another ? The piety and humanity that founded St. Cross—church, almshouses, dole of food to the wayfarer—sad ghosts of these haunt their ancient cloister. The realities have fled away, to find (we will hope so) new and fitter mansions. Here is no visible ruin as yet, for this endowment remains a legal and arithmetical fact, with some significance to the thirteen old men, much to the wealthy nobleman, their ' master.'

William Allingham.
Varieties in Prose.
Longmans, Green and Co., 1893.

A kind Retreat

BELOVED St. Cross ! where all thy charms combine
That warm the canvas or that grace the line ;
Thou kind retreat from sorrow and from care,
With sparkling waters and a balmy air ;
Amid thy meadows green and peaceful shades,
Thy crowning hills and long deep bow'ry glades,
What troubled heart can fail in thee to find
Health for the body, solace to the mind.

Quoted in *A Guide to the Hospital of St. Cross*, by the Rev. L. M. Humbert.
William Savage, 1869.

St. Swithin, the weather-famous, besides his share of patronage in the Cathedral, has a little parish-church of his own, built by King John over the postern of St. Michael. Swithin, Bishop of Winchester, dying *circa* 865, his body (as the story goes) was buried at his own request, out of humility perhaps, not in the Cathedral, as usual with bishops, but in the churchyard, where the drops of rain might wet his grave ; afterwards, when he was canonised, the monks resolved to move his bones into the Cathedral, and the 15th of July was fixed upon for the ceremony ; but on that day, and for forty days in succession, it rained so violently that the plan was given up as displeasing to the saint, and they built, instead, a chapel at his grave, where many miracles were wrought. Such the tradition, with its postscript that, ever since, the weather on St. Swithin's Day, be it wet or dry, will hold for thirty-nine days following.

St. Swithin's Church and its Patron Saint

William Allingham.
Varieties in Prose, ed. by his widow, 1893.
Longmans, Green and Co.

Mr. Harding did not go out to Crabtree Parva. An arrangement was made which . . . put Mr. Harding into possession of a small living within the walls of the city. It is the smallest possible parish, containing a part of the Cathedral Close and a few old houses adjoining. The church is a singular little Gothic building, perched over a gateway, through which the Close is entered, and is approached by a flight of stone steps which leads down under the archway of the gate. It is no bigger than an ordinary room—perhaps twenty-seven feet long by eighteen wide—but still it is a perfect church. It contains an old carved pulpit and reading-desk, a tiny altar under a window filled with dark old-coloured glass, a font, some half-dozen pews, and perhaps a dozen seats for the poor, and also a vestry. The roof is high pitched, and of black old oak, and the three large beams which support it run down to the side walls and terminate in grotesquely carved faces—two devils and an angel on one side, two angels and a devil on the other. Such is

St. Swithin's, Winchester, disguised as St. Cuthbert's, Barchester

the church of St. Cuthbert at Barchester, of which Mr. Harding became rector, with a clear income of seventy-five pounds a year.

Anthony Trollope, *The Warden.*

RUS IN URBE

The Russian gun

WHILE railings run round Russia's gun,
  The city's quiet
Attempts to kerb do but disturb
  And rouse a riot.
Since some have sinned, some must rescind
  Their former fiat.

O. W.
The Wykehamist, June 1908.

Winter around Winchester

FAREWELL those gentler seasons of the year,
  Young Spring, who fill'd with flow'rs the willing soil;
Summer, whose sunbeams nurs'd the foodful ear;
  With Autumn, grateful to the reaper's toil;
For lo, sad change! from yonder gathering cloud
  Stern Winter wildly drives his dark array:
From the keen North the winds are piping loud,
  As through the yielding woods they sweep their way.

. . . .

Where are those rural charms that fed my eyes,
  The cowslip'd meadow, and the hedge-row green?
In one wide waste the snow-clad Landscape lies;
  And Frost with withering hand deforms the scene.
I sought the copse, the joyous thrush's haunt;
  For much I wish'd her melody to hear;
In vain I woo'd her to begin her chaunt,
  Nor joyous thrush, nor melody was there.

In social troops the silent larks are found,
  Picking with busy bill their scanty food;
Ah me, I hear the gun's destructive sound,
  And the snow blushes with their harmless blood!

At ev'ry bush, at ev'ry sudden breeze,
  Starts the lone Trav'ler on his wilder'd way ;
In his own shade a thousand deaths he sees,
  And stops, and pants, and listens in dismay.

Winter, a poem begun at Winchester School, 1757,
by William Lipscomb.

[*N.B.*—Though not directly dealing with Winchester, this youthful verse is so evidently inspired by scenery around Winchester, that its insertion here may perhaps be forgiven.]

WINCHESTER hath 4 tavernes, Joan Prat, Anne Bud, Thomas **Taverns**
Buxton and Cornelius Brexton. At Soake, neere Winchester,
three, William Pope, John Noake, and Walter Travers.

John Taylor, the Water-poet.
A Catalogue of Tavernes in ten Shires, 1636.

§ 3. WINCHESTER IN FICTION

THE city of Wintoncester, that fine old city, aforetime capital of **'Winton-**
Wessex, lay amidst its convex and concave downland in all the **cester'**
brightness and warmth of a July morning. The gabled brick,
tile, and freestone houses had almost dried off for the season
their integument of lichen, the streams in the meadows were
low, and in the sloping High Street, from the West Gateway
to the mediæval cross, and from the mediæval cross to the
bridge, that leisurely dusting and sweeping was in progress
which usually ushers in an old-fashioned market-day.

From the Western gate aforesaid the highway, as every
Wintoncestrian knows, ascends a long and regular incline of
the exact length of a measured mile, leaving the houses gradually
behind. Up this road from the precincts of the city two persons
were walking rapidly, as if unconscious of the trying ascent—
unconscious through preoccupation and not through buoyancy.

They had emerged upon this road through a narrow barred wicket in a high wall a little lower down. They seemed anxious to get out of sight of the houses and of their kind, and this road appeared to offer the quickest means of doing so. Though they were young they walked with bowed heads, which gait of grief the sun's rays smiled on pitilessly.

. . . . . .

When they had nearly reached the top of the great West Hill the clocks in the town struck eight. Each gave a start at the notes, and, walking onward yet a few steps, they reached the first milestone, standing whitely on the green margin of the grass, and backed by the down, which here was open to the road. They entered upon the turf, and impelled by a force which seemed to overrule their will, suddenly stood still, turned, and waited in paralysed suspense beside the stone.

The prospect from this summit was almost unlimited. In the valley beneath lay the city they had just left, its more prominent buildings showing as in an isometric drawing—among them the broad cathedral tower, with its Norman windows and immense length of aisle and nave, the spires of St. Thomas's, the pinnacled tower of the College, and more to the right the tower and gables of the ancient hospice, where to this day the pilgrim may receive his dole of bread and ale. Behind the city swept the rotund upland of St. Catherine's Hill; further off, landscape beyond landscape, till the horizon was lost in the radiance of the sun hanging above it.

Against these far stretches of country rose, in front of the other city edifices, a large red-brick building, with level grey roofs, and rows of short barred windows bespeaking captivity, the whole contrasting greatly by its formalism with the quaint irregularities of the Gothic erections. It was somewhat disguised from the road in passing it by yews and evergreen oaks, but it was visible enough up here. The wicket from which the pair had lately emerged was in the wall of this structure. From the middle of the building an ugly flat-topped octagonal tower ascended against the east horizon, and viewed from this spot, on its shady side and against the light, it seemed the one blot on the city's beauty.   Yet it was with this blot and not with the beauty, that the two gazers were concerned.

Upon the cornice of the tower a tall staff was fixed.   Their eyes were riveted on it.   A few minutes after the hour had struck something moved slowly up the staff, and extended itself upon the breeze.   It was a black flag. . . .

Tess of the D'Urbervilles, by Thomas Hardy.
Macmillan and Co., Ltd.

My lord's little house of Walcote,[1] which he inhabited before he took his title and occupied the house of Castlewood, lies about a mile from Winchester, and his widow had returned to Walcote after my lord's death as a place always dear to her, and where her earliest and happiest days had been spent, cheerfuler than Castlewood, which was too large for her straitened means, and giving her, too, the protection of the ex-Dean, her father.   The young Viscount had had a year's schooling at the famous College there with Mr. Tusher as his governor.   So much news of them Mr. Esmond had had during the past year from the old Viscountess, his own father's widow; from the young one there had never been a word.

Twice or thrice in his benefactor's lifetime, Esmond had been to Walcote; and, now, taking but a couple of hours' rest only at the inn on the road, he was up again long before daybreak, and made such good speed, that he was at Walcote by two o'clock of the day.   He rid to the inn of the village, where he alighted, and sent a man thence to Mr. Tusher with a message that a gentleman from London would speak with him on urgent business.   The messenger came back to say the Doctor was in town, most likely at prayers in the Cathedral.   My Lady Viscountess was there too; she always went to Cathedral prayers every day.   The horses belonged to the post-house at

Esmond's meeting with his 'dear mistress'

[1] Probably Prior's Barton House.

Winchester. Esmond mounted again, and rode on to the George; whence he walked, leaving his grumbling domestick at last happy with a dinner, straight to the Cathedral. The organ was playing: the winter's day was already growing grey: as he passed under the street-arch into the Cathedral-yard and made his way into the ancient solemn edifice.

.   .   .   .   .   .

There was a score of persons in the Cathedral besides the Dean and some of his clergy, and the choristers, young and old, that performed the beautiful evening prayer. But Dr. Tusher was one of the officiants, and read from the eagle, in an authoritative voice and a great black periwig; and in the stalls, still in her black widow's hood, sat Esmond's dear mistress, her son by her side, very much grown, and indeed a noble-looking youth, with his mother's eyes and his father's curling brown hair, that fell over his *point de Venise*—a pretty picture such as Vandyke might have painted. Mons. Rigaud's portrait of my Lord Viscount, done at Paris afterwards, gives but a French version of his manly, frank English face. When he looked up there were two sapphire beams out of his eyes, such as no painter's palette has the colour to match, I think. On this day there was not much chance of seeing that particular beauty of my young lord's countenance; for the truth is, he kept his eyes shut for the most part, and, the anthem being rather long, was asleep.

But the musick ceasing, my lord woke up, looking about him, and his eyes lighting on Mr. Esmond, who was sitting opposite him, gazing with no small tenderness and melancholy upon two persons who had had so much of his heart for so many years; Lord Castlewood, with a start, pulled at his mother's sleeve (her face had scarce been lifted from her book), and said, ' Look, mother ! ' so loud, that Esmond could hear on the other side of the church and the old Dean on his throned stall. Lady Castlewood looked for an instant as her son bade her, and held up a warning finger to Frank ; Esmond felt his whole face flush, and his heart throbbing, as that dear lady beheld him once more. The rest of the prayers were speedily over. Mr. Esmond did not hear them; nor did his mistress, very likely, whose hood went more closely over her face, and who never lifted her head again until the service was over, the blessing given, and Mr. Dean and his procession of ecclesiasticks out of the inner chapel.

Young Castlewood came clambering over the stalls before the clergy were fairly gone, and running up to Esmond, eagerly embraced him. ' My dear, dearest old Harry,' he said, ' are you come back? Have you been to the wars? You 'll take me with you when you go again? Why didn't you write to us? Come to mother.'

Mr. Esmond could hardly say more than a God bless you, my boy, for his heart was very full and grateful at all this tenderness on the lad's part; and he was as much moved at seeing Frank, as he was fearful about that other interview which was now to take place; for he knew not if the widow would reject him as she had done so cruelly a year ago.

' It was kind of you to come back to us, Henry,' Lady Esmond said. ' I thought you might come.' . . . She gave him her hand, her little fair hand: there was only her marriage ring on it. The quarrel was all over. . . . It was a rapture of reconciliation.

' Here comes Squaretoes,' says Frank. ' Here 's Tusher.' Tusher, indeed, now appeared, creaking on his great heels. Mr. Tom had divested himself of his alb or surplice, and came forward habited in his cassock and great black periwig. How had Harry Esmond ever been for a moment jealous of this fellow? ' Give us thy hand, Tom Tusher,' he said. The chaplain made him a very low and stately bow. ' I am charmed to see Captain Esmond,' says he. ' My lord and I have read the *Reddas incolumen precor*, and applied it, I am sure, to you. You come back with Gaditanian laurels: when I heard you were bound thither, I wished, I am sure, I was another Septimius.

My Lord Viscount, your lordship remembers *Septimi, Gades aditure mecum*?'

'There's an angle of earth that I love better than Gades, Tusher,' says Mr. Esmond. ''Tis that one where your Reverence hath a parsonage, and where our youth was brought up.'

'A house that has so many sacred recollections to me,' says Mr. Tusher, . . . 'a house near to that of my respected patron, my most honoured patroness, must ever be a dear abode to me. But, madam, the verger waits to close the gates on your ladyship.'

Thackeray, *Henry Esmond*.

Henry
Esmond
spends New
Year's Eve at
Winchester,
1703

. . . THE family parted long before midnight, Lady Castlewood remembering, no doubt, former New Year's Eves, when healths were drunk, and laughter went round in the company of him to whom years, past and present and future, were to be as one ; and so cared not to sit with her children and hear the Cathedral bells ringing the birth of the year 1703. Esmond heard the chimes as he sate in his own chamber, ruminating by the blazing fire there, and listened to the last notes of them, looking out from his window towards the city, and the great grey towers of the Cathedral lying under the frosty sky, with the keen stars shining above.

Thackeray, *Henry Esmond*.

Cock-fight at
Winchester

'COME along and let's go see the cocking-match at Winchester.'

. . . .

My young Lord Viscount was exceedingly sorry when he heard that Harry could not come to the cock-match with him, and must go to London ; but no doubt my lord consoled himself when the Hampshire cocks won the match ; and he saw every one of the battles, and crowed properly over the conquered Sussex gentlemen.

Thackeray, *Henry Esmond*.

'The Black
Swan'

'*Please be at the Black Swan Hotel at Winchester at midday tomorrow*,' it said. '*Do come ! I am at my wit's end.*—HUNTER.'

' Will you come with me ? ' asked Holmes, glancing up.

' I should wish to.'

' Just look it up, then.'

' There is a train at half-past nine,' said I, glancing over my Bradshaw. ' It is due at Winchester at 11.30.'

' That will do very nicely. . . .'

By eleven o'clock the next day we were well upon our way to the old English capital. . . . All over the countryside, away to the rolling hills around Aldershot, the little red and grey roofs of the farmsteads peeped out from amidst the light green of the new foliage. . . .

' Well, there is the tower of the Cathedral, and we shall soon learn all that Miss Hunter has to tell.'

The ' Black Swan ' is an inn of repute in the High Street, at no distance from the station, and there we found the young lady waiting for us.

' The Copper Beeches,' among the *Adventures of Sherlock Holmes*, by A. Conan Doyle.

George Newnes, 1892.

OLD BOB, in the face, was rather like Socrates ; in form, save as to shoulders, he strongly resembled Punch. . . . He dressed the character of the old schoolmaster, from the shovel-hat and powdered bald head to the gaiters, as correctly as if he proposed to act it in a farce.   ' Old Bob '[1]

. . . In general Old Bob was good-tempered, patient and forbearing, not punishing without fair warning, and then with deliberate dignity. But on peculiar provocation, as by anything like the exhibition of a mutinous spirit, especially on the part of a big boy, he lost all control of himself. His face grew pale, his eyes twinkled ominously, he would puff his cheeks out,

[1] The Hyde Abbey Boys' School, Winchester, was founded about 1760; it ended in 1833 on death of Rev. Chas. Richards (' Old Bob '), who was schoolmaster for fifty years, thirty-one of which he was also vicar of the parish. He retired in 1828, and on his death the whole of the premises were put up to auction.

and his whole form appeared actually to swell.   Then, pulling up his nether garments—a habit with him when in a rage— and his voice shaking with passion, he would exclaim, ' Take care, Sir.   Let me not hear thee say that again.   If thou dost, I 'll whip thee.   I 'd whip thee if thou wast as high as the house !   I 'd whip thee if thou wast as big as Goliath ! ! ' and it was generally understood among us that he would have done so in either case. . . .

' A Sample of the Old School,' in *Household Words*, May 18, 1850.

' Whipping us up Parnassus '

. . . Such implicit confidence had Old Bob in birch that he imagined he could absolutely whip us up Parnassus, and he very often flogged a boy for not being able to do his verses. ' I 'll make thee a poet, my boy,' he used to say, ' or the rod shall.'

Ibid.

' Example is better than Precept '

Old Bob had a very high idea of the force of example.   Incredible as it may appear, it is a fact that he would send a troublesome pupil to see an execution (at Winchester Gaol).   I once witnessed him doing this.   The boy in question was incorrigibly mischievous, and given to roguish pranks.   Addressing him by name, Old Bob said, ' There is a man to be hanged this morning.   Go and see him, my boy.   Thou art a bad boy, and it will do thee good.   You '—turning to an elder boy—' you go with him and take charge of him.'   Truly this was carrying out the principle of ' the good old school.'

Ibid.

PART II

THE CATHEDRAL

§ 1. THE VENERABLE PILE

THERE is a giant massy pile uprears
His head at Winchester ; the very stones
Are History ; the ancient coffined bones
Of Saxon kings, brings back the bygone years
Of Egbert's sovereignty ; the solid tiers
Of pillars, where the organ's solemn tones
Float wondrously, recall the tyrant thrones
Of Norman dynasty ; most fitting chroniclers.
The Western Window, all its tinted glass
Destroyed by Cromwell's soldiery ; the screen
Of richest Gothic carving, once a mass
Of ornament, now shorn of silver sheen
By fierce Iconoclast ; the rich deep glow
Of Eastern Window ; each their story show.

'Winchester Cathedral,' by 'Old Wykehamist.'
In *The Wykehamist*, October 1886.

THE cathedrale chirch and the close lyith on the south side of
the towne, and is in cumpace with the cemitery nere half a
mile ; and one side of it hemmith in the toune as the waul of
it, even almost from the Kinges Gate to the very palace waulle
of Wolvesey.

John Leland's *Itinerary*.

AND now we are in the Cathedral yard, a spot crowded with
historical memories. At the corner we entered, reaching from
Great Minster Street to Market Street, and from the High

'A giant massy pile'

'The Cathedrale Chirch'

Grand and solemn

115

Street to the Square, was the palace of William the Conqueror ; east of that as far as the end of the Cathedral yard, was 'the New Minster'; and beyond that again St. Mary's Abbey of Nuns, the Nunnamestre. The New Minster, so called to distinguish it from the Old—that is, the Cathedral, with its monastery—was founded by King Alfred, under the learned St. Grimbald, for the purpose of the education of priests and young nobles of his court. Within this New Minster Alfred himself was buried.

But now look at the Cathedral west front through the stately vista of limes and the huge nave. No one will deny that it looks heavy in its massiveness, with nothing to break the lines, only a very low tower at the intersection of the transepts in their great Norman simplicity, almost as Bishop Walkelin left them 800 years ago. It is all very grand and solemn in the still churchyard, but the visitor at first sight would hardly put this in the first rank of cathedrals. There is not the grace of Salisbury, nor the rich ornament of Lichfield, nor the stately towers of Canterbury and York, nor the splendid situation of Durham and Lincoln. Massive grandeur, but not beauty, will be his first judgment, but let him suspend that judgment till he gets inside ; meanwhile, we will walk round the exterior. We pass the west front, which has a large Perpendicular window, and doorways of curious sharp-pointed arches. These are the work of Bishop Edyngdon (middle of fourteenth century). Then we come at the south-west corner to a narrow passage, which conducts us round into the Cathedral Close. This passage, called the Slype, was constructed by Bishop Curle (1636), in order to save the Cathedral from the desecration of a footway which went through it. It has these curious inscriptions upon it :—

ILL\ \
☞ >AC   PREC\ \
H/   VI >ATOR AMBULA ☞

Illac precator, hac viator ambula ('Worshipper, go that way ; traveller, this ').

CESSIT COMMUNI PROPRIUM JAM PERGITE QUA FAS.

'Private right has yielded to public, now go by the way which is open to thee.'

S ⟨ ACR / ERV ⟩ A   S ⟩ IT / F   ILL / IST ⟩ A   CH ⟩ ORO / F

'Let the way be sacred to the choir, and this is made handmaid to the market-place.'

> 'Winchester Cathedral,' by Canon Benham, in
> *Our English Minsters.*
>
> Isbister and Co.

. . . THE hour
Of twilight mostly aids the power
Of fancy o'er the dreaming mind.
Then, if your thoughts the leisure find,
Seek ye the venerable pile,
And in the broad nave stand, the while
Creep slowly in the shades of night,
And faint and fainter streams the light
Through the west window's coloured pane,
Which seems in richest hues to stain
The pillars high and ample floor.
Then let your musing eye run o'er
The beauty and the power that lives
Around, to which the dim light gives
A grander, loftier aspect—then
The buried past may breathe again,
And in the deepening gloom of night,
A ruder pile meets fancy's sight,
And war-cries of the conquering Dane
Strike terror through the holy fane ;
And rushing feet, and shrieks of woe,
And prayers to the unsparing foe

'The vast and venerable pile'

Are heard, and prayers to heaven.—In vain :
The demon-rout rush in amain,
And groans of dying men resound,
And monk and priest lie slaughtered round.
Then shouts of fiendish triumph tear
The sacred roof.   But soon a fair
And noble structure o'er the scene
Of carnage rises—Walkelin
Hath built his massy Norman tower ;
The priesthood reign in pomp and power,
And in a gay procession bear
The image of their patron, dear
Saint Swithun, to his ancient shrine.
And now in proud succession shine
The holy prelates—calmer years
Succeed : the noble Wykeham rears
His nave, expanding to the view
Like to a broad-arched avenue.

.   .   .   .   .   .

. . . Hark ! strange words of ire
Startle the echoes of the choir,
With Bible texts uncouthly blended,
And holy rites are to be mended
By mailed priests, the gun-and-sword
Expounders of the Gospel-word.
Yet scarce can their brief rage deface
The beauties of the hallowed place,
Or trouble Wykeham's calm repose
Near tombs which royal dust enclose :
There Christian hearts revere him still ;
Nor will his glory cease to fill
That vast and venerable pile,
The noblest of our Saxon isle.

Christopher Wood.
Reminiscences of Winchester, c. 1860.

THE surroundings of the Cathedral are the embodiment of calmness and cloistral seclusion ; indeed this *religio loci*, this hallowed τεμενος is, perhaps, nowhere so powerfully experienced as at Winchester, whose Close bursts upon the visitor as he turns into it from the busy, cheerful High Street for the first time, in a manner which deeply affects, but does not overwhelm. There is perhaps nothing more strikingly beautiful than the spectacle presented by that noble avenue of limes leading up to the west front of the Cathedral, amid whose long-drawn, silver-grey Perpendicular nave, low Norman tower, deeply projecting transepts, choir and eastern chapels, there resides an indescribable air of English sturdiness and solidity—a contrast to the huge, well-nigh immeasurable piles of Amiens, Bourges, Chartres, or Rheims. To some, this great church may at first sight appear rather as a work of nature than of man. Yet what great name does it not recall ? Swithun, Walkelin, Godfrey de Lucy, Edingdon, Wykeham, Beaufort, Waynflete, Fox.

Turning from the church itself we have the velvety turf surrounding it, prebendal houses—Tudor, Jacobean, Caroline, Georgian, modern, all mixed up together in the most delightfully heterogeneous manner possible, their gardens aglow with midsummer's most brilliant floral tributes ; while the modest mignonette perfumes the air, already heavily laden with the scent of the lime avenue. . . .

T. Francis Bumpus.
Cathedrals of England and Wales.
T. Werner Laurie, 1906.

MAJESTIC 'midst its immemorial limes
   The grey Cathedral rears its massive head ;
No sound, except the cadence of the chimes,
   Breaks through the silence of the sleeping dead,
Save where, beneath the shadows of the trees,
Drones the low melody of countless bees.

The houses cluster round its mighty pile,
　　Lying among the creases of the down,
And over all the great tower seems to smile
　　A calm assurance to the watching town.
Like to some wise old man, whose eye can see
All that has been, and all that is to be.

The chequered centuries beneath it rolled,
　　Each with its mingled tale of peace and war,
And, still unchanged, it waits the time foretold
　　When strife shall cease and battle be no more,
Calm o'er the heat of life where round its base
Man frets and chatters out his noisy space.

The grass grows lank o'er many a lichened grave
　　Crumbling to ruin in the churchyard there ;
And in the cloistered coolness of the nave,
　　With meek hands clasped in an eternal prayer,
Lie those whose purity has won renown,
The bishop's mitre with the prince's crown.

　　　　　　　　　　　'St. Swithun,' in *Poems and Parodies*,
　　　　　　　　　　　　　　by J. L. Crommelin-Brown.
　　　　　　　　　　　　P. and G. Wells, Winchester, 1908.

'The grey, fortress-like Cathedral'

FULL-CLOTHED in freshest verdure tremble the lofty lindens of the Close ; firm as a rock stands the grey, fortress-like Cathedral, its oldest stonework undecayed as though built yesterday. A side-wicket admits to the vast interior, with massy pillars, and roof high-embowed over the coffins of old kings : solemn and monumental the weighty transept arches and plain thick pillars of Norman work. Noble, too, are these clustered columns of the nave ; yet I wish, on the whole, that Bishop William and others had withheld their hands from *perpendicularity*. The nave windows are to me of ugly form, the tracery of the great west window stands an offence, which its fine glass hardly condones.   And this glass is but a patchwork. Upon Cheriton Down, one March day of 1644, the Roundheads smote the Cavaliers, and, leaving many brave men dead and dying on the hill, came grimly down into Winchester and smashed the Cathedral windows and monuments.   The gathered bits of glass, *disjecta membra* of saints, kings, queens, bishops, warriors, a fragment of a motto, a corner of a device, broken as they are, make splendid this tall, greenish-bluish west window....

William Allingham.
Varieties in Prose.
Longmans, Green and Co.

Low in the vale appears, in Gothic state
Yon Temple's pile, magnificently great ;
As though the fretted iles, at dead of night,
Blind Superstition taught the taper'd rite,
Each white-robed priest his chaunting vespers sung,
And the dire dirge thro' echoing arches rung ;
With such, perhaps, amid the awful gloom,
The stoled fathers raised their Rufus' tomb ;
Or ranged in long array and order dread,
Their Alfred's honoured bier slow-pacing led,
And shrin'd each Saxon King in mansions of the dead.

Seen from the King's House

'The Prospect from the King's House, Winchester,' under
'Poetry' in *The Hampshire Repository*, 1798.

THE Cathedral has stood ' twice as long as the great Jewish Temple of old . . . it is a very moving thing to be able to look back eight hundred years and think of those who have trodden these self-same floors and looked on these massive walls.   This church has been visited by almost every prince and many a man of note in English history.   It was built to be to Norman England what the Temple had been to the Jews—the central expression of a nation's faith, the place dedicated to the con-centrated worship of the conquering race.   It was the seat of

The Temple

great Bishops, who advanced their country's welfare in matters of art and learning and religion. The whole early history of England and much of its later history seems bound up with it.'

From a Sermon by Dean Kitchin on the Eight-hundredth
Anniversary.

The Sense of Awe

I REMEMBER well the day when, a mere child, just fresh from home, I was first allowed as a Wykehamist to claim my place Sunday after Sunday in this Cathedral. The sense of awe, of uplifting glory, is as fresh and overpowering now, as it was more than fifty-eight years ago.

Archdeacon Fearon, preaching in Winchester Cathedral,
July 10, 1910.

The venerable Cathedral

ONCE the capital of England, this historical city is strikingly situated on the slopes and at the bottom of the chalk valley through which the river Itchen flows nearly due north and south. Surrounded as it is by chalk downs, there are many beautiful views from them of the venerable Cathedral standing on the more level ground in the centre of the old town, which contains so much of architectural and antiquarian interest.

Wessex, painted by Walter Tyndale, described by Clive Holland.
A. and C. Black, 1906.

'A fatherly and ancient Sovereign'

IF Salisbury, with its striking and beautiful tenuity of forms, its slim windows and its graceful columns, its attractive spire, compelling immediate notice and admiration from every quarter, is (as she deserves to be) crowned the refined and delicate queen of our southern cathedrals, Winchester may be considered their fatherly and ancient Sovereign, and its grave and noble aspect excites the respectful feeling due to patriarchal years and thoughtful wisdom.

Charles Townsend.
Winchester, etc., 1842.

Winchester and Salisbury Cathedrals compared

THE exterior of the Cathedral is remarkable for the plainness of its masonry, the length of its nave, and the solidity of its tower, which rises only about twenty feet above the roof. In these

respects it is so essentially different from the neighbouring
Cathedral of Salisbury, that a comparison may be entered
into of the respective beauties and peculiarities of them. At
the first glance at the exterior of the Cathedral of Salisbury,
we are delighted with its elegant lightness, the appropriateness
of its ornaments, and its perfect uniformity of design, whilst
we gaze with mixed feelings of awe and admiration on its
' heaven-directed spire '; but when we view—steadily view—
the exterior of that of Winchester, though it command not all
those pleasurable emotions, we are struck by its solemn grandeur,
its vastness of extent, and its immovable solidity. When we
enter the nave of the former, we are still pleased with its
elegant grace, and wonder how the slender shafts of its columns
uphold its massive roof ; but the flood of light poured in destroys
those sensations of sublimity which the darker nave of the
latter, with its ponderous pillars, so admirably sustain.   Salisbury
Cathedral must be taken as a whole—Winchester Cathedral
must be examined in all its parts. If the exterior of the one
delights and charms us, the interior of the other commands our
admiration and reverence.   Salisbury appears as if it had sprung
into existence at the touch of the wand of some mighty magician,
as perfect and as beautiful as it now appears to an enraptured
eye : Winchester, on the contrary, bears on its brow the marks
of ages, and presents to the antiquarian the most perfect
specimens of the growth of the pointed style from the period of
unadorned simplicity, till at last it became encumbered, nay
buried, beneath heaps of ornament.

Prouten's Winchester Guide, c. 1850.

§ 2. ST. SWITHUN

WINCHESTER may be justly called the City of the Saints, for
biographers enumerate ten canonised bishops of this see. . . .
It has derived a popular celebrity as the resting-place of St.
Swithin, the removal of whose remains during a heavy rain

The City of
the Saints

has given rise to the belief, that, if it should rain on his feast, it will continue to fall in a deluge for forty days after.

M. E. C. Walcott.
Memorials of Winchester, 1866.

Seynt Swithun

Seynt Swithun his bishopricke to al goodnesse drough,
The towne also of Winchester he amended enough,
For he lette the strong bruge without the towne arere,
And fond thereto lym and ston and the workmen that were there.

Fourteenth-century Poem.

'Twice twenty days'

How, if on Swithin's feast the welkin lours,
And every penthouse streams with hasty showers,
Twice twenty days shall clouds their fleeces drain,
And wash the pavements with incessant rain.

John Gay.
Trivia, Book I. l. 183, *et seq.*

St. Swithun the rainy

ST. SWITHUN's day, if thou dost rain,
For forty days it will remain ;
St. Swithun's day, if thou be faire,
For forty days 'twill raine nae maire.

Proverbial Rhyme.

UNUM BEATI SWITHUNI MIRACULUM

St. Swithun mends the Eggs

INTER SIGNA GLORIOSI SWITHUNI ANTISTITIS
Que per eum rex caelestis hac in vita edidit
Hoc ex multis unum refert prisca fama populi
Conditoris quod in Laude paucis libet promere.

Iidem namque pastor almus & provisor strenuus
Forte pontem extruebat geminasque januas
Per quas urbis Winthoniae adeuntur moenia
Artifices congregati huic instabant operi.

Forum petens casu venit illuc muliercula
  Ova ferens unde vitae mercetur subsidia
  Quae ludendo operantum confregit stultitia
  Atque victum miserandae ademit pauperculae.

Illa pium atque mitem requirit pontificem
  Et plorando illi suum exponit dispendium
  Cui cultor pietatis benignus ac dapsilis
  Per cunctatus mox ovorum duplum reddit precium.

Post haec ille domino plenus caritate profluus
  Puras coelo manus librat effundens oramina
  Et creantis motu cuncta mox ova redintegrat
  Gaudens illa sic discessit domino laudes reddidit.

.   .   .   .

Gratuletur et exultet felix urbs Winthonia
  Que virtute tanti patris meritisque rutilat
  Cujus sacra fovet ossa sentit & miracula
  Incessanter illi plaudat odas cum letitia.

.   .   .   .

A Tenth-century MS. in the British Museum.—MS. Reg. 15.
c. vii. fol. penult.

Prologue: Song of the Itchen

COOL from the veins of the rolling hills   St. Swithun
Flow for ever my laughing rills,
Ripple on ripple eternally,
Rippling away to the infinite sea.
Sons of men ye build on my side,
Field to field ye lay in your pride,—
Think for a moment how many of old,
Made little names with their heaps of gold,
Piling their houses beside my waters ;—
Like leaves and sticks on a stormy day
That I sweep in thousands away and away,

Never again shall men give them a word,
Gone from the mind with their sons and daughters ;—
Still for ever my ripple is heard,
Ripple and ripple, and ripple for aye,—
Stealing along, when never a sound
Pierced the measureless forest around,
Only the anthem of birds in spring,
Only the wild winds' whispering,
Only the wolf with his lonely cry
Seeking his meat of his Master on high,
And still (as in earlier aeons, like dreams
Dimly remembered) the voice of my streams.
Stealing along, when by fairy hands
The city was laid in my meadow lands
(Carried away from the thymy hill,
Where the fairies dance in the moonlight still).
Stealing along, when Cerdic's host
Won for ever our English coast,
When my shallows were troubled and dark with
    blood,
And the heap of the slaughter choked my flood,
When the sons of Woden in steady array,
Strong as my stream when it sweeps to the tide,
Drove the chieftains that turned to bay
Down the sward of the steep hill-side.
Rightly ye judge that your land is great,—
I saw the foundation of all your state,
Not in the glitter of blades alone,
But in trowel and hammer on wood and stone,—
In gentle deeds of the strong and the wise,—
In them that quietly lifted their eyes
Through all the tumult of tongue and of sword
To the glory of peace that should come from the Lord.
Such was he that we honour to-day,
Who spanned with arches my watery way,

Wise in the counsels of warrior kings,
Teacher of rulers mighty and good,
Faithful in great and in little things,
Feeding the poor with the Master's food,
Building his churches beside my wave,—
To the furthest hereafter he speaks from the grave.

.   .   .   .

[St. Swithun builds a wall round the Cathedral and a bridge
across the Itchen.]

Except the Lord with guarding hand
    Shall stay beside our rising wall,
Except the watchman at his stand
    Can on our God for succour call ;
Then all our work is thrown away,
    And strength, and skill, and foresight fail.
Look Thou on what we build to-day,
    That by Thy grace it may prevail.
And when with stone a wall we raise
    To keep our dwelling-place within,
Set Thou about our heart always
    A fence against the storm of sin.
And when with pier and arch we throw
    A road across the foaming stream,
Keep Thou the feet of them that go,
    From sin's delirious wandering dream.
For good it is that man by man
    Should dwell in safety side by side ;
And good it is the bridge should span
    The river that would keep them wide.
But on the builder still the pain
    Of fear and inward doubting falls,
Lest sense, oppression, lust of gain,
    Should taint his houses, foul his walls.

Then let the town for Thee increase,
  For Thee the tide of commerce flow,
Lest secret rapine pass for peace,
  And wealth of one be others' woe.

.   .   .   .

[Saint Swithun old, and troubled at the inroads of the Danes.]

Vain to have watched for weary, weary years,
To see the breaking of the dawn of peace ;
Within, without, are darkness, horror, fears ;
      Father, release.
For all about Thy little fold
The heathen wolves are howling for the prey ;
Fruitless our victories—on our spirits, cold
      Creeping dismay.
Vain to have toiled afoot through night and storm,
To preach, to hallow houses to Thy name ;
Thy Church is wasted by the godless swarm,
      And put to shame.
Only within the walls that I have reared
Our little brotherhood may breathe awhile,
And I, howe'er our wider hopes are seared,
      May work and smile.

[St. Swithun dies, desiring to be buried among the poor.]

Brothers, a long and a last good-night !
  Sleep to the weary is sweet.
Leave me to rest till in infinite light
  Of an endless morning we meet.
Lay me to sleep in the cool soft sod
  By my own Cathedral door,
With the brothers on earth of my Saviour and God,
  The friends that I loved—the poor.

English Verse, *St. Swithun*, by G. R. Benson.
The Wykehamist, July 1883.

HANC portam presens cernis quicumque viator ;
Devocat effunde preces ad celsitonantem.
Pro Christi famulo Swithun antistite quondam ;
Per cujus summam cum sollicitudine curam.
Est hujus ponas constructa operatio pulchra,
Ad Christi laudem, Wentane urbisque decorem ;
Sol octingentos cum rite revolveret annos.
Quinquaginta novem replicaret et insuper annos
Incarnata fuit postquam miseratio Christi.
Tunc erat et vertent indictio septima cursum.

Wentane urbisque decorem

A Tenth-century MS. in the British Museum.—MS. Reg. 15.
c. vii. fol. penult.

No orator was he to sway the State,
  Yet statesmen envied him his simple speech ;
No King upon whose bidding courtiers wait,
  Yet Kings were wont his blessing to beseech.
Unnoticed by the roaring world outside,
Quiet he lived and worked, and quiet died.

The Humble Saint

Such was his sanctity that when he prayed,
  Old sinners hearing, so the stories say,
Trembled as Felix did, and were afraid
  At the more perfect knowledge of the Way.
And yet his people ever found him kind,
Helping the laggards, leading on the blind.

Ah ! humble Saint ! who made a last request
  Before his spirit turned again to God,
That after death his buried bones should rest
  Beneath the eaves, where every passer trod.
And so, within his ancient Abbey's shade,
He who had lived in peace, in peace was laid.

I

And when long after, as the legend goes,
   The monks removed him from this lowly **tomb**
To fitter burial, great clouds arose,
   Blotted the heaven's face with angry gloom,
The cow'ring world with whips of tempest lashed,
While round the thunder buffeted and crashed.

.   .   .   .   .   .

Sleep on, Saint Swithun—not in that poor space
   Which thou didst ask of thy humility ;
Thy holy relics found a worthier place
   And one more fitted to such piety,
Where the great organ, shouting through the pile,
Shakes the dim vista of a listening aisle.

.   .   .   .   .

'St. Swithun' in *Poems and Parodies*,
by J. L. Crommelin-Brown.
P. and G. Wells, Winchester, 1908.

§ 3. FOUNDERS' TOMBS

'That most beautiful Cathedral in Europe'

WITHIN the shrine of Winchester Cathedral are buried the architects who erected that most beautiful Cathedral in Europe ; but not every architect is so happy as to sleep in the structure his hands have builded.

Ward Beecher.

'Praesul praegratus'

EDYNDON natus Wilhelmus hic est tumulatus
Praesul praegratus, in Wintonia cathedratus.
Qui pertransitis, ejus memorare velitis.
Providus et mitis, ausit cum mille peritis.
Pervigil Anglorum fuit adjutor populorum
Dulcis egenorum pater et protector eorum.
M. C. tribus junctum, post L. X. V. sit I. punctum
Octava sanctum notat hunc Octobris injunctum.

Inscription on Edington's tomb.

[William, born at Edington, is here interred.

He was a well-beloved prelate, and Winchester was his see.

You, who pass by his tomb, remember him in your prayers.

He was discreet and mild, yet a match for thousands in knowledge and sagacity.

He was a watchful guardian of the English nation,

A tender father of the poor and the defender of their rights.

To one thousand add three hundred with fifty, ten, five,
and one,

Then the eighth of October will mark the time when he became
a saint.]

Translation given in Milner's *History of Winchester*.

WILHELMINUS dictus Wykeham jacet hic nece victus :   'Largus erat
dapifer'
Istius ecclesiæ presul, reparavit eamque.

Largus erat dapifer ; probat hoc cum divite pauper ;

Consiliis pariter regni fuerat bene dexter.

Hunc docet esse pium fundatio collegiorum :

Oxoniae primum fiat Wintoniaeque secundum.

Jugiter oretis, tumulum quicunque videtis,

Pro tantis meritis ut sit sibi vita perennis.

Inscription on Wykeham's tomb.

[William surnamed Wykeham lies overthrown by death :

He was bishop of this church and repairer of it.

He was unbounded in his hospitality, as the poor and the rich
can equally prove.

He was likewise a sage politician and counsellor of the state.

His piety is manifest by the colleges which he founded :

The first of which is at Oxford, the second at Winchester.

You who look on this monument, cease not to pray

That for such great deserts he may enjoy eternal life.]

Translation given in Milner's *History of Winchester*.

**At the tomb
of Wykeham**

WYKEHAM, around thy venerable tomb
With fond affection still thy children come ;
And tho' no more the loud-voiced hymn they sing,
Still silent prayers and heartfelt wishes bring,
That thy departed Spirit, secure and blest,
May with the destined heirs of glory rest ;
And, for thy pious bounty here bestow'd,
Treasure in Heaven may have, and joy in God !

Lines written at the tomb of William of Wykeham, in
Winchester Cathedral, by William Crowe, 1788.

**The Holy
Spot**

. . . THERE Otway often bowed
In pensive awe, before he went his way
To fame and misery.   He who endowed
His country's lyre with notes that call away
The soul from Earth to Heaven, sad, thoughtful Young,
Hath pondered o'er that tomb.   There too the gay

Somerville, for a musing hour, hath hung
Admiring ; and the gentle bard who mourned
O'er Thomson's grave,[1] there dreamed.   But he who sung

Saint Catherine's Mount in classic numbers, turned
Oftenest to that grave, Winton's own bard,
The learned Warton.—Many more who earned

Renown in the wide world, with meek regard
To the wise prelate, have their tribute paid.
And long will gratitude and reverence guard

The holy spot in which his bones are laid ;
And where his gentle spirit soars above
The cold dull marble, and hath worthier made

[1] Collins.

Souls worthy—inspiring them with earnest love
Of humankind.   His ardent charity
Lives in old Winton's heart.   Still may it prove
Her virtue through the bright days yet to be !

Christopher Wood.
Reminiscences of Winchester, c. 1860.

THIS being *Sunday*, I heard, about 7 o'clock in the morning, a sort of jangling, made by a bell or two in the *Cathedral* . . . hearing the bells of the Cathedral, I took Richard to show him that ancient and most magnificent pile, and particularly to show him the tomb of that famous bishop of Winchester, WILLIAM OF WYKEHAM ; who was the Chancellor and the Minister of the great and glorious King, Edward III., who sprang from poor parents in the little village of Wykham, three miles from Botley ; and who, amongst other great and most munificent deeds, founded the famous College, or School, of Winchester, and also one of the Colleges at Oxford.   I told Richard about this as we went from the inn down to the Cathedral ; and when I *showed him the tomb,* where the bishop lies on his back, in his Catholic robes, with his mitre on his head, his shepherd's crook by his side, with little children at his feet, their hands put together in a praying attitude, he looked with a degree of inquisitive earnestness that pleased me very much.   I took him as far as I could about the Cathedral.

[margin: In his Catholic Robes]

William Cobbett, Rural Rides, 1825.

§ 4. CATHEDRAL MUSIC

SOME idea of part-singing as practised in Winchester in the eleventh century can be formed from these data [the Winchester Organa, undoubtedly used in the Old Minster].   The art was in a state of transition : the earlier writers, such as Isidore, Aurelian, Hucbald, etc., had confined themselves to a bare definition and

[margin: Winchester Music in the Eleventh Century]

classification of concords, but in the writings of the later tenth century we see that a great step forward had been made. . . .

The Winchester Organa exhibit all the three kinds of harmonic motion. In the Sequence-melodies, for example, two clear instances of contrary motion occur in the Allelulia of the first melody, but it is the exception, and the vox organalis proceeds mainly by oblique motion or by similar motion, probably a fourth below the vox principalis. . . . Contrary motion is rare, though it does occur, and it is interesting to note on the syllable eth*ni*ke that the quilisma of the principalis is accompanied by a sort of descending quilisma in the organalis.

W. H. Frere.
The Winchester Troper, Henry Bradshaw Soc., 1894.

The Magic Soother

THOU magic soother of the soul's unrest,
Of nature's gifts the holiest and the best !
What power first called thee, music, from thy cell,
And bade thee in thy living numbers tell
Of mortal joys or griefs, of smiles or tears,
Of heaven-born hopes, and trembling earthly fears,
And bade thee rouse with soul-inspiring art
The fire of passion in the human heart ?

.   .   .   .   .   .

But oh ! thrice blest was he who made thee rise
To God, as man's accepted sacrifice,

.   .   .   .   .   .

Where in the sombre majesty of years
Some huge cathedral-pile its form uprears,
Within whose walls a mellow light is shed
O'er monuments of unforgotten dead,

.   .   .   .   .   .

Now, peals thy voice as, when the clouds are riven
By flying flame, the thunder voice of Heaven,
Now in unutterable harmonies
Murmuring it rises, trembles, sinks and dies,

And now in slower and more solemn tone
Rings o'er that massive majesty of stone
Till grand old arch and monumental mound
Seem the embodiment of stately sound ;

.   .   .   .

Then fades and swoons, so as almost to seem
The music of a half-forgotten dream,
And falls as lightly on the willing air
As Seraph's footfalls on the golden stair,
Then swells in undertone, as flowering trees
Sound with unceasing murmuring of bees,
Whispering far down the vista of the aisle,
And giant pillars of the time-worn pile,
Where fretted arch and vaulted roof look down
On tombs of those who planned for their renown
The noblest shrine that mortal hand can raise,
A home of God, a sanctuary of praise.
Until, beneath the lofty eastern dome,
Where sculptured marble marks great Beaufort's tomb,
With eyes and cold stone hands upraised to heaven,
As even in death he prayed to be forgiven,
The sound might seem, as there we muse alone,
To call a smile on features wrought of stone.

'Cathedral Music,' Prize English Poem, Winchester
College, 1866, by E. D. A. Morsehead.
Published in *The Wykehamist*, October 1866.

§ 5. SOME VISITORS, ETC.

October 3, 1642-3.

I WENT to Winchester where I visited the castle, school, church, **John Evelyn**
and King Arthur's Round Table, but especially the church and **at the Cathedral**
its Saxon kings' monuments, which I esteemed a worthy antiquity.

Evelyn's *Diary*.

September 16, 1685.

HENCE (from the King's House) to see the Cathedral, a reverend pile, and in good repair. There are still coffins of the six Saxon kings, whose bones had been scattered by the sacrilegious rebels of 1641, in expectation, I suppose, of finding some valuable relics, and afterwards gathered up again and put into new chests, which stand above the stalls of the choir.

Evelyn's *Diary*.

Tuesday, October 24, 1738.

A visit to the Cathedral, 1738

As soon as it was light we got away (from Alresford), and before nine o'clock we arrived at Winchester, and in the house of Master Gauntlet. The first thing I did was to write to my Lady Peterborough to let her know I would dine with her the next day if it was convenient. . . . We then took our walk to the Cathedral, which I looked over with more curious eyes than I had done before. I took notice in the choir of a fine old pulpit carved and given by one Silkstead who had been prior of Winchester. I also took notice of the nave of the church, that is where the crosses meet; this was beautiful and repaired by King Charles the First, and there is his picture with his son, King Charles the Second, in his arms. King Charles the First gave the fine canopy over the altar, as also the fine prayer books for the service of the altar. I do not doubt, but you remember the fine steps to the altar, the fine rail, and the extreme curious pavement composed of several sorts of marble. This was done by the will of Dr. William Harris, who died in 1700, and bequeathed to the church £800 for that design, and it is executed with great exactness and beauty. I think this gentleman's name should not be forgot.

I do not know if you took notice in one of the side aisles of a monument (it is only a flat stone upon the floor) of the Countess of Essex. She was married to Sir Thomas Higgins, and he made an oration in the church at the funeral, and, if you please to remember, showed it you in manuscript. We then proceeded to the college, the church, school and library. These places afforded us no manner of new discovery. And here I will end my first letter.

> A Journey through Hampshire in 1738, in the handwriting of the second Earl of Oxford, apparently addressed to his wife (*Hist. MSS. Com.*, Duke of Portland's MSS.).

STRAWBERRY HILL, *September* 18, 1755.

. . . I LIKE the smugness of the cathedral and the profusion of the most beautiful Gothic tombs. That of Cardinal Beaufort is in a style more free and of more taste than anything I have seen of the kind. . . . Besides the monuments of the Saxon kings, of Lucius, William Rufus, his brother, etc., there are those of six such great or considerable men as Beaufort, William of Wickham, him of Wainfleet, the Bishops Fox and Gardiner, and my Lord Treasurer Portland. How much power and ambition under half a dozen stones! I own, I grow to look on tombs as lasting mansions, instead of observing them for curious pieces of architecture. *[margin: The 'smugness' of the Cathedral]*

> Horace Walpole to Richard Bentley.
> *Letters* (Clarendon Press edition), iii. 341-2.

Thursday, October 3, 1771.

THURSDAY, 3rd, at Winchester. I now found time to take a view of the Cathedral. Here the sight of that bad Cardinal's tomb, whom the sculptor has placed in a posture of prayer, brought to my mind those fine lines of Shakespeare, which he put into the mouth of King Henry the Sixth : *[margin: John Wesley in Winchester Cathedral]*

> 'Lord Cardinal,
> If thou hast any hope of Heaven's grace,
> Give us a sign. He dies, and makes no sign.'
>> John Wesley's *Journal.*

> [The only words that remain of the inscription round Beaufort's tomb are : *Tribularer, si nescirem misericordias tuas.*]

Fanny Burney
at Winchester
Cathedral,
1791

WEDNESDAY, August 3. We walked to the Cathedral and saw it completely. Part of it remains from the original Saxon building, though neglected, except by travellers, as the rest of the church is ample for all uses, and alone kept in repair. The bones of eleven Saxon Kings are lodged in seven curious old chests, in which they were deposited after being dug up and disturbed in civil wars and ensuing confusions. The small number of chests is owing to the small proportion remaining of some of the skeletons, which occasioned their being united with others. The Saxon characters are in many inscriptions preserved, though in none entire. They were washing a plaster from the walls, to discern some curious old painting, very miserable, but very entertaining, of old legends, which some antiquaries are now endeavouring to discover.

William of Wykeham, by whom the Cathedral was built in its present form, lies buried, with his effigy and whole monument in very fine alabaster, and probably very like, as it was done, they aver, before he died.

Its companion, equally superb, is Cardinal Beaufort, uncle of Harry VI. William Rufus, slain in the neighbouring forest, is buried in the old choir : his monument is of plain stone, without any inscription or ornament and only shaped like a coffin. Hardyknute had a much more splendid monument preserved for him ; [1] but Harry had other business to attend, I presume, than to decorate the tomb of one brother while despoiling of his kingdom another.

An extremely curious old chapel and monument remain of Archbishop Langton, of venerable Gothic workmanship. The altar, which is highly adorned with gold, was protected in Cromwell's time by the address and skill of the Winton inhabitants who ran up a slight wall before it, and deceived the Reformists, *soi-disants*. I could hardly quit this poor dear old

---

[1] It is inscribed :—

Qui jacet hic regni sceptrum tulit, Hardicanutus
Emmae Cnutonis gnatus et ipse fuit.

                              Ob. A.D. IXLI.

building, so much was I interested with its Saxon chiefs, its queer little niches, quaint images, damp cells, mouldering walls, and mildewed pillars. One chest contains the bones entire of Egbert, our first King. Edred also, I distinguished.

The screen was given to this church by King Charles, and is the work of Inigo Jones. It is very simple in point of ornament, very complete in taste and elegance ; nevertheless, a screen of Grecian architecture in a Cathedral of Gothic workmanship was ill, I think, imagined.

Diary and Letters of Madame D'Arblay, London, 1842-6.

IN the Cathedral, I was gratified at least by the ample dimensions. The length of line exceeds that of any other English church ; being 556 feet by 250 in breadth of transept. I think I prefer this church to all I have seen, except Westminster and York. Here was Canute buried, and here Alfred the Great was crowned and buried, and here the Saxon Kings ; and later, in his own church, William of Wykeham. It is very old ; part of the crypt into which we went down and saw the Saxon and Norman arches of the old church on which the present stands, was built fourteen or fifteen hundred years ago. Sharon Turner says, ' Alfred was buried at Winchester, in the Abbey he had founded there, but his remains were removed by Henry I. to the new Abbey in the meadows at Hyde, on the northern quarter of the city, and laid under the high altar. The building was destroyed at the Reformation, and what is left of Alfred's body now lies covered by modern buildings or buried in the ruins of the old.' William of Wykeham's shrine tomb was unlocked for us, and C. took hold of the recumbent statue's marble hands, and patted them affectionately, for he rightly values the brave man who built Windsor, and this Cathedral and the School here, and New College at Oxford. But it was growing late in the afternoon. Slowly we left the old house, and parting with our host, we took the train for London.

Emerson visits the Cathedral

R. W. Emerson, English Traits, 1856.
Concerning a Journey to England made in 1833 and 1847.

Greville
visits
Winchester

AUGUST 4th (1835). Came to town on Sunday, having slept at Winchester on Saturday night to see the town and the cathedral, and hear the service in the latter, which was very moderate ; the cathedral, however, is worth seeing.

The Greville Memoirs.

Dean Rennell
(Dean of
Winchester,
1805-40)

DEAN RENNELL was a man of very superior abilities, but of great eccentricity, mainly due to extreme absence of mind. It used to be told of him that unless Mrs. Rennell took good care, he was tolerably certain, when he went up to his room to dress for a dinner-party, to go to bed.

.   .   .   .

Among the stories that were current of Rennell I remember one to the effect that when upon one occasion he was posting from Winchester to London he stopped at Egham for luncheon. A huge round of boiled beef, nearly uncut, was placed upon the table.   But the dean found it was, as he thought, far too much boiled ; so without more ado he cut the huge mass into four quarters and helped himself to a morsel from the centre !   The landlady, when the mutilated joint was carried out, was exceedingly indignant, and insisted that a guinea should be paid for the entirety of it.   The dean, much against the grain, as the chronicle goes, paid his guinea, but packed up the four quarters of the round and carried them off with him.

Further indication of his eccentricity might be seen, as I remember, in his habit of wearing in the cathedral pulpit in cold weather, not a skull cap, but a flat square of velvet on his head, with which occasionally he would in the heat of his discourse wipe his face, then clap it on his head again.

T. A. Trollope.
What I Remember, i. 142-3.
R. Bentley and Son, 1887.

ON THE REV. J. DENNIS, LATE MINOR CANON OF
WINCHESTER CATHEDRAL

A Minor
Canon

On Sunday John Dennis will surly grimace
A maze of dry words and, God knows, little grace,

With unmeaning words and circumrotations,
And odd words of Scripture and patched-up quotations
Attempted to prove, but attempted in vain,
That he must run fast who wish'd to obtain.
' Egad,' cried a wag, ' how the times are depraved !
A shepherd must fall whilst his flocks may be sav'd,
For I am sure that, unless by a violent strain,
If John runs as he reads he will never obtain.'

T. Warton.
Add. MS. 29,539, f. 20.

*On the erection of a shabby clock-house on the roof of the spacious
and venerable Cathedral of Winchester*

BENEATH old Venta's antient hall,
Where that famed Table decks the wall
At which sat Arthur and his Knights
To celebrate promiscuous rites,
To hold stern council for the state,
Or, like our modern knights, to eat ;
Lo ! there th' unconscious labourer's spade
Did good King Arthur's hoard invade,
And, by a thousand ruthless knocks,
Produced to light a *Pepper-box* ;
Not such as serves our pigmy age,
'Twas big as any parrot's cage,
Or might have been enlarg'd with ease
To hold an infant swarm of bees ;

.   .   .   .   .   .

Soon as this treasure-trove was known
The Chapter claim'd it as their own,
Proving, by old records new found,
The Hall was built on hallow'd ground ;
And, since that ' Tempus null' occurrit
Ecclesiæ,' it should make a Turret.

The Pepper-
box

And now behold, oh grievous grief !
The Box that season'd Arthur's Beef

. . . . . .

Restor'd from dark Oblivion's bed,
Bedawb'd with white, and capp'd with lead,
Expos'd to laughter, stands on high
That children for the Toy might cry ;
And, least it should escape the sneer,
A tell-tale Clock cries, ' Look ! tis here.'

A Wiccamical Chaplet, by George Huddesford, 1804.

May 12, 1722.

A virulent Preacher

HAVE you seen a book called the *Miseries and Hardships of the Inferior Clergy* chiefly about London ? It is a notable book, but the author, we are told, is very profligate. But one of the same tribe was so spirited up by it, that lately in the Cathedral of Winchester he preached very virulently against all other clergymen that had better preferment than he had. The Dean and prebendaries present sent the verger to him to tell him to come down ; but his assurance failed him not, and he went on. And he could not be silenced till the organs opened against him.

Dr. William Stratford of Christ Church, Oxford, to Edward Harley (*Hist. MSS. Com.*, Duke of Portland's MSS. vii. 323)

BOOK II

THE COLLEGE

SCHOOL DAYS AND SCHOOL WAYS

§ 1. THE GENIUS LOCI

BUT dearest far to all of us,
Our *College* ! we confess thee :
Scarce can our simple love address thee ;
Silent, we greet thee thus.
 While far above,
 With perfect love,
Thy vanished children bless thee.

 . . . . . .

Winchester ! Home to whom our hearts,
Full of glad memories, take us :
Let all else fail, thou wilt forsake us
Never : and though time parts
 Us from thy side,
 We still abide
The lovers, thou didst make us.

 . . . . . .

Now once more let the old words come,
The old *Eia ! quid silemus ?*
Now, *Dulce Domum resonemus !*
For love of thee, Sweet Home !
 Vivas et stes
 Te indies
Amantius amemus.

'Winchester,' in *Ireland and Other Poems,*
by Lionel Johnson, 1889.
Elkin Mathews, 1897.

Quid
silemus ?

K

HAIL Learning's best belovéd home !
Thy praise is past, and yet to come.
Night's clouds are sailing o'er thy tower,
No leaf, no riplet, mars the hour—
Hushed moments when thy Genius falls
On carven roofs and shadowy walls.

.   .   .   .   .   .

No rising sun unwatched by him
Has touched thy pinnacles ; nor ray,
Bright usher of a festal day,
Melting the dense enfolding cloud
Of Catherine's steep, when from the crowd
Of Winton silver clarions fling
Their welcome for a youthful king,
Fair Richard ; or that holier head,
Thy lover, from the broader spread
Of Tamise waters. . . .

> The Rev. William Moore.
> *Venta and Other Poems.*
> D. Nutt, 1882.

DEDICATION OF A BOOK IN MANUSCRIPT

To the fairest !
              Then to thee
Consecrate and bounden be
Winchester ! this verse of mine.
Ah, that loveliness of thine !
To have lived enchanted years,
Like to life in dreamworld spheres,
Where thy Tower's noon shadow falls
Over those proud buttressed walls,
Where a purpling glory pours
From high heaven's inheritors
Blazoned 'neath the arching stone !
To have wandered, hushed, alone,
Gently round thy fair, fern-grown

Chantry of the Lilies lying,
Where the soft night winds go sighing
Round thy cloisters in moonlight
Branching dark or dashed with white :
Round old, chill aisles, where moon-smitten
Blanches the *Orate* written
Under each worn, old-world face
Graven on Death's holy place !

To the noblest !
           None but thee.
Blest our living eyes, that see
Half-a-thousand years fulfilled
Of that age, which Wykeham willed
Thee to live, yet all unworn
As upon that first March morn ;
When thine honoured city saw
Thy young beauty without flaw
Born within her water-flowing
Ancient hollows, by wind-blowing
Hills enfolded evermore.
Thee that lord of royal lore,
Orient from old Hellas' shore,
Grocyn, had to mother : thee
Monumental majesty
Of most old philosophy
Honours, in thy wizard Browne.
Tender Otway's dear renown,
Mover of a perfect pity,
Victim of the iron city,
Thine to cherish is : and thee,
Champion of old Liberty ;
Harper of the Highland faith,
Elf and faëry, and wan wraith ;
Chaunting softly, chaunting slowly,
Minstrel of all melancholy ;

Passion's poet, Evening's voice ;
Collins glorifies.   Rejoice,
Mother ! in thy song : for all
Love thine immemorial
Name, august and musical.

To the dearest !
                    Ah to thee !
Hast thou not in all to me
Mother, more than mother, been !
Well toward thee may Mary Queen
Bow her with a mother's mien.
Who so rarely dost express
An inspiring tenderness,
Woven into thy sterner strain,
Prelude of the world's full pain.
But two years, and still my feet
Found thy very stones more sweet
Than the richest fields elsewhere :
Two years, and thy sacred air
Still poured balm upon me, when
Nearer drew the world of men :
Two years have I lived, still thine,
Lost, thy presence !   Gone, that shrine,
Where six years, what years ! were mine !
Ah, long twilights, linden-scented,
Sunsets lingeringly lamented,
In the purple West, prevented,
Ere they fell, by evening star !
Ah, long nights of winter ! far
Leaps and roars the faggot-fire ;
Circling faces glow, all eyes
Take the light : deep radiance flies.
Merrily flushing overhead
Names of brothers long since fled,

And fresh clusters in their stead
Jubilant round fierce forest flame.

Love alone of gifts no shame
Marreth, and I love thee ; yet
Sound it but of echoes, let
Thine my maiden music be,
Of the love I bear to thee,
Witness and interpreter,
Mother mine, loved Winchester !

L. P. J. (Lionel P. Johnson).
In *The Wykehamist*, December 18, 1888.

THERE are in like maner diuerse collegiat churches as Windsor, **'Poore Scholers'** Wincester . . . and in those a great number of poore scholers, dailie mainteened by the liberalitie of the founders, with meat, bookes, and apparell, from whence after they haue beene well entered in the knowledge of the Latine and Greeke toongs and rules of versifieing (the triall whereof is made by certeine apposers yearelie appointed to examine them), they are sent to certeine especiall houses in each universitie, where they are receiued [and] trained up, in the points of higher knowledge in their priuat hals, till they be adjudged meet to shew their faces in the schooles, as I haue said alreadie.

Harrison's *Description of England, apud* Holinshed's *Chronicle*,
c. 1577, sub. ' Universities.'

THERE is, indeed, a peculiar *genius loci* which seems to a con- **Five centuries at Winchester** siderable extent to account for the powerful grip which the old school takes on the affection of her children. She and her daughter Eton stand alone among our public schools in this respect—that they are essentially mediæval, not modern institutions. The touch of the vanished hand of the Middle Ages is upon Winchester. As one passes into the old quad-rangle, mingles with the boys in college, and listens to their talk stuffed full with old-world words,—'notions,' as they call them—which passed out of general use centuries ago, but which would bring a smile of recognition to the face of Chaucer, Spenser, or of Shakespeare if they could hear them, one realises with unaccustomed force the continuity and unity of English history. This community of persons, living in the same buildings, under the same rules, and speaking the same language as their predecessors did in the fourteenth century, should remind the Englishman of the Victorian age of the deep-down connection, in the very roots of the race, between the England of to-day and that faint and far-away England of the Middle Ages of which Winchester is an almost unique survival. It is, indeed, the peculiar glory of Winchester that she has practically never changed her system. She has contrived to preserve almost all the old, and yet to assimilate all that is best in the new civilisation from age to age, so as to be at the present time as powerful an educational force as she was in the first flush of her youth. . . . Well may she look back with pride upon her five long centuries of life, and well may her sons respond with gratitude to the call, ' Let us now praise famous men and our fathers who begat us.'

The Daily Graphic, July 25, 1893.

The Wyke-hamist's Mecca

THAT which is the Wykehamist's Mecca, the centre of his remembrances—which is as beautiful in the glow of a summer evening as it is on a moonlight night—is Chamber Court. The walls of Chapel and hall on its southern side have gained so rich a colour from the weather, the material and the size of the other three sides have been adjusted with so nice a perception of proportion, that it has a strange fascination for those who love it. The grey flint is stern and strong, but time has done much to soften the severity of the outline, and Wykeham's plan has gained much by age, though it has lost something by alteration.

Illustrated London News, January 31, 1891.

O STATELY Mother, long by circumstance
Firm wedded to the pleasant meadow leas,
Whose calm to unravel from thy chasten'd spell
Our hearts in vain essay !   With what a chain
Of sweet remembrance dost thou bind thy sons.
We took the gifts thou gavest unawares,
But ne'er forgot them, when at eventime,
With universal hush thy darkening fields
Felt holy twilight whose o'erbrooding calm
Drave far all alien spirits.   Through black
    tops
Of wintry elms glittered pale sky, and where
Day sank beneath the jetty ridge of down,
Calm pulsed the evening star in mellow air.
Or when beneath the moon's great open eye
Slept all the lands untroubled, and the woods,
Rapt deep in lapping slumbers, quite forgot
The lidless glare of noon : when shrouded mists
Spread all enamoured round each dripping stem,
And took the long black shadow, that was cast
From one lone pinnacle, whose carven height
Fretted that holy presence ; was not this
The Spirit in thee that can never die ?
Or when, together met in yon dim fane,
We heard the pealing organ strain to fill
The cold vast aisles that melted into gloom,
Mocking their yellow tapers : when there came
A silent lull, and in some distant aisle
An echo lingered strangely ; was not this
That even-pulsed joy, which liveth still
When veil'd and dim are pleasure's heated eyes ?
To what an heritage thou growest heir,
Thy children know not : only this we know,
For five long centuries. . . .

The Wykehamist, July 1893.

Reserve and
Reticence
To the visitor who has made his way from the bright spacious-
ness of the Cathedral Close, the first impression, as he stands
fronting the ancient gateway in College Street, is one of austerity.
The sunless street, the high fronting wall of flint and stone,
pierced only here and there by a chance window, the massive
oaken door, the grime of ages that has settled everywhere, all
combine to strike a note of unrelieved gloom : it is the same
suggestion of reserve and reticence which meets us in the high-
walled approach to the sister college at Oxford, as if to make the
beauty of the interior all the more striking from its contrast
with the plain outside.

The Rev. W. P. Smith on Winchester College, in Memorials of
Old Hampshire, ed. G. E. Jeans.
Bemrose and Sons, 1906.

Fifty years
ago
IN lulling music will I rest awhile,
And watch the streamers of the water weed
Dark-waving, and anon the dusky trout
Steering beneath them in the shadow cool,
Or down amid the cresses ; while the stream
Makes and withdraws in haste a myriad pouts,
Then flows in silence darkling to the mill.
Beneath these level poised leaves I see
Quick sparkling gnats above the water brooks
Sunlit : and kine yon luscious herbage crop,
Through rich wet pasture, striped with sun and shade
And set with willow coppices ; beyond
There smokes the road, by dusty poplars lined,
And here the river, whirling cropped grass,
And tangled weeds, with sweet and juicy stalks,
Fresh, sickle-severed in the misty morn,
Comes winding silently along the leas.
Hark, from the distant towers in mellow tone
Chime answers dreamy chime, while I hear
And thus regard thine all untroubled sleep,
Steeped in noon's yellow sunlight, like a dream,

Deep in my heart the Angel memory
Unravels all this weary circumstance
Which age has wov'n about me. Yet a thought
Chains me again to sorrow. I am grey,
And old, and long forgotten. It was said
That some of lovely soul or golden tongue
Chance upon fame and live for ever. These
Are for all time, and many such there be.
But some, though haply with small wit endowed,
Yet to their powers breathe out their little souls
In salving somewhat in an o'erfretted world
That else had cried in vain : their work is done,
Down in the dust they lie, and their poor names
Are quite immersed in this lapsing time.
Oh, give me back my years that I may laugh
With cheeks unwrinkled, and a heart as yet
By age unfrozen. Swift the years have fled,
And men awake, and all the hills are white.

The Wykehamist, July 1893.

To the Rev. Dr. Lowth, on his Life of
William of Wykeham

O LOWTH, while Wykeham's various worth you trace
   And bid to distant times his annals shine,
Indulge another bard of Wykeham's race
   In the fond wish to add his name to thine.

A tribute
from the
poet
Whitehead

From the same fount, with reverence, let me boast
   The classic streams with early thirst I caught ;
What time, they say, the Muses revel'd most,
   When Bigg presided and when Burton taught.

.   .   .   .   .   .

Yes, ye sweet fields, beside your osier'd stream
Full many an Attic hour my youth enjoy'd ;
Full many a friendship form'd, life's happiest dream,
And treasured many a bliss which never cloy'd.

William Whitehead, 1715-1784.

A Dedication   To St. Mary's College, Winton, in whose classic halls I matured
that love of literature which has been the joy and consolation
of my life, and on the hills in whose vicinity I learned to fight
my ' decisive battles,' this volume is inscribed with reverence
and affection.

Dedication of Colonel Malleson's *The Decisive Battles of India.*
Allen and Co., London, 1883.

§ 2. COLLEGE CONSTITUTION

DE COLLEGIO SEU POTIUS COLLEGIATA SCHOLA WICCAMICA WINTONIENSI

De Collegio

INTER turrigeras, quas Anglia continet, urbes
Urbs antiqua suo minitatur culmine nubes ;
Venta prius dicta est ; Wintonia deinde vocata :
Regalis platea est, si vulgi more loquamur.
Wiccamus, insignis mitrâque pedoque Suithini,
Condidit his sacris Sacraria digna Camœnis ;
Hic, hic pauperibus κουρότροφον ille locavit ;
Et ne dirueret saevus fundamina Daemon,
Tutelae domus haec Divae est sacrata Mariae.

Collegiata Schola Wiccamica Wintoniensi,[1] in *The College of
St. Mary, Winton,* ed. by C. W. (C. Wordsworth) 1848.

Numbers in College

ET ne civili domus haec arderet ab igne,
Est positus Custos, qui praesidet omnibus unus.
Sunt duo, cura vagae quibus est commissa Juventae,
Atque decem Socii, qui dicti a plebe Magistri.

[1] The author of this poem has been proved not to be the headmaster,
Christopher Johnson (1560-71), as Wordsworth believed. It was evidently
written at a much later date under the headmastership of John Potenger
(1642-1653). See *The Wykehamist,* July 1899.

Inde Capellani, qui constant ordine trino ;
Vindicat et trinum numerum sibi Clericus ; unus
Organa qui facili percurrit dissona dextrâ :
Sed pueros numerus bene septuagesimus arctat.
Praefecti octodecim seniores rite vocantur ;
Exemplo monituque Scholae moderamina servant :
Si tamen obstiterint rabidi, nimiumque protervi,
Nomina sunt chartae, charta est data deinde Magistro,
Qui quadripartitâ benè corrigit omnia virgâ.
Sex-decimus numerus jubet ut sit meta Choristis ;
Hi resonant sacros argutis vocibus hymnos
In Templo ; ex Templo Sociis, Puerisque ministrant :
His quoque discipulis patet almi janua Ludi.
Nomine seu Pueri vociteris, sivi Choristae,
Non caput obtegitur pilio, crassove galero,
Cimmeriisque togis vestiti inceditis omnes.
Sex Camerae Pueris signantur, et una Choristis.
Ut magis hic mores serventur et ordo decorus,
Praefecti camerâ tres praeponuntur in unâ.

Collegiata Schola Wiccamica Wintoniensi, in *The College of
St. Mary, Winton*, ed. by C. W. (C. Wordsworth) 1848.

LOWTH, and most other writers who speak of this College, mention the number and respective degrees of its members ; but none of them, since Harpsfield, seem to be aware of the mysterious meaning of these determinate numbers and qualities. We may venture, then, to say, after the hint of this author, who was himself a distinguished Wykehamist at the beginning of the sixteenth century, that the warden and ten priests, who were perpetual fellows, represented the College of the apostles, Judas Iscariot, of course, not being represented ; that the head-master and second-master, with seventy scholars, denoted the seventy-two disciples ; that the three chaplains and three inferior clerks marked the six faithful deacons ; Nicholas, one of that number, having apostatised, has therefore no representative ;

Mysterious meaning in numbers of College community

finally, that the sixteen choristers represented the four greater and the twelve minor prophets.

Historical and Descriptive Guide to Winchester, 1829.

First peal

PURPUREAS Aurora fores ubi pandit ab ortu
Eoö, et quintâ cum linea tangitur umbrâ,
Stridula spirantes campana reverberat auras.
Inde sonus subito somnosus perferat aures :
' Surgite,' Praefectus clamat ; ' Num stertitis,' ohe !
Jam campana sonat ; vos surgite, surgite, pigri.

Collegiata Schola Wiccamica Wintoniensi, in *The College of St. Mary, Winton*, ed. by C. W., 1848.

School

MUSA, Scholam memora, quae vera est mamma Minervae,
Quae pleno pueros lactentes ubere nutrit.
Quatuor iliceis fulcris schola nostra quiescit ;
Lux tribus hanc lustrat bipatentibus alma fenestris,
In quibus octodecim Praefectis structa superne,
Ut bene praesideant aliis, subsellia dantur.
Haec Australis habet paries ; Borealis apertam
Totius mundi tabulam ; qui tendit ad ortum
Ostendit, fieri quae, Quintiliane, requiris ;
Murus ad occasum capit hoc insigne decorum,
AUT DISCE, AUT DISCEDE, MANET SORS TERTIA CAEDI.

Ibid.

TRELAWNY, BISHOP OF WINCHESTER, TO DR. JOHN RADCLIFFE, THE FAMOUS PHYSICIAN

Unruly
Fellows

DEAR SIR,—This is no visiting day, and to-morrow I am obliged to go fifteen or sixteen miles to confirm, and yet what I have to say to you is of such importance to me that I must not delay it, for feare lest you should happen unwarily to do me a mischief, which I am sure you would not willingly do.

I have reason to believe that some of the Fellows of Winchester College may, some how or other, have made friends to you to engage my Lord Treasurer to countenance them so far as to get an order of council to put a stop to my proceedings in my inquiry into the reasons of their disobeying the injunctions of the Warden and powers of New College.

From the steps which I have already made in this matter, they distrusting the merits of theyr cause, appealed to the Archbishop, insinuating that I only visited them as diocesan ; but his Grace, by the Dean of Arches, being satisfied that I acted not as Bishop but as Visitor of the College, dismissed theyr appeal as being sensible he had nothing to do with it.

From him they apply'd to the Lord Keeper for a Commission of Delegacy ; but his lordship went out of town without doing anything in it, as convinced, I believe, that this matter was only fit for Westminster Hall, there being no one instance, as the lawyers tell me, of its being referred to a Court of Delegates to determine whether a person be Visitor or not, which surely a certain gentleman was not aware of, who broke in upon my Lord Keeper last Wednesday with rudeness and impudence, to hope to have awd his Lordship into a grant of such a Commission, for some men of late days give themselves strange opinions of theyr having made the late change in the Ministry, and upon that account think they may use them at present with familiarity, perhaps command ; and I wish they may not think my Lord Treasurer himself to be one of theyr creatures ; but be theyr interest and success what it will, having justice and the laws of the land on my side, I am resolved to go on, and, if I go beyond my powers, no doubt but Westminster Hall will make me sensible of it.

   .   .   .   .

I have been now neare four years, and made three journies on purpose, persuading the Warden and Fellows of Winchester College to make up theyr differences among themselves, and if that could not be done to take in the assistance of the Dean and Prebendaries of Winchester, telling them they did not know what mischief they might do themselves by forcing me on a

Visitation. Sometimes they gave me hopes that things should be amicably made up; but now, by an encouragement which perhaps they will not be thankfull for, they make it necessary for me.

I should not have given you this trouble, but that I foresee that your interest will be apply'd for by one of the fellows who is your patient, which I am sorry for, becaus if you knew him as well as I do, you could not think him fit to live. . . .

July 29, 1711.

Trelawny Papers, *Camden Miscellany*, vol. ii.

Three absolute Rulers

IT was said by them of old time that there were three absolute rulers in the world : the Great Mogul, the captain of a man of war, and the prefect of hall at Winchester.

W. Tuckwell.
Winchester Fifty Years Ago.
Macmillan and Co., 1893.

The old order changeth

THE Winchester College of to-day differs far more from the same college of ten years ago than that of ten years ago can have differed from that of a couple of centuries since. Till recently the sacrifices made to the requirements of public opinion consisted in such improvements as the substitution of plates for trenchers, of meat for a gristly imitation of the same, of large airy and hideously ugly reading and dining halls for those glorious old edifices of the good old days in which our fathers hardened themselves for the trials of life by ' jockeying ' for milk, or impaling on their toasting forks the incautious rat who shared the nursery of learning in copartnery with themselves.

All this is utterly changed, and in every one's opinion, save the rats, changed for the better. Old Commoners have been absolutely abolished, and the Commoners or non-foundation boys of Winchester now reside in the nine Masters' houses, where they are brought up in a style and comfort which our fathers would have condemned, while they quoted the case of Jeshurun. The number of Commoners is little short of three hundred, while we believe that within the last twelve years it stood as low as sixty. The College has undergone no less marvellous changes. The number of College boys has been increased from seventy to seventy-five. Sixth and Seventh Chambers—the objects of time-honoured and uncomfortable associations to many a Wykehamist, since the time when first the ' serge-clad scholars drank of the crystal water beneath the plane-tree's bough,' to the present enlightened age of improved swipes— Sixth and Seventh Chambers have been transformed from sleeping apartments into sitting-rooms for College boys. The wall which separated Commoners from College has been taken away, and Commoner and College-boy now no longer look on one another as natural enemies.

The Globe, November 12, 1870.

§ 3. COMMONERS

Verses on the Death of Dr. Burton

Bathe not for me, dear youths ! your mournful lays
In bitter tears.   O'er blooming Beauty's grave
Let Pity wring her hands : I full of years,
Of honours full, satiate of life, retire
Like an o'er-wearied pilgrim to his home,
Nor at my lot repine.   Yet the last prayer,
That from my struggling bosom parts, shall rise
Fervent for you !   May Wickham's much-loved walls
Be still with Science, Fame and Virtue blest,
And distant times and regions hail his name.

Dr. Joseph Warton.

A Founder of Old Commoners

How many noble associations do we owe to Wykeham's bounty ? The glorious old city, still royal in its decay ; the breezy heights of St. Catherine's with its solitary tuft of firs ; the old school-room with its ' books,' and ' scobs,' and quaint mural painting ; the noble chapel, where the sun would stream gloriously through

The debt of Commoners to Wykeham

the Jesse window ; where we listened to more than one beloved
voice, which ' though dead, still speaketh ' ; the yet grander
cathedral, whither, Sunday after Sunday, we were wont in our
simple procession to repair ; the sweet strain of *Dulce domum*,
sung in the summer twilight,—these are ours, as truly as though
our names had been duly enrolled in the Warden's books, and
we had faced in awe and trembling the magnates of election
chamber.

H. C. Adams.
Wykehamica, 1878.

The supposed Adventures of a Gentleman Commoner in the eighteenth century

PEREGRINE, who was now turned of twelve, had made such
advances under the instruction of Jennings, that he often
disputed upon grammar, and was sometimes thought to have
the better in his contests with the parish-priest, who, notwith-
standing this acknowledged superiority of his antagonist,
did great justice to his genius, which he assured Mr. Trunnion
[Peregrine's uncle] would be lost for want of cultivation, if the
boy was not immediately sent to prosecute his studies at some
proper seminary of learning.

This maxim had been more than once inculcated upon the
Commodore by Mrs. Trunnion, who, over and above the deference
she paid to the parson's opinion, had a reason of her own for
wishing to see the house clear of Peregrine, at whose prying
disposition she began to be very uneasy. Induced by these
motives, which were joined by the solicitation of the youth
himself, who ardently longed to see a little more of the world,
his uncle determined to send him forthwith to Winchester,
under the immediate care and inspection of a governor, to whom
he allowed a very handsome appointment for that purpose.
This gentleman, whose name was Mr. Jacob Jolter, had been
school-fellow with the parson of the parish, who recommended
him to Mrs. Trunnion as a person of great worth and learning,
in every respect qualified for the office of tutor. He likewise
added, by way of eulogium, that he was a man of exemplary

piety, and particularly zealous for the honour of the Church of which he was a member, having been many years in holy orders, though he did not then exercise any function of the priesthood. Indeed, Mr. Jolter's zeal was so exceedingly fervent as, on some occasions, to get the better of his discretion : for, being a high churchman, and of consequence a malcontent, his resentment was habituated into an insurmountable prejudice against the present disposition of affairs, which, by confounding the nation with the ministry, sometimes led him into erroneous, not to say absurd, calculations ; otherwise, a man of good morals, well versed in mathematics and school divinity, studies which had not at all contributed to sweeten and unbend the natural sourness and severity of his complexion.

This gentleman being destined to the charge of superintending Perry's education, everything was prepared for their departure ; and Tom Pipes, in consequence of his own petition, put into livery, and appointed footman to the young squire. . . .

As for the lieutenant [Jack Hatchway] he accompanied them in the coach ; and such was the friendship he had contracted for Perry, that when the Commodore proposed to return, after having accomplished the intent of his journey, Jack absolutely refused to attend him, and signified his resolution to stay where he was. . . . ' I have some thoughts of going to school myself to learn your Latin lingo ; for as the saying is " *Better late mend than never.*" And I am informed as how one can get more for the money here than anywhere else.'

In vain did Trunnion endeavour to convince him of the folly of going to school at his years, by representing that the boys would make game of him, and that he would become a laughing-stock to all the world ; he persisted in his resolution to stay, and the Commodore was fain to have recourse to the mediation of Pipes and Perry, who employed their influence with Jack, and at last prevailed upon him to return to the garrison. . . .

Thus left to the prosecution of his studies, Peregrine was in a little time a distinguished character, not only for his acuteness of apprehension, but also for that mischievous fertility of fancy, of which we have already given such pregnant examples. But as there was a great number of such luminaries in this new sphere to which he belonged, his talents were not so conspicuous while they shone in his single capacity, as they afterwards appeared, when they concentrated and reflected the rays of the whole constellation.

At first he confined himself to piddling game, exercising his genius upon his own tutor, who attracted his attention by endeavouring to season his mind with certain political maxims, the fallacy of which he had discernment enough to perceive. Scarce a day passed in which he did not find means to render Mr. Jolter the object of ridicule ; his violent prejudices, ludicrous vanity, awkward solemnity and ignorance of mankind, afforded continual food for the raillery, petulance, and satire of his pupil, who never neglected an opportunity of laughing and making others laugh at his expense.

Sometimes in their parties, by mixing brandy in his wine, he decoyed this pedagogue into a debauch, during which his caution forsook him and he exposed himself to the censure of the company. . . . All the remains of authority which he had hitherto preserved over Peregrine soon vanished ; so that, for the future, no sort of ceremony subsisted between them, and all Mr. Jolter's precepts were conveyed in hints of friendly advice, which the other might either follow or neglect at his own pleasure. No wonder then that Peregrine gave a loose to his inclinations, and by dint of genius and an enterprising temper, made a figure among the younger class of heroes in the school.

Before he had been a full year at Winchester, he had signalised himself in so many achievements, in defiance to the laws and regulations of the place, that he was looked upon with admiration, and actually chosen *Dux*, or leader, by a large body of his contemporaries. It was not long before his fame reached the ears of the master, who sent for Mr. Jolter, communicated to him the informations he had received, and ordered him to

redouble his vigilance in time to come, else he should be obliged
to make a public example of his pupil for the benefit of the
school. . . . [The governor, after expostulating with Peregrine,
suggested the study of mathematics] ' as yielding more rational
and sensible pleasures to a youthful fancy than any other
subject of contemplation ' ; and actually began to read Euclid
with him the same afternoon.

Peregrine entered upon this branch of learning with all that
warmth of application which boys commonly yield on the first
change of study ; but he had scarce advanced beyond the
Pons Asinorum, when his ardour abated, the test of truth by
demonstration did not elevate him to those transports of joy
with which his preceptor had regaled his expectation ; and
before he arrived at the forty-seventh proposition he began to
yawn drearily, make abundance of wry faces, and thought
himself but indifferently paid for his attention . . . and he
returned with double relish to his former avocations. . . .
His behaviour was now no other than a series of licence and
effrontery ; prank succeeded prank and outrage followed
outrage, with surprising velocity. Complaints were every day
preferred against him ; in vain were admonitions bestowed by
the governor in private, and menaces discharged by the masters
in public ; he disregarded the first, despised the latter, divested
himself of all manner of restraint, and proceeded in his career
to such a pitch of audacity, that a consultation was held upon
the subject, in which it was determined that this untoward
spirit should be humbled by a severe and ignominious flogging
for the very next offence he should commit. In the meantime
Mr. Jolter was desired to write in the master's name to the
Commodore, requesting him to remove Tom Pipes from the
person of his nephew, the said Pipes being a principal actor
and abettor in all his malversations ; and to put a stop to the
monthly visitations of the mutilated lieutenant [Jack Hatchway],
who had never once failed to use his permission, but came
punctual to a day, always fraught with some new invention.

Indeed, by this time Mr. Hatchway was as well known, and much better beloved, by every boy in the school than the master who instructed him, and always received by a number of scholars, who used to attend Peregrine when he went forth to meet his friend, and conduct him to his lodging with public testimonies of joy and applause.

As for Tom Pipes, he was not so properly the attendant of Peregrine, as master of the revels to the whole school. He mingled in all their parties, and superintended the diversions, deciding between boy and boy, as if he acted by commission under the great seal. He regulated their motions by his whistle, instructed the young boys in the games of hustle-cap, leap-frog, and chuck-farthing; imparted to those of a more advanced age the sciences of cribbage and all-fours, together with the method of storming the castle, acting the comedy of Prince Arthur, and other pantomimes, as they are commonly exhibited at sea; and instructed the seniors, who were distinguished by the appellation of bloods, in cudgel-playing, dancing the St. Giles's hornpipe, drinking flip, and smoking tobacco. These qualifications had rendered him so necessary and acceptable to the scholars that, exclusive of Perry's concern in the affair, his dismissal, in all probability, would have produced some dangerous convulsion in the community. Jolter, therefore, knowing his importance, informed his pupil of the directions he had received, and very candidly asked how he should demean himself in the execution; for he durst not write to the Commodore without this previous notice, fearing that the young gentleman, as soon as he should get an inkling of the affair, would follow the example, and make his uncle acquainted with certain anecdotes which it was the governor's interest to keep concealed. Peregrine was of opinion that he should spare himself the trouble of conveying any complaints to the Commodore, and if questioned by the master, assure him he had complied with his desire; at the same time he promised faithfully to conduct himself with such circumspection for the future, that the masters should have no temptation to revive the inquiry. But the resolution attending this extorted promise was too frail to last, and in less than a fortnight our young hero found himself entangled in an adventure from which he was not extricated with his usual good fortune.

He and some of his companions one day entered a garden in the suburbs, and having indulged their appetites desired to know what satisfaction they must make for the fruit they had pulled. The gardener demanded what (in their opinion) was an exorbitant price, and they, with many opprobrious terms, refused to pay it. The peasant being surly and untractable, insisted upon his right ; neither was he deficient or sparing in the eloquence of vulgar abuse. . . . [A scuffle followed, in which the fortune of the day was decided by the superior strength of Tom Pipes ; the gardener was left ' in the embraces of his Mother Earth,' and was afterwards ' conveyed to his bed, from which he was not able to stir during a whole month.'] His family coming upon the parish, a formal complaint was made to the master of the school, and Peregrine represented as the ringleader of those who committed this barbarous assault. An inquiry was immediately set on foot, and the articles of impeachment being fully proved, our hero was sentenced to be severely chastised in the face of the whole school. This was a disgrace the thoughts of which his proud heart could not brook. He resolved to make his elopement rather than undergo the punishment to which he was doomed ; and having signified his sentiments to his confederates, they promised, one and all, to stand by him, and either screen him from chastisement, or share his fate.

Confiding in this friendly protestation, he appeared unconcerned on the day that was appointed for his punishment ; and when he was called to his destiny, advanced towards the scene, attended by the greatest part of the scholars, who intimated their determination to the master, and proposed that Peregrine should be forgiven. The superior behaved with that dignity of demeanour which became his place, represented the folly and presumption of their demand, reprehended them for their audacious proceeding, and ordered every boy to his respective station.   They obeyed his command, and our unfortunate hero was publicly horsed, *in terrorem* of all whom it might concern.

This disgrace had a very sensible effect upon the mind of Peregrine, who having by this time passed the fourteenth year of his age, began to adopt the pride and sentiments of a man. Thus dishonourably stigmatised, he was ashamed to appear in public as usual : he was incensed against his companions for their infidelity and irresolution, and plunged into a profound reverie that lasted several weeks, during which he shook off his boyish connections and fixed his view upon objects which he thought more worthy of his attention. . . . Being one evening at a ball which is always given to the ladies at the time of the races, the person who acted as master of the ceremonies, knowing how fond Mr. Pickle was of every opportunity to display himself, came up and told him that there was a fine young creature at the other end of the room, who seemed to have a great inclination to dance a minuet, but wanted a partner, the gentleman who attended her being in boots.

Peregine's vanity being aroused at this intimation, he went up to reconnoitre the young lady, and was struck with admiration at her beauty . . . her whole appearance [was] so captivating, that our young Adonis looked and was overcome. . . . [The next day he found out from the young lady] that her habitation was about sixteen miles from Winchester, in a village which she named, and where (as he could easily gather from her discourse) he would be no unwelcome guest. . . . Having received a supply of money from the Commodore who acted towards him with great generosity, he ordered Pipes to put up some linen and other necessaries in a sort of knapsack which he could conveniently carry, and thus attended set out early one morning on foot for the village where his charmer lived, at which he arrived before two o'clock in the afternoon ; having chosen this method of travelling, that his route might not be so easily discovered, as it must have been had he hired horses, or taken a place in a stage coach. . . . While he remained under the influence of this sweet intoxication, his absence produced great disturbance at Winchester. Mr. Jolter was grievously afflicted at his abrupt departure, which alarmed him the more as it happened after a long fit of melancholy which he had perceived in his pupil. He communicated his apprehensions to the master of the school, who advised him to apprise the Commodore of his nephew's disappearance, and in the meantime inquire at all the inns in town whether he had hired horses, or any sort of carriage. . . . Mr. Trunnion was wellnigh distracted at the news of his flight : . . . he immediately dispatched expresses to all the seaport towns on that coast, that he might be prevented from leaving the kingdom ; and the lieutenant, at his own desire, was sent across the country, in quest of the young fugitive.

Four days had he unsuccessfully carried on his inquiries with great accuracy, when, resolving to return by Winchester, where he hoped to meet with some hints of intelligence, by which he might profit in his future search, he struck off the common road to take the benefit of a nearer cut ; and finding himself benighted near a village, took up his lodgings at the first inn to which his horse directed him. . . . [Here he chances to meet Tom Pipes and the hero, whom he persuaded of the] danger of incensing the Commodore . . . and, in short, conveyed his arguments . . . in such expressions of friendship and respect, that Peregrine yielded to his remonstrances, and promised to accompany him next day to Winchester. . . . [Accordingly the next day they set out from the inn and] arrived about two o'clock in Winchester, where Mr. Jolter was overwhelmed with joy at their appearance.

The nature of this adventure being unknown to all except those who could be depended upon, everybody who inquired about the cause of Peregrine's absence was told that he had been with a relation in the country, and the master condescended to overlook his indiscretion. . . . [However] the Commodore fearing that Perry was in danger of involving himself in some pernicious engagement, resolved, by advice of Mr. Jolter and his friend, the parish priest, to recall him from the place where he had contracted such imprudent connections, and send him to the University where his education might be completed, and his fancy weaned from all puerile amusements. . . . Meanwhile, preparations were made for Peregrine's departure to the University, and in a few weeks he set out, in the seventeenth year of his age, accompanied by the same attendants who lived with him at Winchester.

Tobias Smollett.
The Adventures of Peregrine Pickle, 1751.

DAVID, LORD ELCHO, AT WINCHESTER

The real Adventures of a Gentleman Commoner at Winchester College in the eighteenth century

IT was . . . towards something tangible [*i.e.* Jacobitism], and not the pursuit of a forlorn hope, that Elcho's education was directed. Before the age of nine he had been taught by a non-juring minister of the English Church that allegiance was due not to the usurper at St. James's, but to the King over the water, and that the Episcopalian ritual in no way suffered by the omission of the prayers for the House of Hanover.

Thus initiated and prepared he set out [from Wemyss Castle] in 1734 for Winchester, in the company of his father. In those days, if all went well, such a journey occupied from twelve to sixteen days, and was performed by persons of wealth and position in a coach drawn either by six or four horses. . . . At Winchester, where he was placed under the care of a Jacobite tutor, Elcho found that the school, like the rest of the world, was divided into Hanoverians (or 'Georgites,' as he calls them) and supporters of the Stuarts. Thus the headmaster, Burton, was a Jacobite, the second master a Georgite, and on one occasion, when Elcho himself was in difficulty over a set of verses and sought assistance from a fellow-pupil, he was met by the question: 'Are you Georgite or Jacobite?' The answer proving satisfactory, the help was rendered, accompanied by the threat that if ever he was seen making friends with any of the Hanoverians, he would have to go elsewhere for his verses. Partisanship indeed seems to have played a larger part than education in the school world of that day. Learning was mainly restricted to the seventy scholars resident at the College ; the wealthier boys boarded in the town with their tutors, and by gambling, cock-fighting, and tavern life acquired a ' polite taste for pleasurable vice.' No wonder that Elcho became one of that mob of gentlemen who spelt with difficulty in the eighteenth century. But if books were neglected, no pains were spared to bring home to the boys a due sense of their earthly prerogatives and temporal distinctions. At church on Sundays peers and the sons of peers were conspicuous in robes of blue, red, or green, baronets and knights in black, while the ' untitled gentlemen ' sat apart in the ordinary dress of the time.

The everyday life of the school was marked less by titular than by racial differences, and young Elcho, with nationality aflame in his blood, was driven to a course of boxing as the best means of combating the charge that his origin was Scottish. Here again the school was a reflection of the greater world without—a reflection multiplied by youth and the ardours of personal conflict. . . . At Winchester the common taunt was that in Scotland they grew no wheat. . . . He [Lord Elcho] had indeed a precocious relish for combats of all kinds, and at Winchester, when not vindicating his accent with his fists, was a constant spectator at cock-fights or encounters between rustics ' for a hat presented by the Lord of the village.'

Lord Elcho.

Affairs of Scotland, 1744-1746 (ed. 1907), Memoir by the
Hon. Evan Charteris, pp. 8-11.

David Douglas, Edinburgh.

SHORTLY after [John] Murray's introduction to James, the same honour was also asked by a young man then wintering at Rome, whose family had always been most loyal to the Jacobite cause.

Lord Elcho
at Winchester

Lord Elcho, the eldest son of the Earl of Wemyss, had just completed his studies at Winchester School, and, as with Murray, was giving his education a finishing touch by foreign travel. The old Earl had been repeatedly offered posts under the Hanoverian Government, but invariably refused to take the oath of allegiance, preferring the society of Paris to that of his own country. As soon as his son reached boyhood he sent him to Winchester, where, if we can credit the Diary of Lord Elcho, the discipline enforced was not of the strictest character. The boys played cards, haunted taverns, and their morals were anything but carefully looked after. ' We did not learn,' frankly writes Lord Elcho, ' Latin and Greek as well as we should have done had we been placed with a private tutor, but we were taught how to live as men of the world, and made acquaintances, which, if cultivated, could be very useful to us in after life.' Among these useful acquaintances were the sons of the Dukes of Hamilton, Devonshire, and Queensborough,[1] and the Earls of Exeter and Coventry. As in the outer world, the school was divided into Jacobites and Hanoverians, and frequent conflicts ensued between those who supported ' King Jamie ' and those who gave in their adherence to the ' Wee, wee German lairdie.'

Alex. Chas. Ewald.
The Life and Times of Prince Charles Stuart.
Chatto and Windus, 1904.

§ 4. THE MAKING OF 'MEN'

PROGRESS OF LEARNING

'The blubb'ring youth'

THE fatal morn arrives, and oh
To school the blubb'ring youth must go,
Before the Muse's hallow'd shrine
Each joy domestic to resign ;
No more, as erst at break of day,
To brush the early dew away,

[1] Evidently Queensberry.

But in ideal range to fly
O'er fancied fields of Poetry,
Again to cull the mystic stores
Of Phrases, Tropes, and Metaphores,
Now gives Mama her last caressing,
And fond Papa bestows his blessing.
These sweet endearments scarcely o'er,
The chaise drives rattling to the door.

.   .   .   .   .   .

But to be brief we 'll be content
With only saying ' Off he went.'

.   .   .   .   .   .

Our youth, the joys of home forgot,
Now grows contented with his lot ;
On Virgil's sweets can dwell with Pleasure,
With Sully pass the hours of Leisure,
In verses act with skill his part—
Nay, say the *Iliad* all by heart.

.   .   .   .   .   .

He 's not (if authors rightly tell us)
One of those harum-scarum fellows
Who seek to know no other pleasure
Than those of eating and of leisure ;
Who thinks the beauties of the Classic
Enough to make a very ass sick,
And own no joys beyond the chase,
No recreations but a race.
By him far nobler joys are found
In Sully's arguments profound,
No dainties please him like the sweets
Of Homer's compound epithets.
At length on Isis banks he views
The walls belov'd by ev'ry Muse.

.   .   .   .   .   .

But fast the rolling years glide on,
And life's far better half is gone.
He now to other things aspires,
Accepts a living and retires.

.   .   .   .   .   .

Long time his flock beheld him shine
A zealous and a wise divine,
Until as ebbing life retires
A Dean'ry crowns his last desires.
Behold him now, devoid of care,
Snug seated in his elbow chair;
He cracks his jokes and eats his fill,
On Sunday preaches if he will,
Solves doubts as soon as others start 'em
By argument secundum artem;
Now puzzles o'er in warm debate
Each weighty point of Church and State,
Or tells o'er now in merry strain
The pranks of early life again,
Recalls to mem'ry school disasters,
Unfinished tasks and angry masters.
    As erst to him, O heavenly Maid,
Learning, to me impart thy aid;
O teach my feet like his to stray
Along preferment's flow'ry way!
And if thy hallow'd shrine before
I e'er thy ready aid implore,
O make me, Sphere-descended Queen,
A Bishop or at least a Dean!

D. N. Shuttleworth
(when a College Commoner, 1800).
Add. MS. 29,539, ff. 29A, 31d.

[*N.B.*—Shuttleworth became Warden of New College and
Bishop of Chichester. There is a note at the beginning of
the volume of task-poems, in which this is contained, in

the hand of Mr. Mackenzie Walcott, who presented the
volume to the British Museum:—

'At Winchester Commoners used to keep MS. task-books,
containing verse tasks and prize poems gained in the
school. Probably this is the only one which survived the
dispersion consequent on Old Commoners being destroyed.
I never saw one after that time. Probably all the toys
were cleared out.—December 15, 1873.']

COMITIA WICCAMICA [1]

En sperata Dies ! annus redit actus in orbem.
Cognatus Custos, binis cum Fratribus, aedes
Wykami visit ; comitum longissimus ordo
Addunt se socios, et recto tramite tendunt.
Proxima mirantur venientem compita pompam.
Ut notas portas tetigêre hinc inde patentes,
Magni descendunt equites ; in limine primo
Quisque suo vario sermone salutat amicum.
Stans dudum Orator, turbâ comitante togatâ,
Insolitum tremit, et dubiâ formidine pallens
Custodem exspectat venientem ; passibus aequis
Pone legunt fratres vestigia tarda minores ;
Invitos signat majestas seria vultus.
Cuique suas simul attribuit facundia laudes,
Scinditur in varias partes diffusa corona ;
Hos juvat antiquas sedes exquirere Matris,
Atria nota terunt, adeunt penetrale Minervae
Nec scriptae Leges, nec Virgae terret Imago ;
Illos dulcis amor, Pietas materna moratur,
Turba frequens latâ huc illuc spatiantur Arenâ.

The Wykehamist, November 1906.

*The coming
of the
Posers*

We reached Winchester late in the evening of the day before
the election [July 1820], putting up, not at ' The George,' or at

*The arrival
of a 'Candle-
stick'*

[1] This poem is shown by Mr. Herbert Chitty to be in all probability
the work of one John Daniel Cotton, scholar, 1744-8. See *The
Wykehamist*, December 1906.

'The White Hart,' as most people would have done, but at the 'Fleur de Lys,' pronounced 'Flower de Luce,' a very ancient, but then third-rate hostelry, which my father preferred, partly probably because he thought the charges might be less there, but mainly because it is situated in the vicinity of the College, and he had known and used it of old. We spent the evening at the house of Dr. Gabell, the headmaster, an old friend of my father's, where his eldest daughter, an intimate friend of my mother's, who had often been a visitor in Keppel Street, made much of me.

And the next day I became a Wykehamist !

T. A. Trollope.
What I Remember, i. 95-6.
R. Bentley and Son, 1887.

The ordeal   . . . DULY instructed as to the part we were to play, we went marvelling up the ancient stone corkscrew stair to the mysterious chamber situated over the ' middle gate,' *i.e.* the gateway between the outer court and the second quadrangle where the chapel, the hall, and the chambers are. The 'election chamber' always maintained a certain character of mystery to us, because it was never opened or used save on the great occasion of the annual election. In that chamber we found the six solemn electors in their gowns waiting for us ; especially the Bishop of Hereford, who was then Warden of Winchester College, an aged man with his peculiar wig and gown, was an object of awe. No Bishop had in those days dreamed as yet of discarding the episcopal wig.

And then the examination began, as follows : ' Well, boy, can you sing ? ' ' Yes, sir.' ' Let us hear you ' ' " All people that on earth do dwell," ' responded the neophyte—duly instructed previously in his part of the proceeding—without attempting in the smallest degree to modify in any way his ordinary speech. ' Very well, boy. That will do ! ' returned the examiner. The examination was over, and you were a member of William of Wykeham's College, *Sanctæ Mariæ de*

Winton prope Winton. '*Prope* Winton,' observe, for the College is situated outside the ancient city walls.

T. A. Trollope.
What I Remember, i. 97.
R. Bentley and Son, 1887.

WINCHESTER had been selected, for his uncle, now Colonel Deane, was himself an old Wykehamist, and had all the affection for his old school characteristic of the tribe. The Colonel was home on leave, and proposed to take Christopher up for the occasion. . . . Those three days were perhaps the pleasantest Christopher had ever spent. The long summer evenings were spent in wandering about the old town, down the river, up St. Giles' Hill, or that other, sacred to all Wykehamists under the name of ' Hills.' . . .

The names of the candidates, posted every morning in Mr. Wells' little shop in College Street, grew steadily fewer in number as the watchful examiners weeded out the incapable, but Christopher's name remained on the board until the end— the dread morning of *viva voce* examination by the headmaster. The little band of aspirants, sadly shrunk now, attended at the porter's lodge to learn the hour fixed for their appearance for their last ordeal. . . .

Christopher was put on to construe first, and acquitted himself creditably enough. The ordeal, severe as it was, was soon over, for time was limited, and there were several more batches to be catechised. It was with a feeling of relief that he felt himself in the open air once more, his work finished, and nothing further to do but to wait for the result. The occasion demanded celebration, and on his way back to his uncle at the ' George ' he treated himself to a feast of strawberries and cream. . . .

Late one evening a telegram came for the Colonel. . . . The result was out and Christopher was tenth on the roll. It was in the papers next day. The family slept with lighter hearts that night, all but Christopher himself, who lay awake revolving all sorts of possibilities for the future, picturing himself

The making of a 'Man'

in that solemn courtyard, in chapel, in one of those quaint
old chambers on the ground floor, wearing a scholar's gown
like those he had envied a few days before—no longer a boy,
but a man and a Wykehamist.

E. H. Lacon Watson.
Christopher Deane.
John Murray.

**To a
Candidate for
Elections**

O FORTUNE, an thou givest me a choice
(' An ' is poetical for if—quite ' a la Milton ')
'Twixt eloquence—a swerve—an alto voice,
All the sweet fancies that my hopes have built on,
    It will surprise thee, may be,
That I would be this gaping little baby.

Yes, I was once like this deluded child,
I wandered rather vaguely to ' Elections,'
Mild as a cherub, yes, and sweetly mild,
When I was told that they had strong objections
    To my poor mathematics,
And other things in my cerebral attics.

I would too stand and reverently cap
The masters (yes, and all the college ' chappies ').
I too was nursed in Fortune's ample lap,
If you 're aware what Fortune's ample lap is.
    I failed in French, and eke
In Latin, and in English, and in Greek.

You have, like many another candidate,
Sought vainly, when you 've heard our erring clock, it 's
Elusive face ; you 've tried to imitate
Our walk, and our affection for our pockets.
    You have no doubt decided
That it 's a ' spiffing place.'   Yes, that 's what I did.

You have, no doubt, been shown the ' pliant ash,'
And braved delightfully that first sweet ' gutter ' ;

You 've spoiled your Verses with a ' Fourpenny Mash,'
And (in a deep bass voice) have striv'n to utter,
    With most sublime emotions,
Small fragmentary particles of Notions.

.   .   .   .

These joys are mine no more : and I opine
That I must go (how sad it is to think we
Must part for ever) : but they will be thine
For five long years (in Latin *annos quinque*),
    And thou wilt take, alas !
My place (that is, supposing that you pass).

A. P. Herbert.
Poor Poems and Rotten Rhymes.
P. and G. Wells, Winchester, 1910.

ELECTION week was the grand festival of the Wykehamical year. **'Stuckling'**
For three days high feast was held in the noble old hall. The
' high table ' was spread on the dais, and all old Wykehamists
were welcome at it. The boys in the lower part of the hall were
regaled with mutton pies and ' stuckling.' . . . I do not think
anybody ate much ' stuckling ' beyond a mouthful *pro forma*.
It was a sort of flat pastry made of chopped apples and currants.
And the speciality of it was that the apples must be that year's
apples. They used to be sent up from Devonshire or Cornwall,
and sometimes were with difficulty obtained.

T. A. Trollope.
What I Remember.
R. Bentley and Son, 1887.

§ 5. ENCHANTED YEARS

O *Cloister Time,* beyond compare,   **'That was to**
    On *Hills,* down *Meads,* down *River* !   **live'**
When summer magic could deliver
Thy soul from every care !
    That was to live :
    And thanks we give
    To *Winchester*, the giver.

M

Days of May blossom and June heat,
  When all the ways were fragrant,
  How good it was to play the vagrant
Over the country sweet !

.   .   .   .

When *Term* dies down to *Domum Day*,
  And last farewells draw nearer :
  Fairer grows *Winchester*, and dearer,
To those who must away.
    Gather then round !
    Send the old sound
To the heart of every hearer.

Calm glide the streams through *Water Meads* ;
  Calmly stand *Hills* above them.
  Hark to the song of those who love them !
How the old music pleads !
    Come, what may come :
    No sweeter Home
To deeper love shall move them.

But limes are rich in flower, and bees
  Make hum, and August follows :
  Away we go, like *Daulian* swallows,
Far from our towers and trees.
    Past the way flies,
    Where *College* lies,
Alone in her ancient hollows.

Back too, like birds from overseas,
  Birds of a common feather,
  Gladly we flock again together,
Back to our towers and trees.
    College in sight !
    Hills ! gently bright
In the golden autumn weather

And then, each heartening winter day :
 When patriot zeal arouses,
  In *College, Commoners* and *Houses,*
The spirit of the fray !
  Time to begin,
  Ah, what glad din
 Beneath the wintry boughs is !

Only nine years, but nine ago ;
 Could dearer rank befall me ?
 With joy I won the right to call me
A *College Junior* : so
  All those good things,
  Tom Warton sings,
 Were waiting to enthrall me.

How fair the ancient city shone
 That best of red Septembers !
 How well my haunted heart remembers
That evening, nine years gone !
  O faces bright
  With ruddy light !
 O dreams beside the embers !

. . . . . .

Lionel Johnson.
'Winchester,' in *Ireland and Other Poems.*
Elkin Mathews, 1897.

THE JUNIOR OF 6 CHAMBER

HITHER ye jocund Muses haste,
And if ye love a theme of taste
Begin with me in tuneful strife
To sing a Junior's happy life.
A thousand cares at times molest
The sage Prepostor's thoughtful breast :

*The College
Junior*

Cares of election chamber vex,
And pupils every hour perplex,
Tho' many a blow imprint my pate
For salt or trenchers brought too late;
But when we get to dear New College,
Profoundly skilled in Classic Knowledge,
Whether in coat of Jenimy cut
Or one so spruce we boys shall strut,
Yet still with pleasure shall we think on
The Junior's happy life at Winton—
Pies, hotcakes, lozenges and snacks,
Saws, hogsheads, dispars, goiners, Jacks.
What tho' our Seniors rule the roast,
Pray then what else have they to boast?
Like us our Seniors are but Boys,
Nor aim at more exalted joys;
Like us they deal with Peggy Brunning,
Like us exposed to constant dunning,
Like us on home their thoughts are running,
Like us impatient for a ride,
Eager they wait for Whitsuntide.
Think not I mean this idle strain
The fiction of a thoughtless brain,
In me behold the very thing,
The self-same character I sing,
Of no poetic club a member,
But humble Junior of 6 Chamber.

T. Warton.
Add. MS. 29,539, fol. 19*b*.

School days

HERE is the old grey tower, here the meads
　　　Through which we strolled,
Unmindful of the world, its cares and creeds,
　　　In days of old.

Dost thou remember, how, on summer eves,
> The dying sun
Peeped at us, blinking through the chequered leaves,—
> Our freedom won ?

And how we sate and talked beneath the trees
> As evening fell,
Until there sounded, lingering on the breeze,
> The chapel bell ;

Or, arm in arm, we wandered by the brink
> Of that clear stream,
That binds the meadows with its silver link,
> Lost in a dream,—

And spoke of subjects ranging far and wide,
> As boyhood may,
Of love and life, and that last cricket-side,
> And work and play.

Ah ! that was Friendship.   Not this world again
> Can e'er renew
The freshness of that bygone love ; in vain
> We search life through.

> E. H. Lacon Watson.
> 'School Days,' from *Verses, Original and Suggested.*
> London, Innes and Co., 1896.

> *December* 16, 1816.

. . . I GIVE you joy of having left Winchester. Now you may **Jane Austen's** own how miserable you were there ; now it will gradually all **humour** come out, your crimes and your miseries—how often you went up by the Mail to London and threw away fifty guineas at a tavern, and how often you were on the point of hanging yourself, restrained only, as some ill-natured aspersion upon poor old Winton has it, by the want of a tree within some miles of the city.

Jane Austen to her nephew on his leaving Winchester College.
J. E. Austen-Leigh's *Memoir of Jane Austen*.
Richard Bentley, 1870.

At School

THE wind that swept across the open down,
And kissed the waving hare-bells and the grass ;
The silver streams, that did in music pass
Along the winding vale below the town ;

The sun that lit the landscape into gold ;
The singing of the wild birds, the flower perfume ;
The greenness, and the freshness, and the bloom,
These were the friends that held my heart of old.

R. C. K. Ensor.
' At School,' in *Modern Poems*.
Brimley Johnson, 1903.

§ 6. CHAPEL

Second peal

CONVOCAT ad Templum tandem campana secunda,
In medio recte quae quintam dividit horam.
Jam Templum petitur ; reseret vigil ostia functor ;
Et curæ sibi sit ne clavem perdat aduncam.

.   .   .   .

Nunc duo Praefecti, quibus est haec cura, sagaci
Prospiciant pueros oculo, ne forte loquantur,
Ne propriis careant libris, recitentve profanum,
Ne sine concessâ veniâ sit quilibet absens.

Collegiata Schola Wiccamica Wintoniensi, in *The College of
St. Mary, Winton*, ed. by C. W. Wordsworth, 1848.

**Evening
Chapel**

. . . THERE sounds upon the summer night
That vesper chime which legions never heard

In all their clarions; and the scene is changed.
Two candles burning in the vestibule
Cast a brief halo on the storied walls:
Tho' all within, the perpendicular shafts
That case the viewless colours of the glass
And tree of Jesse in the eastern light,
Soar up in solemn darkness; there they kneel,
One family, the prefect and the fag,
And pray their Heavenly Father's will be done
As angels do it.
                    Ere they pass without
In single file, the muster-roll is called:
But lowly now, not clamorous, as at morn.
Yes; all are there, save one, perchance a child
Weary or overtasked.

The Rev. W. Moore.
'Evening Hills,' in *New Poems*.
Kegan Paul, Trench, Trübner and Co., 1904.

AH! Piety, thou art not dead!   **'Their brief
Here is the footfall of thy tread;   and wingèd
Here, where yon kindling Eastern beam,   prayer'**
In many a purple-tinted stream,
Lights the long line of Wykeham's sons;
Christ flames upon their orisons;
And eyes, that will, can find Him there,
In trembling gleams of morning, where
Breeze-shaken leaves lift quiveringly
The flooding glory!   Jesse's tree
Mounts up in branching royalty
On those old panes, till Bethlehem flings
True Day Spring on the Jewish Kings.
And now the topmost spray, that grows
From roots where Wykeham's life-blood flows,

Is drinking from a newer sun
Undying hope, fresh strength to run
Life's first fleet-footed stadia.   Hear,
Saviour ! their brief and wingèd prayer !

The Rev. W. Moore.
Venta and Other Poems.
D. Nutt, 1882.

The Jesse Window

AT once to raise our Rev'rence and Delight,
To elevate the Mind and please the Sight ;
To pour in Virtue at th' attentive Eye,
And waft the Soul on Wings of Ecstasie :
For this the Painter's Art with Nature vies,
And bids the visionary Saint arise.
Who views the sacred Forms, in Thought aspires,
Catches pure zeal, and as he gazes, fires,
Feels the same ardour to his Breast convey'd,
Is what he sees, and emulates the shade.
Thy strokes, great Artist, so sublime appear,
They check our Pleasure with an awful Fear,
While, thro' the Mortal Line, the God you trace,
Author Himself, and Heir of Jesse's Race,
In Raptures we admire thy bold Design,
And, as the subject, own the Hand divine.
While through thy work the rising Day shall stream
So long shall last thine Honour, Praise, and Name.
And may thy Labours to the Muse impart
Some Emanation from her Sister Art.
To animate the Verse, and bid it shine
In Colours easy, bright, and strong, as Thine.
Supine on Earth an awful Figure lies,
While softest slumbers seem to seal his Eyes,
The hoary Sire Heav'n's Guardian Care demands,
And at his Feet the watchful Angel stands.

The Form august and large, the Mien Divine,
Betray the Founder of Messiah's Line.
Lo ! from his Loins the promis'd Stem ascends,
And high to Heav'n its sacred Boughs extends :
Each Limb productive of some Hero springs,
And blooms Luxuriant with a Race of Kings.
Th' eternal Plant wide spreads its arms around,
And with the mighty BRANCH the mystick Top is crowned.

.   .   .   .

And oh ! 'till Earth and Seas and Heav'n decay,
Ne'er may that fair Creation fade away ;
May Winds and Storms those beauteous Colours spare,
Still may they bloom as permanent as fair,
All the vain Rage of wasting Time repell,
And his Tribunal see whose cross they paint so well.

*The Genealogy of Christ, as it is represented in the East Window
in the College Chapel at Winchester*, by a young gentleman
of Winchester School.   Robert Lowth, 1729.

GREY tower of Wykeham ! thou whose eyes have seen
A hundred generations throng thy gate,
Each busy with the moulding of his fate,
Have watched them come and go, and pass between
The clustering Chambers and the stretch of green,
And sent them out as units in the State,
Each character distinct and separate,
Yet all combining parts of one Machine,
And priding in the School has borne its part,
But thou wouldst seem to be its very soul ;
Than all thou clingest closer to the heart.
The Chambers see our work, the Meads our play,
Yet most we love thee, who hast heard us pray.

**Winchester
College
Chapel**

J. L. Crommelin-Brown.
Poems and Parodies.
P. and G. Wells, Winchester, 1908.

On being late
for Chapel

ON the tower of chapel lingers
    All the glow of evening light,
And the twilight's drowsy fingers
    Warn us of approaching night.

While outside the bats are wheeling,
    As in verse they always will,
And the pale-rimmed moon is stealing
    Gradually above the Hill.

Pealing anthems down the fretted
    Vault resound the note of praise.
(For this last I am indebted
    To an Elegy of Gray's.)

Now do Betsy, Jane, and Sally
    Don their latest Sunday hat,
Now, along the lonely alley
    Prowls the melancholy cat.

Now the twinkling stars incite to
    Wonder Dr. Watts's mind.
Every crow has winged its flight to
    Bed—and I am left behind.

I suppose that as I listen
    To the organ's ' pealing ' note,
In my eye a tear should glisten
    And a lump come in my throat.

Then I should ' restrain the rising
    Sob,' and sadly turn away,
As in novels, moralising
    On the evil of the day.

Yet, 'tis strange, the organ's thunder
    Wakes no kindred chord in me ;
And the only thing I wonder
    Is what length my lines will be.

J. L. Crommelin-Brown.
Poems and Parodies.
P. and G. Wells, Winchester, 1908.

§ 7. NIGHT IN COLLEGE

HER towers are bright beneath the moon,
High fleecy clouds seem stretched upon
The pinnacles, or, torn and rent,
Creep through the archéd battlement,
Lacing the grey with silver thread.
The golden stars are overhead,
Their eyes on murmuring Itchen, save
Where bending laurels quaff the wave.
Many a night serene as this,
Hath poured the balm of midnight bliss
On Wykeham's towers ; e'en such a night
Bathed walls new-chiselled in her light,
When first within yon windows dim
Was heard the chant, the vesper hymn
Of long-haired children, and they lay
Dreaming the wonders of the day,
That first bright day, when Wykeham's halls
From idlesse of proud castle walls,
Gathered young flowers of Albion,
In Learning's newer race to run.

**Night in
Chamber
Court**

The Rev. W. Moore.
(Author of *Pericula Urbis*) *Venta and Other Poems.*
D. Nutt, 1882.

The Hour of
Prayer

                                                AND now the hour
Sounds nine since burning noon ; and as it sounds,
One cherished custom more ! . . .
These chambers now are changed to oratories ;
As if an angel's wand had touched each floor
And traced a circle round each kneeling boy,
Whispering ' Here unmolested let him be ;
Here let him hide, a pardoned prodigal,
Beneath the almighty wings.'
                                          And yet this calm,
So sudden in the reckless throng, was wrought
Not by an angel but a man ; a man,
By angel's dispensation, and now passed
From earth ; yet wheresoever his converse now,
Surely the record of that hour is writ
When he with zeal consumed for youthful souls
Called the precursors of these prefects proud ;
Adjuring them by memorable things,
By the sweet lessons of their homes ; by this
Their grander home ; by this entrusted power,
Lest it should ever turn into a curse ;
By all they ever hoped to be ; to swear
These minutes on the stroke of nine should be
For ever sacred.

                          The Rev. W. Moore.
                ' Evening Hills,' in *New Poems*.
        Kegan Paul, Trench, Trübner and Co., 1904.

A brave
example

GEORGE RIDDING was twelve years old when he entered College
[1840]. . . . His first night in College, of which he never spoke,
was a sharp test of that goodness. When bedtime came, he
saw that none of the other nine boys in his chamber knelt to say
their prayers. He quietly knelt down, was laughed at, roughly
interrupted and pelted with abuse and solid weapons, but he
took no notice, and knelt on. The second night he did the

same under the same difficulties ; but on the third night, when he again knelt down, the contemporary, who told this story of him, knelt down also ; and very soon his brave example was followed by most of the boys in his chamber. Five years later, when he was head of the school, the practice of kneeling by their bedsides to pray was universal among the scholars.

Lady Laura Ridding.
George Ridding, Schoolmaster and Bishop.
Edward Arnold, 1908.

Night in
'Chambers'

So to their deep sleep
The weary sink ; e'en students' lights are out ;
Only the tallow tapers, duly trimmed,
Watch dimly o'er each hearthstone ; or a spark,
A tiny spark, in some grey ember burns ;
Only a moonbeam steals on letters cut
In a black marble o'er an oaken bed,
The blazon of its tenant long ago.
Only the brook in the garden, gushing by,
Lends its low music to the voices heard
In many a youthful dream.

     O, Lady, dear
To many children, e'en in garish day
The stones of all thy pinnacles announce
The greatness of thy lineage ; but the night,
The midmost night in all thy chambers hushed,
Speaks best of thee ; there is no speech nor cry,
Yet voices of the past are in them all.
The conscious marble tells its tale ; what eyes
Beneath those oaken canopies have watched
That flickering flame ; or seen the embers fade ;
What ears have heard the babble of that brook.

. . . .

So let them sleep ;—then mould them as thou wilt ;—
Sleep on, when from the gateways of the east

Along the everlasting downs the breeze
Blows its far trumpets o'er the wood ; sleep on,

. . . .

Till many a crimson sunbeam on the Tower
Falling has roused it, Memnon-like, to song,
Pealing the hour of five.   Then let them rise,
Strong for each minute of a live-long day.

The Rev. W. Moore.
' Evening Hills,' in New Poems.
Kegan Paul, Trench, Trübner and Co., 1904.

§ 8. 'HILLS'

'Juga Viridantia'

Ad juga sublimis viridantia montis eundum est :
Incedat sociata cohors, sociata recedat ;
Atque ita donec apex montis tangatur, eamus.
Hunc humilis montem vallis quasi cingulus arctat ;
Haec meta est pedibus non transilienda ; nec aude,
Ne tibi sunt tremulae febres, discumbere terræ.
Hic tamen ejecto discas bene ludere disco,
Seu pila delectat palmaria, sive per auras
Saepe repercusso pila te juvat icto bacillo,
Seu pedibus calcata tuis, his lusibus uti
Innocuis fas est ; . . .

Collegiata Schola Wiccamica Wintoniensi.

'Morning Hills'

St. Catherine's Hill is a notably isolated down in the immediate neighbourhood of Winchester, and just above the charming little village of St. Cross.   There is a clump of firs on the top, and the unusually well-marked circumvallation of a Roman (or British ?) camp around the circle of the hill.   The ditch of this circumvallation formed our ' bounds.'   The straying beyond them, however, in the direction of the open downs away from the city, and from St. Cross, was deemed a very venial offence by either the prefect of hall or the masters.   But not so in the direction of the town. It was the duty of the three 'juniors' in college—one of whom I was during my first half-year—to 'call *domum*.' . . . All year round we went to 'morning hills' before breakfast, and to afternoon hills about three. In the summer we went, . . . every evening after 'hall,' but not to the top of the hill, only to the water-meads at the foot of it, the object being to bathe in the Itchen.

T. A. Trollope.
What I Remember, i. 107.
R. Bentley and Son, 1887.

WINCHESTER COLLEGE HALL,
6.30 P.M.

O THE strange eve of June, so long ago :   **'Evening**
Its ardour, cause of toil and transient joy,   **Hills'**
Burns in the heart for ever ;

As it burnt
In bars of brilliance then, through casement oped
High as the raftered roof, and smote below
The table's snowy cloth or wooden ware ;
Or lit a battered pewter or a head
Flaxen or auburn in the gown-boy's throng ;
Or e'en some brazen button on the coat
Of one who stood and served them.

Then a voice
Above all cries of the refectory
Has shouted ' Hills ' ; strange word, not void of fear
To those who wot not all that it might be.
The grace is said ; and pell-mell down the stairs
The seventy children of great Wykeham rush
To don the beaver and be prompt to take
Their places on the destined pilgrimage ;
Lest laggard feel the throng-compelling wand.

.   .   .   .

And now with shout and jeer   **In Chamber**
And jest the column of the Commoners comes ;   **Court**

And giants lead those lines; or so they seemed
To those three artless infants of the gown;
As now, the order of the onset given,
All move through the quadrangle.

                                    Verily
Pilgrims a moment that procession seems
Then, when all cries are hushed, and bared all heads,
Where Mary, from her sculptured canopy
Above the inner gate, for ever smiles,
As if to win them to some gentleness.
But that is passed, and the utmost gateway passed:
And then, the holy precincts left behind,
The inextinguishable merriment
Of boyhood with felt manhood in the blood
Lets itself loose and runs its racy course.

.   .   .   .

                        . . . Fitfully
The ashen wand leaps out to dress the line;
Yet all the paven way with laughter rings,
The bully's sally and the victim's cry

The Warden's Garden

Unnoticed.   But, hard by, the flanking wall
Of that long causeway harbours wondrous peace,
In glooms of clustered verdure, close-shorn lawns
Where sunlight sleeps; and through the garden sealed
Itchen, low murmuring on his silver bed,
Enhances more the cloistral calm.

                                    But now
Those walls are passed; and from the broad green dale

Water-meadows

Sparkling with summer on its limpid streams,
Breezes of evening greet them airily
Fanning the sultriness; and far away,
High o'er a quarry gleaming on a hill,
A clump of pine-trees crowns a trenchèd slope

St. Catherine's

Once sable sentinels of Catherine's shrine.
What thousand eyes in far-off centuries

Have looked uplifted to that hill ; what feet
Have scaled that holy height : and e'en to us
Its base is goal this eve ; no pilgrims, we ;
And yet we tread where such have trod. . . .

.   .   .   .

Higher and narrower wended now the path ;
Sheer on the right the vale hight Tempe yawned ;   'Tempe'
Leafy and cool and sweet-perfumed we knew
That vale in Thessaly ; and leafy this ;
But not so sweet, we found, as falling there
We lay midst shreds and carrions of the ditch.
For one of those said giants, patience lost
At the slow progress of the hated van,
Quick to the Moloch of his wrath had hurled
Two infants down the precipice : who thence
Clomb and emerged on upper air to find
The path now clear of all save him who wields
That ashen indiscriminating wand.
But Wykeham's serge is kindly strong to meet
His castigating rods ; and childhood's tears
Are April showers.
                          So when at last, beyond
Expanse of corn green-waving and two stiles,
The lines disband, those rough derisive words
And e'en that sudden shock are half forgot ;
And lo, like Lethe at their feet, the stream   Itchen
Seems lending all its lucid deeps to heal
All sorrow ; though its tasselled banners wave
O'er shallower reaches of the gleaming bed
Than here might aid the swimmer's art. . . .

.   .   .   .

                          . . . 'Twere sweet
After the fourteen hours of toil and stress
To sink one moment on the holy sod
Where the slight milkwort droops at close of day ;

N

To look afar on those grey pinnacles
So peaceful now above their silent courts,
Backed by the solemn spireless minster mass.
But hark ! the tumult of the bath begins :
The keys are creaking in the lock to ope
The sluice : and cataracts thunder in the void ;
See ! a lithe form already stripped has flashed
O'er the huge beam that guards the water-gate ;
And straight as arrow to the targe has plunged
Into the depth unseen. . . .

.   .   .   .

Domum

                            'Tis come, the hour,
The clamorous hour, when all return to ranks.
Down glassy vistas of the lower stream,
Into the ravine of the eternal down,
Far up the mystic slope, it reaches, where,
In cool and chalky cavern, Arethuse,
From Dorian founts sweet emissary, sits,
And listening smiles to the ageless evening star
Reflected on her ageless pool, to think
Her Dorian boys in Enna long ago
Ne'er shouted so ; nor e'er did Sparta build
A home like that now summoned to.   Again
' Home ' rings down some close pathway of the vale,
Where, maybe, two are walking and are sad,
Conscious this home is little longer theirs,
Yon walls, these sparkling greeneries.   And now
The wand brings order from the jostling crowd,
There, on that tell-tale oyster-paven spot :
Again the hated gown-boys in the van,
Again in flowing serge decorous each ;
Again the laic column on the rear,
The self-same giants leading ; and again
That vale of Tempe : but no mishap now ;

Again those garden walls where peaceably
Men dwell, and lowlier the shrouded brook
Murmurs, and ghostlier the twilit forms
Of verdure haunt the alleys ; and again
That still quadrangle and the form benign ;
And those seven chambers where the weary sleep ;
Or soon shall sleep, when hunger unappeased
No more shall need their ministries. . . .

The Rev. W. Moore.
' Evening Hills,' in *New Poems*.
Kegan Paul, Trench, Trübner and Co., Limited, 1904.

§ 9. BATHING IN ITCHEN

. . . We panted, until evening released us to wander forth **Bathing and** along the water-meadows by Itchen and bathe, and, having **Poaching** bathed, to lie naked amid the mints and grasses for a while before returning in the twilight.

This bathing went on, not in one or two great crowds, but in groups, and often in pairs only, scattered along the river-bank almost all the way to Hills ; it being our custom again at Winchester (and I believe it still continues) to *socius* or walk with one companion ; and only at one or two favoured pools would several of these couples meet together for the sport. On the evening of which I am about to tell, my companion was a boy named Fiennes, of about my own age, and we bathed alone, though not far away to right and left the bank teemed with outcries and laughter and naked boys running all silvery as their voices in the dusk.

With all this uproar the trout of Itchen, as you may suppose, had gone into hiding ; but doubtless some fine fellows lay snug under the stones, and—the stream running shallow after the heats—as we stretched ourselves on the grass Fiennes challenged me to tickle for one ; it may be because he had heard me boast

of my angling feats at home.   There seemed a likely pool under
the farther bank ; convenient, except that to take up the best
position beside it I must get the level sun full in my face.
I crept across, however, Fiennes keeping silence, laid myself
flat on my belly, and peered down into the pool, shading my
eyes with one hand.   For a long while I saw no fish, until
the sun rays, striking aslant, touched the edge of a golden
fin very prettily bestowed in a hole of the bank, and well
within an overlap of green weed.   Now and again the fin
quivered, but for the most part my gentleman lay quiet as a
stone, head to stream, and waited for relief from these noisy
Wykehamists.   Experience, perhaps, had taught him to despise
them ; at any rate, when gently—very gently—I lowered my
hand and began to tickle, he showed neither alarm nor
resentment.   ' Is it a trout ? ' demanded Fiennes in an excited
whisper from the farther shore.   But of course I made no
answer, and presently I supposed that he must have crept
off to his clothes, for some way up the stream I heard the
Second Master's voice warning the bathers to dress and
return, and with his usual formula, *Ite domum saturæ, venit
Hesperus, ite capellæ!*   Being short-sighted, he missed to
spy me, and I felt, rather than saw or heard, him pass
on ; for with one hand I yet shaded my eyes while with the
other I tickled.

Yet another two minutes went by, and then with a jerk I
had my trout, my thumb and forefinger deep under his gills ;
brought down my other clutch upon him and, lifting, flung him
back over me among the meadow grass, my posture being such
that I could neither hold him struggling nor recover my own
balance save by rolling sideways over on my shoulder-pin ;
which I did, and, running to him where he gleamed and doubled,
flipping the grasses, caught him in both hands and held him
aloft.

A. T. Quiller Couch (' Q.').
Sir John Constantine.
Smith, Elder and Co., 1906.

LINES WRITTEN ON THE DEATH OF BINGHAM, DROWNED AT
WINCHESTER [IN POT OR FIRST LOCK]

HAPLESS flow'r ! by fate prevented,   Drowned in
   Tho' to blossom scarce begun,   'Pot'
Early is thy urn lamented,
   For full soon thy course is run.

Water nymphs with flow'rets strew him,
   And your coral wreaths present,
Itchen, for 'twas thou that slew him,
   Itchen, o'er his tomb lament.

Lately we beheld him leading
   Wykeham's sons o'er yonder plain,
Now another youth succeeding
   Leads the gay unthinking train.

Each of us perhaps to-morrow
   Like our friend may meet our doom,
Freely then indulge your sorrow
   O'er his much-lamented tomb.

     By 'Huddesford' or 'Hill.'—Add. MS. 29,539, fol. 2.
[Huddesford was Fellow of New College, editor of *Salmagundi*.]

WALKING along the canal from Twyford not long ago I came   'Milkhole'
to what in former days was known as a 'milkhole' and 'pot,'   and 'Pot'
and I was irresistibly reminded of a scene I witnessed there
when I was a College Junior ever so many years ago. 'Pot'
is very different now from what it was in those days. The
canal and the locks were then in working order, and 'pot'
was our chief and favourite bathing-place, and when the lower
gates were shut and the lock was filling fast with clear green
water, twisting and twirling and bubbling, you might go a
long way before you would beat that glorious header into the
middle of it. . . .

I think it must have been at evening Hills that the episode I refer to occurred.   A number of us were collected there, those who were good enough swimmers taking headers into ' pot ' itself, others bathing in the shallow at the tail of ' milkhole,' and some on the bank looking on. . . .

All of a sudden there was a commotion and a cry from the group of boys in the water below ' milkhole,' and it appeared that one of them had somehow got into deep water and was being carried under by the back rush.   A dangerous place it was for those who could not swim, as there was a strong undertow setting towards the gates and nothing there to stand upon or hold on by. . . .

Fortunately, however, the catastrophe had been made known to the aristocrats who were bathing in ' pot ' just above, and one of them ran down, and without a moment's hesitation plunged into ' milkhole ' and swam across, just as the undertow had carried the drowning boy up to the gate.   Even when he grasped the boy it was no easy matter to get him up to the surface and back to the bank, for there was no purchase on those slippery gates.   But he managed it at last—our hero—as we knew he would. . . .

Look up at the Crimean Memorial as you enter chapel, and there . . . you will see the name of Lieut. Fred G. Barker, who was killed at the battle of Inkerman, Nov. 5th, 1854, aged 21 years.   He was the hero of my tale.   *Qualis ab incepto.*

The Wykehamist, February 1894.

The Junior's Christening

> . . . On to the brink !
> Scan the vast cistern, measure all its side
> Boiling and frothing with the weedy wave.
> There thou must plunge, and with a bound like that,
> E'en ere it brims the pathway.
>
> So : 'tis done :
> And on the wave which swarms with swimmers now

Thou risest corklike from the gurgling gulf :
But ere thou take thy pastime with the rest
Some strong unpriestly hand is on thy head,
And trine immersion by the unaltering rite
Is, as for all before thee, thine.   Ah ! well :
'Twas purgatorial, yet 'twas saving too,
This baptism : the body's generous glow
Is somehow mantling o'er the mind ; and fresh
As in the slumbering chambers rang at morn
The slave-boy's cry, the same shall be this eve
To call the loiterers home.

> The Rev. W. Moore.
> 'Evening Hills,' in *New Poems*.
> Kegan Paul, Trench, Trübner and Co., 1904.

§ 10. DOMUM

It chanced some twelve-score years ago
　In Wykeham's ancient School,
The genial summer brought relief
　From the stern Master's rule.

The scholars doffed their bands and gowns,
　Closed every classic tome,
And donned their gomers, as they termed
　The garments of their home.

And all were joyful, all save one,
　That morn condemned to wait
The life-long holidays alone
　Within the College Gate.

A ring with precious diamonds set
　Was missing, woe betide !
Stol'n from a chamber free to him
　But closed to all beside.

A 'Domum'
Legend

He marked his comrades' look askance,
  He heard their parting glee;
Would none believe his innocence
  Or hear his heartfelt plea?

Then on him closed the prison door,
  Where 'twas his doom to stay;
He might not see his sweet, sweet home,
  But he could think and say—
      Domum, domum, etc.

    .   .   .   .   .   .

There on the cold grey stone he lay
  Beneath the Cloister's shade,
And on the mouldering walls around
  That plaintive music played.

And from a nest perched high o'erhead
  There fell the long-lost ring,
And soft birds' voices piped these notes
  His requiem to sing—
      Domum, domum, etc.

          The Wykehamist, February 1893.

'Concinamus,
O sodales!'

CONCINAMUS, O sodales!
  Eja! quid silemus?
Nobile canticum
Dulce melos, Domum
  Dulce Domum, resonemus.

    Domum, Domum, Dulce Domum,
    Domum, Domum, Dulce Domum,
    Dulce, Dulce, Dulce Domum,
    Dulce Domum resonemus.

Appropinquat ecce felix!
  Hora gaudiorum;

Post grave tedium
Advenit omnium
  Meta petita laborum.

Musa, libros mitte, fessa ;
  Mitte pensa dura,
Mitte negotium,
Jam datur otium,
  Me mea mittito cura.

Ridet annus, prata rident ;
  Nosque rideamus :
Jam repetit domum
Daulias advena ;
  Nosque domum repetamus.

Heus ! Rogere, fer caballos ;
  Eja, nunc eamus ;
Limen amabile,
Matris et oscula
  Suaviter et repetamus.

Concinamus ad Penates,
  Vox et audiatur ;
Phosphore ! quid jubar,
Segnius emicans,
  Gaudia nostra moratur ?

[COMRADES, join our tuneful measure ;
  Wherefore should we silent be ?
Noblest theme ! and dearest treasure,
  Home sweet home, we 'll sing of thee.

    Home sweet home, we 'll sing of thee ;
    Home sweet home, our theme shall be ;
    Home sweet home, rare melody ;
    Home sweet home, rare melody.

Wingèd hours onward stealing,
    Waft us fleetly towards the goal ;
Toil is o'er, and rapturous feeling
    Wakens in the weary soul.

Muse of learning, gently smiling,
    Lay aside thy musty tomes ;
Listen to our lay's beguiling,
    Banish care from happy homes.

Nature radiant is all laughing ;
    Homewards Philomel doth speed ;
We our fill of joy are quaffing,
    Home our guerdon, home our meed.

Roger, quick ! for time is pressing,
    Lead the horses to the door ;
Home, a mother's fond caressing
    Waits us, we can stay no more.

All the live-long night till morning
    Carol forth our roundelay ;
Phœbus ! why so slow in dawning ?
    Joy like ours brooks no delay.]

An English version of *Domum*, by ' Orpheus.'
The Wykehamist, April 1869.

Ad Meos

O PARS magna mei, quot intus olim
Et curæ et mihi gaudio fuistis,
Ut patri suboles amans amanti,
(Prosit vos subolem vocâsse amantem !)
Si quondam tolerastis imperantem,
Nunc concurrite nomina invocanti.

Si Domûs procul urget exsulantes
Vos desiderium, mei quod instar ?
Quot olim mihi congregatus ordo
Illic discipulos tulit magistro !
Ignotus repeto domum, nec ullus
Interesse suâ putat scholaris
Qualis umbra vager prioris aevi.

Prolem Wiccamicam tamen saluto
Donatus rude jam senex, sodales
Nunc, qui discipuli fuistis olim.

Quingentesimus annus ecce ! felix
Est natalium et hora gaudiorum :
Huc adeste, Domum, quot estis, omnes,
Domum, nobile canticum, sonemus.
Jam negotia Musa mittat omnis :
Et Musis datur otium : remittant
Cum Musis pueri senusque curas.
Cum ridentibus annus ecce ! pratis
Ridet : advena Daulias profugit
Domum : nos quoque jam domum petamus.
Nos amabile limen osculisque
Mater excipiet Domum ; Rogerus
Quanquam nullus adest ferens caballos,
At nos ocius eia ! nunc eamus.
Unâ voce canamus ad Penates
Dulcem Wiccamicamque cantilenam.
Sic, cum finis erit nec emicabit
Segnis Phosphorus et domum reducet,
Tum, nec post grave taedium moranti,
Cuique meta petita sit laborum :
Domum, dulce melos, canant sodales.

George Southwell.
The Wykehamist, July 1893.

WHITSUNTIDE

*Written at Winchester College on the immediate approach
of the Holidays*

'The strain
of joy and
liberty'

HENCE, thou fur-clad Winter, fly!
Sire of shivering Poverty!
Who, as thou creep'st with chilblains lame
To the crowded charcoal flame,
With chattering teeth and ague cold,
Scarce thy shaking sides canst hold
While thou draw'st the deep cough out :
God of Football's noisy rout,
Tumult loud and boist'rous play,
The dangerous slide, the snow-ball fray.

But come, thou genial Son of Spring,
Whitsuntide! and with thee bring
Cricket, nimble boy and light,
In slippers red and drawers white,
Who o'er the nicely-measur'd land
Ranges around his comely band,
Alert to intercept each blow,
Each motion of the wary foe.
Or patient take thy quiet stand,
The angle trembling in thy hand,
And mark, with penetrative eye,
Kissing the wave the frequent fly,
Where the trout, with eager spring,
Forms the many-circled ring,
And, leaping from the silver tide,
Turns to the sun his speckled side.

Or lead where Health, a naiad fair,
With rosy cheek and dripping hair,
From the sultry noon-tide beam,
Laves in Itchin's crystal-stream.

Thy votaries, rang'd in order due,
To-morrow's wish'd-for dawn shall view,
Greeting the radiant star of light
With Matin Hymn and early rite :
E'en now, these hallow'd haunts among,
To thee we raise the Choral Song ;
And swell with echoing minstrelsy
The strain of joy and liberty.
If pleasures such as these await
Thy genial reign, with heart elate
For thee I throw my gown aside
And hail thy coming, Whitsuntide.

[A poem by ' the late Thomas Warton, junior,' among those in
Salmagundi, edited by George Huddesford, 1801.]

WE have laughed in the sun, we have struggled and won,   **Domum Night**
    We have lived through a glorious year ;
We have known at the last of the worth of the past
    When the days of our passing were near ;
We have learned to be leaders and losers,
    And tried as they taught us to try,
And we gather to-night in despair and delight
    For the song that must be a good-bye.

We have treasured each day as it flitted away,
    We have lingered our last on the hill,
But we 'll roll our refrain through the valley again,
    For to-night we are treasuring still ;

Though we part with a sigh and a sadness
  From the friends of our happiest years,
We may surely forget to look back with regret
  With the happiest song in our ears.

We have homes that are dear, but the home which
    is here
  Is the mother of all we are worth,
And the honour we know from the world we shall owe
  To the place which has given us birth ;
In the suns of an Indian summer,
  When we work for an emperor's needs,
We shall think of the school which has taught us
    to rule,
  And the midsummer magic of Meads.

Oh, the minutes are short in the echoing Court,
  But this night shall remain with you long.
You shall feel us about in the hour of your doubt,
  Joining hands in the shadowy throng ;
And far off in the misty hereafter,
  More sweet than the music of Fame,
Shall ring in your ears the wonderful cheers
  Of the friends who would honour your name.

Though a tenderer race will be chiefs in our place
  And grow great in the popular eye,
Though the names we have made will so easily fade
  By the names of another July,
Yet the hearts of the men who have made us
  Will bear us a record of truth,
And remember us still for the good or the ill
  That we worked with the riches of youth.

A.

The Wykehamist, August 1911.

Honouring
Saint Mary
of Winton

AT Winchester, which we boys (though we fared hardly) never
doubted to be the first school in the world, as it was the most
ancient in England, we had a song we called *Domum* : and
because our common pride in her—as the best pride will—
belittled itself in speech, I trust that our song honoured Saint
Mary of Winton the more in that it celebrated only the joys of
leaving her.

The tale went, it had been composed (in Latin too) by a boy
detained at school for punishment during the summer holidays.
Another fable improved on this by chaining him to a tree. A
third imprisoned him in cloisters whence, through the arcades
and from the ossuaries of dead fellows and scholars, he poured
out his soul to the swallows haunting the green garth :—

> ' Jam repetit domum
> Daulias advena,
> Nosque domum repetamus.'

Whatever its origin, our custom was to sing it as the holidays—
especially the summer holidays—drew near, and to repeat it
as they drew nearer, until every voice was hoarse. As I
remember, we kept up this custom with no decrease of fervour
through the heats of June 1756, though they were such that
our *hostiarius* Dr. Warton, then a new broom, swept us out of
school, and for a fortnight heard our books (as the old practice
had been) in cloisters, where we sat upon cool stone and in the
cool airs, and between our tasks watched the swallows at play.

A. T. Quiller Couch ('Q.').
Sir John Constantine.
Smith, Elder and Co., 1906.

ON RETURNING HOME FROM WINCHESTER, 1761

IN vain, O native fields, ye strive to please,
   In vain to joy your various scenes invite :
Nor can ye give my soul its wonted ease ;
   Nor can ye give my Fair-one to my sight !

Reminis-
cences of a
Domum Ball

Joy is not here : fly, sweet Remembrance, fly,
    Fly where I revell'd late in Pleasure's train ;
Recall the fleeting form to Fancy's eye ;
    And live o'er all the blissful hours again.

Mine was the lot, from ev'ry youth to bear
    The prize how envy'd, how desir'd by all !
Mine was the lot, where hundred nymphs were fair,
    To lead the fairest through the mazy Ball.

.   .   .   .   .   .

William Lipscomb.

To hear Dulce Domum sung

THE visitor should come in July and hear the Dulce Domum sung, and witness that most characteristic gathering of Wykehamists, old and young, proud of their royal school, the most ancient of any in these dominions, and one which has contributed at the very least its proportion of worthies in Church and State.

M. E. C. Walcott.
Memorials of Winchester, 1866.

§ 11. GAMES

Winchester v. Eton

IT was a competition between the schools of Eton and Winchester ; and the earnestness and life that beamed from every countenance were most beautiful to witness : about the wide field you saw not, as usually, the straggling idle visitor, or the money-seeking gamester, but fathers and mothers, brothers and sisters, were there, in numerous and cheerful parties, bringing with them all the hopes and fears of family and personal affection. . . .

Charles Townsend.
Winchester, etc., 1842.

A Win for Winchester

THE match was over, and we had won ! Winchester had won ! United Winchester made a combined rush for the hero of the day, and bore him struggling to the pavilion ; thence, still unsatisfied, to College. There were thoughts of carrying him round the town. Grey-bearded men waved their hats and cheered with the rest. It was a mad spectacle.

There were feasts in College that night, and for many succeeding nights. For, among the crowd of old Wykehamists who pressed forward to shake hands with the pioneer of victory [Christopher Deane], more than one had left behind a five pound note. A stream of liberality flowed that day. Some even fell upon myself. For days afterwards College Street reaped a golden harvest. Those were great times.

E. H. Lacon Watson.
Christopher Deane.
John Murray.

WHITE on the ground the hoar frost lies,
 And white are the bare-branched trees ;
The sun shines clear from the blue hazed skies
 Through fleeting mists that freeze.

Sixes

Above, the grey old chapel tower,
 Below, the red and brown ;
A breathless hush, then strikes the hour,
 And the heads of the ' hot ' go down.

The long low kick that cheers the soul,
 The ' own side ' followed through,
The clearing ' bust ' which saves a goal,
 The ' flyer ' clean and true.

The man who checks a headlong rush,
 The cheers that shout his name ;
A plant, a dash, a moment's hush,
 Then the goal that wins the game.

o

Go where the sward lies green below,
  And the well-oiled willow clicks;
Go where the eight-oared racers row,
  But leave me to watch a six.

Between the branches' fretworked grace,
  The chapel's grey background,
Clear-cut against the blue of space,
  The ' canvas ' face-ringed round.

When through the mist of forty years,
  We sadly look behind,
This is the scene which first appears,
  Deep-printed in our mind.   B. C. L.

         The Wykehamist, November 29, 1905.

**A Health to
Houses Six!**

HERE 's a health to Our Game, the best game upon earth,
And a health to the men who acknowledge its worth;
Here 's a health, too, to Houses, the pick of the three—
The best home of the brave, the best nurse of the free.

Chorus

The Romans have said, ' Stet Fortuna Domus ';
' Stet Fortuna Domorum 's ' the motto for us;
' Stet Fortuna Domorum ' for ever and aye,
For we 'll conquer again, as we conquered to-day.

Here 's a health to Our Captain, who hots them all down;
To that King of Footballers, the King of the Brown;
To the jolly brown leather he steers through the hot;
To each sally and rally and difficult shot.

Chorus

Hoist him up on your shoulders, and bear him along,
And shout out, till you 're hoarse, this victorious song,

' Stet Fortuna Domorum,' for ever and aye,
For we 'll conquer again, as we conquered to-day.

Here 's a health to Our Ups, who are trusty and true,
Who can bear down the Red and can bear down the Blue,
Who can speed like the hare, and kick like—well—the rest,
For each one is so good you could ne'er tell the best.

Chorus

Hoist them up on, etc.

Here 's a health to Our Hotwatch, who kicks it so clean,
And a health to the Commoners he gets it between,
To the sprint that he makes to the end of the ground,
To the goal that he gets, the wide cheers that resound.

Chorus

Hoist him up, etc.

Here 's a health to Our Kicks who are stalwart and strong,
To each ' flier ' and ' bust ' they send spinning along,
To the rush that they face, to the charge that they stop,
To their lusty ' six-posters,' that quiver and drop.

Chorus

Hoist them up, etc.

Here 's a health to all Wykehamists—Blue, Red or Brown.
May they ne'er meet in life one who *can* hot them down !
For they 'll rally round Canvas as oft as they may,
And still love the old school, with its work and its play.

Chorus

Hoist them up, etc.

R. W. Seton Watson.
Scotland for Ever, etc.
Edinburgh, David Douglas, 1898.

Songs without Singers

ONLY a day in dreary November,
  Sixty quick minutes of feverish play ;
This is the day for a man to remember,
  Treasured within him for ever and aye.
Out with it, on with it, you are the chosen ones ;
Shove it along, then, and pity the frozen ones ;
Doing and daring for what you are wearing,
  Are you not happy, my brothers, to-day ?

You that have lost your reward at the latest,
  Though you have striven as stoutly as they,
You shall be numbered next year with the greatest,
  Nobly triumphant or bravely at bay ;
Only to see how they bustle and worry 'em,
Only to shout as they hustle and hurry 'em !
Out and away with it, look how they stay with it—
  Are you not happy, my brothers, to-day ?

They that must gaze on your rocketing fliers,
  Tasting the past in the feel of the fray,
Love you for losers and cheer you for triers,
  Smile in your triumphs, and share your dismay.
What would they give to be out in the thick of it,
Just for a moment, to show you the trick of it,
Just to be boys again, hear the old noise again—
  What would they give to be with you to-day !

So may we run in the field of to-morrow,
  Steady and straight in the Winchester way,
Losing but laughing, and sad without sorrow,
  Eager at learning and quick to obey !

Here 's to the game which our fathers have made for us,
Here 's to the men who have panted and played for us,
Hardy as Britons, and gentle as kittens—
　　Yes, we are all of us happy to-day !

　　　　　　　　　　　　　　　　　　A.
　　　　　　The Wykehamist, November 1911.

WHAT do you see, Walt Whitman ?

I see a mass of arms clad in brown and white and blue and white
　　jerseys,

Of legs clad in cut-shorts that once were white,

Arms that struggle, and legs that kick convulsively, that is
　　what I see ;

And I see hands that grasp the empty air,

Or if not the air then their next-door neighbour,

Or if not their neighbour then the netting which pens the players
　　in ;

And there are two watchers with note-books and pencils,

Note-books to write in, and pencils to rap the grasping
　　hands,

(There is mud on the hands, and their knuckles are white with
　　the tension of grasping),

The play of the muscles, the curve of the back stooping to
　　push,

Faces glistening with sweat, sinews in the neck taut with the
　　effort of extrication, that is what I see.

I see a ring of eager faces ;

Mouths that open, and anxious eyes.

And ever the grey tower above showing through the trees,

(The trees stripped of their foliage, and the tower shows through
　　their tracery),

Slender, silent tower.

　　　　　　　　　J. L. Crommelin-Brown.
　　　　　　　　　Poems and Parodies.
　　　　　　P. and G. Wells, Winchester, 1908.

(margin note) Walt Whitman watches Fifteens

The sprite of
Winton
football

'TWAS New Year's Eve : on Chapel Tower
The sprite of Winton football sat,
And filled with tears, a copious shower,
    His hat.

He gazed across deserted Meads :
' They ne'er will take me back again :
Ne'er will they see such mighty deeds,
    Such pain.

Good-bye, dear Canvas, never dry :
Your ancient game rejected squirms :
Good-bye, dear ropes, dear posts, good-bye,
    Dear worms.

It is the first stage to my death :
I will begone : I am no more,
Soccer in Short——! ' beneath his breath
    He swore.

A. P. Herbert.
Poor Poems and Rotten Rhymes.
P. and G. Wells, 1910.

'Pruff
Ridding'

HIS pluck and extraordinary disregard of pain made him a
formidable football player—' a marvellous up in canvass, with
a splendid alertness, courage, and skill in the game.' Once as
a ' Hotter ' he received a kick upon his head, audible to all
around. He heard it, and went on playing with a chuckle :
' Junket over that fellow.'

Lady Laura Ridding.
George Ridding, Schoolmaster and Bishop.
Edward Arnold, 1908.

§ 12. FAGGING AND FLOGGING

To the 'Fag'

. . . QUICK, ye slaves,
On with the pots ; and let them all be hot
Amidst the red tongues flickering in the gloom ;
Out with the tables, let your master sup.
For crumbs and bones and home-brew of the Hall
Ill stay the stomach of a hero who
Into that bubbling caldron 'neath the hills
Seven headers took ; whose volleys in the mead
Ye have been hunting half the day.   O speed
Your perilous task for him whose lightest wish
Is iron law.   Kings, truly, must respect
Their pages' hour of rest ; 'tis written too,
The passing sadness of a cupbearer
Once moved the Persian despot ; but these ten,
These kings uncrowned who sup beneath the moon
In restful glory, conscious of the state,
And deeds that served it, have no villeins' wrongs
To deal with nor relentings of their own.
All that they do is right ; the subject learns
To obey, and other lessons when he may.
Still from those lordly tables there are crumbs ;
And dogs may eat them.

The Rev. W. Moore.
' Evening Hills ' in New Poems.
Kegan Paul, Trench, Trübner and Co., Limited, 1904.

I PASS under the college archway and courts grey with time, **'Fagging'** green with new foliage, and see, with a natural sigh, the fine lads strolling careless in cap and gown.   But, surely, regrets for the past, if natural, are vain—if vain, not to be dwelt on ; if dwelt on, foolish.   Are these boys all happy, too ?   Many a ' fag ' (the fagging is severe, and often cruel) is longing for manhood and freedom.   Even in play hours he must submit to the will and caprice of an oldster.   ' Good for him on the whole—prepares him for the battle of life.'   Perhaps so ; but perhaps (along with ' cram,' chapel, and other things) it prepares him to *make* life a battle—a scene of fierce, unscrupulous rivalry, instead of peaceful effort and mutual help. Life brings its combats, its battles, to be well fought out when each crisis comes ; but it ought not to *be* a battle. The laws of war are not the laws of life.

The book-shop outside the gate is full of college boys ; at the next-door pastry cook's the younger ones swarm like bees. Up those steps, the dining-hall still sets its tables with the old-world square wooden trencher, but also nowadays with knife and fork ; and tea flows morn and even, where beer in their fathers' time was the only lawful liquor. A famous novelist of our day (who deals much in cathedrals [1]) said to me, ' We had no tea or coffee '—he was a Wykehamist,—' but beer, as much as you liked—beer at breakfast, beer at dinner, beer at supper, beer under your bed.' Beer sounds barbarous for boys ; but clean home-brewed is a different thing from the tavern-keeper's mixtures. Our novelist is a burly man, and so was Cobbett, who detested ' slops.'

Some of the big lads are at cricket, and with a will. Terribly swift the athletic bowler swings in his heavy ball overhand ; his well-greaved opponent sends it whizzing off the bat. The sport is now made a serious business. . . . To many, perhaps to most of our boys, cricket and boat-racing are the serious parts of school life.

William Allingham.
Varieties in Prose.
Longmans, Green and Co., 1893.

'Fagging' defended

ON looking back to my career at Winchester I have always acknowledged the immense advantage of a public-school education. The school discipline of fagging was to a young and rather sensitive boy very severe, but it was just that which was wanting to brace one up to face the realities of life ; and in spite of some cruelty amongst the head boys, and of the dis-

[1] Probably Anthony Trollope.

advantage of their not being all treated by the headmaster on the principle of honour, the tone of the school as a whole was that of highly honourable young lads.   There might have been something better if there had been more confidence, and something higher in the best sense.   The religious element, indeed, which happily is now more highly developed in almost all schools, was perhaps more than commonly kept back by the want of confidence between the master and the boys.   Still it will always be to the credit of Winchester that Arnold was brought up there, and that (at a later period than that which I am now discussing) he sent his sons thither.

W. R. W. Stephens.
Memoir of Lord Hatherley.
R. Bentley and Son, 1883.

' *Dorsum, qui meruit, ferat !* '

OLD friend, I greet thee with a hearty shake,
And lay once more in mine thy knotty palm,
Whose silent pressure e'en to tears could wake
The stricken soul, or raise a bruisèd arm.
Thou tyrant-guardian of my early days
I give thee greeting now and well-earned praise !

Time was I feared thy gaunt and supple form,
The anger of thy ashen countenance,
Thy presence fled, as from impending storm,
And quailed before thy stern unpleasing glance,
That, like some hawk when some poor victim stoops,
Poises—then on with shrieking fury swoops.

They say thou still dost sing the same old song,
And sleep upon the same old oaken bed ;
But thou, who ofttimes for some fancied wrong,
Didst cut me living, now hast cut me dead—
Though strangers now, these hands shall raise a mound,
And plant thine ashes in their native ground.

A. J. in *The Wykehamist*, February 1894.

Ode to a Ground Ash

Flogging at Winchester

I FEEL convinced in my mind that I have been flogged oftener than any human being alive. It was just possible to obtain five scourgings in one day at Winchester, and I have often boasted that I obtained them all. Looking back over half a century, I am not quite sure whether the boast is true ; but if I did not, nobody ever did.

Anthony Trollope.
An Autobiography, 1815-82.
William Blackwood and Son, Edinburgh and London, 1883.

'A mere form'

THE real and unanswerable objection to the infliction of ' corporal punishment,' as it was used in my day at Winchester, was that it was a mere form and farce. It caused neither pain nor disgrace, and assuredly morally degraded nobody. I have been scourged five times in the day ; not because, as might be supposed, I was so incorrigible that the master found it necessary to go on scourging me, but simply because it so chanced. . . . But this was a rare *tour de force*, scarcely likely to occur again. I was rather proud of it, and wholly unconscious of any ' moral degradation.'

T. A. Trollope.
What I Remember, i. 117.
R. Bentley and Son, 1887.

'Veneris lux sanguino-lenta'

PROH ! dolor, heu ! Veneris lux sanguinolenta propinquat ;
Sanguineamque voco, nam si peccaveris hujus
Hebdomadae spatio, poenas patiere cruentas :
Flecte genu, puerique duo, qui rite vocantur,
Dimittent ligulas, manibusque ligamina solvent.

Collegiata Schola Wiccamica Wintoniensi, from *The College of St. Mary, Winton*, ed. by C. W. (C. Wordsworth).

'Birch in thine aveng-ing hand'

THREE times running shirked he sheerly
Morning lines and Chapel too,
Though he 'd been instructed clearly
That such conduct wouldn't do.

Then outspake his ' patient pastor,'
  ' Order thy proud name, Sir Childe ;
Thou shalt go to the Head Master ' ;
  Naturally getting ' riled.'

Shent with shame, in speechless sorrow,
  Sad he sought the door of school,
Pausing there in hope to borrow
  Courage, and his brow to cool.

  .   .   .   .   .   .

Green with fright as six ' green bakers,'
  At the door the victim stands,
All his courage, like Bob Acres',
  Oozing from his clammy hands.

O Magister Informator !
  Flesh of man may not withstand
Either envious stroke of Fate, or
  Birch in thine avenging hand.

Oh ! unmentionable beginning,
  Oh ! the kneeling on the floor,
Oh ! sarcastic Prefect grinning,
  Oh ! but I can tell no more.

  .   .   .   .   .   .

But, young reader, whosoever
  Drop'st salt water on these whines,
By thy head, and tail,—oh ! never,
  Never, shirk thy morning lines !

E. G. B.
The Wykehamist, February 1874.

§ 13. *NOCTES SHAKSPERIANAE*

PROLOGUE ON THE OLD WINCHESTER PLAYHOUSE OVER THE BUTCHERS' SHAMBLES

Prologue to Otway's 'Monimia'

WHOE'ER our stage examines, must excuse
The wondrous shifts of the dramatic Muse ;
Then kindly listen, while the prologue rambles
From wit to beef, from Shakespeare to the shambles !
Divided only by one flight of stairs
The monarch swaggers, and the butcher swears !
Quick the transition when the curtain drops,
From meek Monimia's moans to mutton chops !
While for Lothario's loss Lavinia cries,
Old women scold, and dealers d—n your eyes !
Here Juliet listens to the gentle lark,
There in harsh chorus hungry bull-dogs bark.
Cleavers and scymitars give blow for blow,
And heroes bleed above, and sheep below !
While tragic thunders shake the pit and box,
Rebellows to the roar the staggering ox.
Cow-horns and trumpets mix their martial tones,
Kidneys and Kings, mouthing and marrow bones.
Suet and sighs, blank verse and blood abound,
And form a tragi-comedy around.
With weeping lovers, dying calves complain,
Confusion reigns—chaos is come again !
Hither your steelyards, butchers, bring to weigh
The pound of flesh, Antonio's bond must pay !
Hither your knives, ye Christians, clad in blue,
Bring to be whetted by the ruthless Jew !
Hard is our lot, who, seldom doom'd to eat,
Cast a sheep's-eye on this forbidden meat—
Gaze on sirloins, which, ah ! we cannot carve,
And in the midst of legs of mutton—starve !

But would you to our house in crowds repair,
Ye gen'rous captains and ye blooming fair,
The fate of Tantalus we should not fear,
Nor pine for a repast that is so near.

Thomas Warton.

Prologue to 'Venice Preserved'

As some clean housewife's hospitable care
Serves to her guest good wholesome country fare,
Such as her own domestic stores afford,
With willing hand she spreads the homely board,
Where neatness and simplicity impart
A taste unknown to luxury and art :
Such is our aim to-night ; by means like these,
'Tis our ambition's humble care to please.
To pomp and shew we make no vain pretence,
We feast you here, with nature, and with sense :
With *Otway's* scenes, with early genius blest,
Here first the muse the tender bard possess'd ;
And here, where first the pow'rful impulse came,
He learnt to guide the heav'n-descended flame :
Yet easy still, nor o'er-refined by art,
He speaks the native language of the heart.
Attend ! these scenes your just regard demand :
See treason's sons, a dire infernal band,
Loose to the sacred ties of human kind,
In dark society of guilt combined !
Whom lawless lust of pow'r and brutal rage,
And black revenge, in horrid league engage,
T' invade their peaceful country's sacred rest ;
To plunge their ruthless daggers in her breast ;
To whelm in ruin the Venetian state :
Attend ; and tremble for Britannia's fate.

'Venice
Preserved'
acted by
young gentle-
men at
Winchester
School, 1755

'By Bishop Lowth, communicated by Dr. Warton,'
The Hampshire Repository, 1799.

BUT the highest advantage of a public school remains yet to be noticed. It is there that the friendships of life are formed, and in this respect I was singularly blessed. In the very year of my arrival at Winchester (1812) I formed a friendship with Walter Farquhar Hook which has lasted through life. From 1812 till the present time scarcely a month has intervened without correspondence between us. Hook was three years older than myself, but he had devoted himself so much to English literature that he fell below me in the school. In this respect we became mutually useful to each other. Hook was passionately fond of reading Shakspeare and Milton when I first knew him, and a small order of knighthood, called after them the Order of Saints Shakspeare and Milton, was founded by him, of which he and I were styled the Knights Grand Masters. The other Elizabethan classics, however, were gradually drawn within the circle of the studies, or rather the recreation, of our leisure hours. Beaumont and Fletcher, Massinger and the *Fairy Queen* were made to contribute to our amusement ; and though, of course, much more was read than we digested, still the benefit derived from these studies has been lasting. We even read through Hoole's *Tasso and Ariosto*, a work of some labour owing to the extreme dulness of the translation. Dr. Gabell himself encouraged English reading. He would frequently repeat Pope's *Imitations of Horace* to the boys at their lessons, and expected them to read the *Spectator*, Johnson's *Lives of the Poets*, and some of the English historians. The time, however, was short for this ; but being rather quick over my work, I was able to help my older friend forward in Greek and Latin in return for the improvement I derived from his maturer judgment and larger powers of thought in English and classical reading.

W. R. W. Stephens.
Memoir of Lord Hatherley, i. 15-17.
R. Bentley and Son, 1883.

ON one memorable occasion, when the early meetings of the Winchester College Shakspeare Society were held in the headmaster's house, John Desborough Walford was taking the rôle of the Ghost in *Hamlet*. The line ' Rest, rest, perturbed spirit ' became ironically applicable to him, for his only answer to his exorciser was ' an airy but audible snore.'

College tradition, mentioned in Noctes Shaksperianae
(ed. C. H. Hawkins).

PATRONS and friends that join to view to-day
What ancient worth may crown our modern play,
List ! while I speak our protean change of scene :
Look what it is, and learn what it has been.
Time was (and yet may be) when each and all
Deemed stern Minerva mistress of this hall ;—
Not spoken parts, but parts of speech were rife,
And sense with syntax vainly fought for life.
But now, ' no verbs and nouns ' shall try your patience,
No concords three conjoined with conjugations,
Declensions we decline—without pretence
Our schoolboy-hate for tenses is intense—
A new ' optative mood ' I can engage,
A scenic ardour, and a Roscian rage.
Since you last viewed our play, and spoke us well,
Without debate we to debating fell—
Fell short by one of giving Beales a soothing,
Proved the Jamaica case an airy nothing,
And ruled in spite of all the maudlin phil-
Anthropists, that some game needs hanging still [1] :
And then to give our youthful follies name,
We printed—' older children do the same '—
Virtue 's the truest fame : and next, I think,
Comes immortality in—printer's ink !

[1] These allusions are to some subjects then lately discussed at the New Winchester Debating Society : *e.g.* ' The Reform Demonstrations,' ' The Jamaica Question,' and ' Capital Punishment.'

This of ourselves we speak ; one word I claim
In humble memory of a well-loved name ;
This name beneath whose care and kindly rule
All learnt to love the Master and the School,
Him we have lost—to him we give to-day—
For love that no such tribute can repay—
All we can give, the meed of grateful minds
Linked by a bond that not e'en time unbinds.[1]
Such are our projects, friends ! on you we call ;
Make play and paper periodical !
Macbeth, while yet he 'scaped the toils of fate,
While loyal still, yet could not *check* his *mate*.
To check-mate us needs but one breath from you,
Grant therefore novices th' allowance due ;
We have *divided Houses* ere to-day ;
Let then this House *unite* to praise our Play.

E. D. A. Morsehead.

Prologue spoken before the Winchester Play, September 5, 1867.
Printed in *The Wykehamist*, November 1867.

F. R. Benson
and his
'strolling
players'

THE even tenor of our life at Winchester has, during the past
fortnight, been disturbed by a company of strolling players.
It may seem strange that the arrival of such persons could have
had any effect upon such a body as our School ; we believe that
never before has such a thing happened, that in spite of travelling
companies and alluring advertisements, the School has tacitly
bound itself by a ' self-denying ordinance,' has guarded itself
closely within the strict pale of routine and custom, and has
' itself found in itself ' all that it required for amusement or
entertainment.

Mr. Benson has changed all this : he has started (let the
Irishism be excused) a new precedent. On the 30th October
he performed before the School the comedy called *Money*.

The Wykehamist, November 1883.

---

[1] Reference to retirement of Dr. Moberly from Headmastership after
thirty-one years.

Lines recited at College tow-row, 1907 [1]

FIRST we bid you hearty welcome, ladies, lords, and gentles all,
Welcome to this stately building, welcome to the Founder's Hall;
Kings and Queens of old came hither; princes quaffed the
    College *Huff*,
Till the Manciple grew weary or the Warden cried ' enough.'
Silk and velvet, furs and sable, ranged and ranked in due degree,
Graced the board, where wit and wisdom clashed in decent revelry.
' *Stoupes* ' and *Beakers*, *Salts* and *Flagons*, *Standing-cups* and
    Goblets old,
Gleamed amid a hundred candles : silver shone on plate of gold.
Then, methinks, rich mellow voices linked in lovely madrigals
Rose to heaven in swelling chorus, sank to earth in softer falls :
All the world was full of music ; merry England's master-notes
Rang and echoed round the rafters from Elizabethan throats.
Such the feast-days of old England, put to bed with good Queen
    Bess :
Days of mirth gigantic wedded to gigantic storm and stress—
Is this dreamland ?   Still the burden of that music far away
Seems to mock our puny efforts, children of a later day,
Yet we venture : soft recorders blend with viol and with lute,
To perform a willing service for their gentle lady flute ;—
Flute that erst, akin to madness, bade the frantic passions rise :
Now a softer touch can summon tears from frailer human eyes.
We have ventured—Valse and Trio, sailor-songs and roundelays
Raise the heart and fire the fancy with a dream of olden days,
We have ventured home-born dances, while some panting notes
    from far
Throbbed and quivered, roared and thundered one terrific
    Kaaba.[2]

       But here where Wykeham's solemn frown
       Upon our mirth looks stately down ;—
       Here, where the saintly soul of Ken
       Breathes mild reproof on modern men ;—

[1] Selections from *A Midsummer Night's Dream* were given at this tow-row.   [2] A chorus of Dervishes.

Where Curle and Morley, Bilson, Foxe,
Serenely shake their mitred [1] locks ;—
Where twenty Wardens bend a brow
Of question on our poor *tow-row,*—
Where massy walls and timbers stout
Have seen five centuries flicker out,
And beechen *trenchers,* seats of stone,
Are set to make us think and moan :—
Dare we present a gross dull play,
A rude mechanics' holiday ?
Yes we dare ; for Wykeham's laws [2]
After supper bid us pause,
Spend an idle hour in song
Or disputes which mean no wrong,
We may talk of sober things,
Stars and earthquakes, queens and kings.
Once, in Bess's golden days,
College gave a leash of plays ;
Links and joists and stage and scene—
All was rich and well beseen—
Once the lantern on the stairs
Needed radical repairs :
Once an oaken table splits
Into half a thousand bits ;
Such the temper, such the fist,
Of a Tudor Wykehamist.
We are weaker men and can't
Bursar, break your precious plant.

So, good guests, look kindly on us from your chairs and from
    your frames,
If we dare to tax your patience, gentle dons and gentle dames :

[1] All bishops, whose portraits hang in Hall.
[2] See Kirby, *Annals of Winchester College.*

Thou, I ween, good Mistress Taylor,[1] wilt not gird at rustic mirth;
For thy Sunday veal proclaims thee half of heaven but half of
    earth.
And methinks, one lately taken [2] reaches out with kindly hand,
Deeply loved and deeply loving, blessings from the Shadowland—
Thou dear friend, so late our Falstaff,[3] will not envy Bottom's
    skill :
Still thy presence dwells among us, generous and unselfish still.

Now, if lion roar too loudly, please forgive the royal calf ;
Edward IV. once sent a lion [4] just to make the scholars laugh.
If his gait be proud and prancing, if his spleen your temper vex,
Think him sent for your diversion by our own Edwardus rex.
And if *Philostrate* [5] be pompous, with a bland superior smile ;
He can race you any distance from a ' hundred ' to a mile.
And if *Thisbe* [6] flit and flutter, skirts a-sail and flounces high,
Please remember she can caper sixty inches to the sky.
And if *Bottom*[7] press his humour, racing down the stage and up,
Please forgive him, College-lovers ; for he won you Taylor Cup.

M. J. R.

[M. J. Rendall, then Second, and now Headmaster of
Winchester College.]

§ 14. TOWN *v.* GOWN

SATURDAY, *February* 23, 1770.

THIS post brought Mr. Bowles a letter from his son at Winchester,   **A great riot**
giving an account of a great riot in that school ; it began on

---

[1] Mrs. Taylor, the supposed benefactress of veal once a week in Lent
to the College.
[2] ' Mrs. Dick.'
[3] Rev. George Richardson, who often read Falstaff in *Henry IV.*
[4] In 1474 ; Kirby, *op. cit.*
[5] C. M. Pope, second in Quarter, Half-Mile and Mile.
[6] J. A. Stainton, winner of High Jump with 5 ft. ½ in.
[7] C. Howard Smith, winner of Hundred Yards, the Quarter, and the
Half-Mile.   College West had just won Taylor Cup for athletic sports.

some affront given, I think Monday, by the townsmen to some of the commoners. Tuesday evening a detachment of commoners set out, armed with bludgeons and some with pistols. Dr. Warton, on hearing this, locked up what boys remained in the Commoners' Hall, but they forced the door open, and would join their friends ; the College was also locked, but they also grew outrageous, and they were let out to join in the fray. About eight they were got home all of them, and put to bed. One townsman was wounded by a shot in his leg. Wednesday night they sallied forth again, armed with weapons of all kinds, and fought in the churchyard ; the riot was so great that the magistrates were obliged to interfere, and the Riot Act was read. At length they dispersed, and I do not hear of any further mischief than bruises. Master Bowles was not in it, but by his manner of writing he seems greatly terrified. I am sorry for all this, as the school had got into great repute, and it must give Dr. Warton infinite concern, but the spirit of riot is gone forth into all degrees.

Mrs. Harris to her son at Madrid.
Harris, *Letters of the First Earl of Malmesbury*, ed. 1870.

SALISBURY, *March* 3, 1770.

A formidable thing

THE riot I mentioned in my last, at Winchester, is all over and no one expelled. It was a formidable thing, for they had several brace of pistols. It began, as I hear, by the landlord of the White Hart desiring some of the commoners who were drinking at his house, not to drink any more, but to go home ; this gave such offence, that the next day some went and broke his windows, the man was obliged to call his neighbours to his assistance, so that brought on the battle between the townsmen and the scholars. The great hero's name is Hare, he had been expelled from Eton.

Mrs. Harris to her son at Madrid.
Harris, *Letters of the First Earl of Malmesbury*, ed. 1870.

November 13, 1774.

THERE has been a foolish riot at Winchester, and forty of the A foolish riot middle class of the commoners have set off. Our neighbour Seaman, Dr. Warton locked up. Lord Shaftesbury stayed at school, Knatchbull went to your uncle Harris's and is still there. Seaman desired to be sent for home, and so he was. He tells me it all arose from some boy dressing up like the housekeeper who has a humpback, and she desired the assistant Huntingford to order them all to bed before their usual time. That they would not comply with, then Dr. Warton came into the hall ; the boys hissed him, and said either Huntingford or they must quit the house ; so all this trouble is owing to a silly old woman, who now, too late, repents her complaining.

Mrs. Harris to her son in Berlin.
Harris, Letters of the First Earl of Malmesbury, ed. 1870.

THERE had been mutterings of a coming storm for some time, Town *versus* Gown, c. 1800 typified by occasional sets-to between some individual boys and snobs, and forays by the latter on the clothes or towels of solitary small bathers. The town party chose their time for a demonstration with peculiar prudence. They waited till Commoners had gone, which they did on the Saturday before Election week. On the Monday following, the boys (now reduced in number to seventy, of whom at least twenty remained in College preparing for the coming examination) went on to Hills. They had not been there long before it became known that there was a gathering of the enemy at Twyford ; and expresses being sent back to College that ' Snobs were on,' and for the reserve to come up, we took the initiative, and went to Twyford to anticipate the attack. We hadn't long to wait, and there was some very pretty fighting both in the way of general skirmishes and individual mills. We got the best of it : and some of the bigger boys, elated with success, determined to push up to the stronghold of the enemy in the town. I was much too small for this part of the campaign, and with the other little boys,

retired behind the breastworks of College, where, by the by, we
arrived very considerably later than the regulation hour. I have
heard heart-stirring accounts of the heroic deeds of the heavy
brigade, but not having been present I cannot particularly
describe them.   I believe that they carried on the attack bravely
in the town for some time till overcome by numbers.   The boys
retreated to a path which leads out of High Street down by the
river-side to College, at the head of which (where there were
two posts to prevent carts passing) they took their stand, and
for a considerable time held their own gallantly.   But at last
they were obliged to break and fly, making good their retreat
into College, however, without anything like serious damage.
On numbering their forces, one boy was found missing, and
grave apprehension was entertained for his safety, which,
however, was soon dissipated by his unexpected appearance from
the Warden's house.   In the flight he had tripped and fallen
into Bungy's ditch, where he wisely lay quiet till the throng of
pursuers had rushed past, when he gently strolled towards
College, and opportunely meeting with a well-known barrister
who was taking his evening's walk, he got him to give him a
lift over the wall of Warden's garden, and was safe.

School Life at Winchester College, by the author of
The Log of the Water Lily, 1866.

§ 15. ROYALTIES AND MEDALS

On the
occasion of
George III.'s
visit to
Winchester
College, 1778

FORGIVE th' officious Muse, that with weak voice
And trembling accents rude, attempts to hail
Her Royal Guest ! who from yon tented field,
Britain's defence and boast, has deigned to smile
On Wykeham's sons : the gentler arts of Peace
And Science, ever prompt to praise, and Mars
To join with Pallas ! 'Tis the Muse's task
And office but to consecrate to Fame
Heroes and virtuous kings : the generous youths

My loved compeers, hence with redoubled toils
Shall strive to merit such auspicious smiles :
And through life's various walks, in arts or arms,
Or tuneful numbers, with their country's love,
And with true loyalty enflamed, t' adorn
This happy realm ; while thy paternal care
To time remote, and distant lands, shall spread
Peace, justice, riches, science, freedom, fame.

Spoken by Lord Shaftesbury on account of the Commoners, and composed by Dr. Warton (see Wooll's *Life of Warton*).

EPIGRAM ON LORD AILESBURY'S WITHDRAWAL OF HIS PRIZES FROM WINCHESTER SCHOOL UPON THE RETIREMENT OF DR. WARTON

WHEN Warton from his Mastership retired
With him the patronage of Bruce expired :
The noble patron's prizes thus we find,
Not for the *boys*, but *master*, were designed.
But the more noble Prince [of Wales] the want supplied,
And gave to genius all that Bruce denied.

The Hampshire Repository, i. 53, March 1799.

To the Prince
of Wales, 1797

Thou too, GREAT PRINCE, in whom serenely shine
The genuine splendours of the *Brunswick Line*,
Thou with fresh glory (were it ours to give)
Shouldst still with them thro' distant ages live,
By thee be shar'd imperial *Edward's* praise,
'Twas His, the FOUNDER OF THESE WALLS to raise ;
His worth to recompense with liberal hand,
And aid the work, his patriot bounty plann'd.
Then was this stately fabrick rear'd !—'Tis THINE
To add new lustre to the grand design :
To kindle virtuous emulation's flame,
And bid the youthful bosom pant for fame ;

Whilst WYKEHAM (as he sits enthron'd above,
And views his offspring with a parent's love),
With conscious pride elated, smiles to see
Their FRIEND, their PATRON, and their PRINCE, in THEE.
Deign then, ILLUSTRIOUS PATRON, to receive
Such thanks, as WYKEHAM's grateful sons can give :
And (though the great, the glorious theme require
A *Dryden's* force, a *Milton's* matchless fire)
Accept these humble lays, nor O ! refuse
The rude effusions of an artless muse,
Whose feeble voice, in numbers weak, essays
To join the full-ton'd choir, and swell the note of praise.

> To 'His Royal Highness the Prince of Wales, having been
> graciously pleased, in 1797, to give annual Prizes *of Gold
> and Silver Medals* for Composition and Elocution, to the
> Scholars and Commoners of Winchester College. . . .'
>
> *The Hampshire Repository*, 1798.

MANNERS AND MEN

§ 1. THE FOUNDER

COLLEGIUM WINTONIENSE

Pater Collegii

PRIMA scholas Europae inter Wintonia : cujus
Pars ego, quae mea laus maxima, parva fui.
Hunc tibi primatum non Zoilus ipse negabit
Si tibi Wickamum noverit esse patrem.

> Epigram by John Owen, 'The British Martial,' printed in
> *The Wykehamist*, April 1886.

**'Thy Colleges
stand fast'**

Qui condis dextrâ, condis collegia laevâ ;
   Nemo tuarum unam vicit utrâque manu.
Hunccine tam cultas tibi qui sacraverit aedes,
   Extincto pateris nomine, musa, mori ?
Musa, perire veta ; vetuit te, musa, perire
   Wykehamus, et quamvis ipse sepultus alit.

> Lines above and beneath Wykeham's Portrait.

Right hand and left thy colleges stand fast :
None hath with both hands' labour one surpassed.
Him shall the Muse, who gave her gifts like these,
Leave unremembered in a dumb repose ?
Nay, but she gives fresh life to him, who gave
Fresh life to her, and feeds her from the grave.

Translation made by H. W. B. Joseph, Tutor and
Junior Bursar of New College, Oxford.

PERHAPS few travellers who alight at Winchester fully realise **The Name of**
the long historical story possessed by this old town ; still in the **Wykeham**
minds of most people the name of William of Wykeham at once
rises, with more or less distinctness, when they make their way
to the Cathedral—bearing on the whole of its long nave the
impress of his mind—and to the College, which owes its existence
to him.

A. R. Bramston and A. C. Leroy.
A City of Memories.
P. and G. Wells, Winchester, 1893.

'TIS Winton's day of solemn state,   **Founder's**
To Wykeham's memory consecrate :   **Day**
Her scattered sons from far she calls
Once more to tread her ancient halls ;
To cast, upon their Founder's day,
The weary load of years away ;
And breathe again, for that brief time,
The freshness of their boyhood's prime.

The morning bells have chimed to prayer
In the old order, two and two,
The youthful throng that worships there
Has passed the reverend portal through ;
And through the gorgeous Eastern pane,
The Summer sun looks down again

Upon the well-remembered show,
That decks the crowded aisle below—
On Boyhood's glowing cheek and eye,
Open and clear as morning sky :—
On Youth, in all its flush of prime,
Life's fairest, freshest, goodliest time—
On forms by years and labours bowed,
Strange contrast to that boyish crowd !
Men, it may be, whose steps have gained
The loftiest heights by worth attained ;
Whose names to England justly dear,
Ring like a trump in every ear ;
'Mid joyous urchins, in whose eyes
No palm transcends the schoolboy's prize !

Yet the same thoughts and feelings sway
Boyhood and Youth, and Age to-day :
For cares of State and dreams of Pride
Within these walls are cast aside ;
And all are Wykeham's sons once more,
As true and guileless as of yore.
The heirship of his mighty name
Makes old and young in heart the same.
And almost could their fancy feign,
That, as they kneel where then they knelt,
Relenting Time had given again
The lightsome step, the bounding vein,
Which in those vanished years they felt.

. . . . . .

Cold were the heart for whom that hour
Had no sweet spell, no quickening power ;
And on that evening, as I strayed,
Beneath the Cloister's hoary shade,
When ' summer's twilight ' 'gan to gloam,
To hear the old ' sweet song of home, '

Back on my thoughts those words returned,
At sight of that exulting throng ;
Like fire within my soul they burned,
And shaped its fancies into song.

William of Wykeham, by H. C. Adams, 1858.

In a grey old town, that our hearts know well,
   Rises a grey stone tower ;
Ever and ever its swinging bell
   Speaks with the voice of power :
For it tells the world of a bishop great,
   In a minster lying low,
Who moulded at will both Church and State,
   Five hundred years ago.

'A bishop great'

  .   .   .   .   .   .

A poem by N. in *The Wykehamist*, July 1893.

Who loves not thee, Wykeham ?   Thy cherished name
Is like a symbol of mild charity,
And holiness, and wisdom—in thy fame
Glories old Winton, who once sheltered thee,
A lorn and nameless child of poverty,
And was the foster-parent of thy mind.
High-placed and powerful 'twas thy lot to be ;
Yet filial fondness did thee ever bind
To those grey walls which to thy earliest years were kind.

'Manners makyth man'

  .   .   .   .

Thy Saxon city far outgrows her walls,
And busier crowds her lengthening streets do throng,
And the hoarse voice of steam loud roaring calls
Her citizens' life's widening streams along.
Still to thy gentle spirit do belong

The spots where thou didst live thy early span ;
And he who, musing, roams these haunts among
Will still meet thee, and read, if read he can,
The lesson thy life taught, that *Manners makyth man.*

Christopher Wood.
Reminiscences of Winchester, c. 1860.

The Glories of Wykeham

' THERE are among the sons of men,' the wise old Hebrew said,
' Whose memory, like the forms they wore, is numbered with the dead.
Whose names, though foremost in the throng that trod with them the scene,
In after ages have become as they had never been.'
But Thou—thy memory doth not die, the magic of thy name
Lives on, where all things else decay, the same and still the same,
While thrones are crumbled into dust, and earth's profoundest schemes
Pass with their founders into nought, as pass the morning dreams ;
While laws that were a nation's life, grow obsolete and strange,
While ancient things are hurried down the ceaseless tide of change ;
The fire that in thy children's hearts, thou in thy day didst light,
Brightly and pure as first it burned, still burns as pure and bright.

.   .   .   .

The noblest names of England's rolls, on which she loves to dwell ;
Which are, to each true English heart, a watchword and a spell—
Who bore her flag through storms of fight, who swayed her helm of state,
Drank at thy fountain of the draught, that made their manhood great !

Through noontide years of noble toil, in Age's calm decline,
With moistened eye, and kindling voice, they told that they
    were thine.
They loved across the track of years, the backward glance to
    cast ;
Through memory's softening haze, to catch sweet glimpses of
    the Past.

.   .   .   .

O surely in that solemn hour, to thee so long delayed,
When to the ripened corn at length the Reaper's hand was laid ;
.   .   .   .

Thy wish would sure have been that thus thy cherished work
    might stand,
Outspreading like some stately tree, its branches through the
    land !
That where in life thy knee was bent, thy children still might
    bend,
Their hope, their creed, their heart the same, unchanging to
    the end !
That still thy memory might have power, like some proud battle-
    cry,
To bring the flush to Boyhood's cheek, the fire to Age's eye.
That on their lips, and in their hearts, the magic of thy name
Should live when all things else decay—*the same and still the
    same !*

William of Wykeham, by H. C. Adams.

SHADE of Wykeham ! where the dim grey arches   **An Invocation**
    Echo round· thee to the voice of praise,
Doth the step of Time that loudly marches
    Reach thee through the changeless change of days ?
Lo ! of things that perish, little reckoning
    Lives there, they are past hours of the night ;
Men are drawn to where a hand is beckoning
    Down far vistas to an orient light,

Onward is the motto of the ages
　　Shrieked by clamorous voices in the crowd,
Branded in the breast by burning pages,
　　Thunder-pealing from the riven cloud.
Sleepest Thou ? and is it that for ever ?
　　Rests thy soul as silent as the grave ?
Or that, for the calmness of the river
　　Runs a fiercer current in the wave ?
One the will that guides it to the ocean,
　　One the even channel of its way,
Countless are the sparks of bright devotion
　　Flashing on the waters every day.
Sons of thine, towards the future turning,
　　Minded with the ages to advance,
Still have found some lessons worth the learning
　　Which ' from out the storied past ' might chance.
Still to thee, the fount of Inspiration,
　　Proudly all their noble deeds they trace,
Nothing have they called their own creation,
　　God, through thee, has given them the grace.

·　　·　　·　　·　　·　　·　　·

By ' Semper Idem ' in *The Wykehamist*, April 1867.

' MANNERS MAKYTH MAN '

' Winton's
brooding
wing '

BROTHERS ! from Winton's brooding wing
　　In some short years we pass—
How shall we prove our metal's ring
　　When current in the mass ?

On Alma Mater's trial stage,—
　　Or wider theatre still,
How shall the Wykehamist engage
　　His careful part to fill ?

I hold most worthy Wykeham's name,
The man whose thoughts and deeds
Are first for others, and their claim,
The whilst dear self recedes !

. . . .

By 'Ora e Sempre' in The Wykehamist, July 1872.

WILLIAM OF WICKHAM: A SONG FOR THE WICCAMICAL ANNIVERSARY, HELD AT THE CROWN AND ANCHOR TAVERN

I SING not your heroes of ancient romance :
Capadocian George, or Saint Dennis of France ;
    No chronicler I am
    Of Troy and King Priam,
And those crafty old Greeks who to fritters did fry 'em :
But your voices, brave boys, one and all I bespeak 'em,
In due celebration of William of Wickham.

A Boisterous Song

Chorus

Let Wickham's brave boys at the Crown and the Anchor
The flask never quit 'till clean out they have drank her ;
And united maintain, whether sober or mellow,
That old Billy Wickham was a very fine fellow.

Hear the Lover, you 'll learn, from his tragical stories,
Of hard-hearted Phœbe, Corinna and Chloris,
    For some sempstress or starcher
    That rascally archer
Call'd Cupid, has made him as mad as a March hare :
But at Wickham's brave boys should he brandish his dart
We 'll drown the blind rogue in a Winchester quart.

Chorus

For Wickham's *brave boys,* etc.

. . . .

Let Whig Rhetoricians our rulers defame,
And hungry Sedition's republican flame
    Foment, and throw chips on,
    Independence their lips on,
While they incense a mob, and exist by subscription :
Here of Liberty's Tree if for scyons they search,
They 'll instead catch a tartar,—Wiccamical Birch.

Chorus

For Wickham's *brave boys*, etc.

Ye Poetical tribe, on Parnassus who forage,
Who prate of Jove's nectar and Helicon-porridge,
    Yet, for beef-stakes and brandy,
    Set each Jack-a-dandy
On a level with Frederick, or Prince Ferdinandy :
What 's the sword of King Arthur, or Admiral Hosier,
To William of Wickham and his jolly old Crosier ?

Chorus

Let Wickham's *brave boys*, etc.

Poem in *Salmagundi*, edited by George Huddesford, 1801.

§ 2. THE SECOND FOUNDER

A Triumphant Progress, 1866-84   THE supreme change which the reign of Dr. Ridding accomplished cannot be described in truer words than those in which Dr. Abbott defined Winchester when speaking at the Second Headmasters' Conference held there in 1888, when the changes which Dr. Ridding's Headmastership had made had stood the test of some years. 'Winchester College was,' he said, 'a place where everything was antique and nothing was antiquated.'

What Dr. Ridding accomplished was most remarkable. The difficulties, obstacles, and prejudices that had to be overcome would have daunted many strong spirits, but they crumbled away under the resistless attack of his ' constructive genius, strength of will, and munificence.' It was this result which made his seventeen years of rule at Winchester a great triumphant progress.

.   .   .   .

The venerable Dr. Sewell [in 1887] . . . spoke of the past suspicions of all the changes—changes which he now felt were gain and not loss : ' I said Ridding was going to ruin the School ; now I say he is our Second Founder.'

Lady Laura Ridding's *George Ridding, Schoolmaster and Bishop*.
Edward Arnold, 1908.

PATIENT Contender for the True and Just,
  With grief acquainted but still unsubdued,
Winner of many a young heart's love and trust
  Ere Winchester from thee her parting rued.

.   .   .   .

The wrestling winds of thought thy mind had felt,
  Gnarled was the slow-grown fibre of thy speech,
Yet in thy sterling voice Truth's spirit dwelt,
  And the deep places of our soul could reach.

With face uplifted as a swimmer's thou
  Wast ever striking for the further shore ;
Ah ! since thy feet have touched it, leave us now
  One message ere we see thy face no more.

—*To take the joy God sends you think not scorn,*
  Watchful but free Youth's revelling moment spend,
Then girt with strength upon the coming morn,
  Your battle fight and fight it to the end.

'George Ridding,' a poem by W. H. Draper, from Lady Laura Ridding's *George Ridding, Schoolmaster and Bishop*.
Edward Arnold, 1908.

' Patient Contender for the True and Just '

The Peg'

THE sparkling eyes and grin of pleasure with which the Headmaster [Dr. Ridding] met the victorious [rifle] team [which had won the Ashburton Shield] in Flint Court on their return late at night on the first occasion of their victory [1871] are still remembered.

'Moberly Library is shut up! Will you allow me to be Peg for to-night?' was his hospitable greeting.

'Three cheers for the Peg!' was shouted in reply. And henceforth he added the name of *The Peg* to *Ja Ra*.

Lady Laura Ridding's *George Ridding*, etc.
Edward Arnold, 1908.

'The Peg' in Fiction

DR. SPEDDING, at that time headmaster of Winchester, was not physically a big man, but he was the fortunate possessor of a singularly powerful face. He may have been short-sighted—it is a fact that he habitually used a single eye-glass—but the expression of his black eyes was so piercingly acute that few would care to presume upon any supposed deficiency in their power. Nose, mouth, and chin were all indicative of strength and resolution. It added to the terror inspired by him in the youthful breast that he spoke habitually in a succession of short, sharp sentences, and that it was impossible to gather (at all events without long experience of his manner) whether he were satisfied with any answer or grievously displeased. Unhappy boys, ignorant of his peculiar method, would sail on merrily amid a gathering cloud of errors, fancying that they were acquitting themselves to the admiration of all. 'Yes, yes, my boy—and what do you say, next?' would be his only comment at the close, and the passage would go through a whole division with no further indication on his part of what was wrong. It was necessary for the keenest wits to keep on the alert before such a sphinx as this.

Christopher Deane, by E. H. Lacon Watson.
John Murray.

MUST thou go, my glorious chief?
Partings are severe, but brief;
Future years forget the grief
    We are grieving.
Thine indeed a glorious sequel;
But, O where to find thine equal!
We must mourn, while others speak well
    Of thy leaving.

On Dr.
Ridding's
leaving

How I loved thee!   How I feared thee!
How I awfully revered thee!
How I trembled when I neared the
    Study portal!
Which was then the foremost feeling
O'er my aching senses stealing?
Hair on end and blood congealing
    Pangs immortal!

But these days of fateful meeting
Now are visions dimly fleeting;
Now I fear no birch's greeting
    When I enter;
Wish not to shrink up inside me,
In my buttoned gown to hide me,
When thy piercing glance has eyed me
    To the centre.

'Monthly fevers' ne'er affect me,
As they used; I recollect me,
When that dread 'brow ague' wrecked me
    At convenience.
Now I fear no 'detuli
Jussa cuius domini,'
Nor the pangs those words imply
    Without lenience.

Yet I 'd gladly creep once more—
Bible-clerk, stride on before—
To thy Study's doomful door,
      At thy bidding,
If my martyrdom could gain thee,
If by that I could detain thee,
If by that thou couldst remain the
      Doctor Ridding.

Vain alas !   Another station
Claims thy present occupation ;
In lamenting resignation
      With one mouth we 'll
Cry : ' Oh ! blest the world to choose thee !
Wretched Winchester to lose thee !
Farewell !   We may not refuse thee !
      Bishop Southwell ! '

The Mushri-English Pronouncing Dictionary, Appendix
to *College Lyrics*, 1882.

§ 3. A WARDEN AND SOME HEADMASTERS

'Tupto'

HUNTINGFORD, Bishop of Hereford, was Warden during the whole of my college career. He was an aged man, and somewhat of a valetudinarian. And to the imagination of us boys, who rarely saw him, he assumed something of the mystic, awe-inspiring character of a 'veiled prophet of Khorassan.' . . . The Warden's nickname, borne among sundry generations of Wykehamists, was *Tupto* ($\tau\acute{\upsilon}\pi\tau\omega$), as we always supposed from that Greek verb used as the example in the Greek grammar. But I have heard from those of an earlier generation that it was *quasi dicas* 'tiptoe,' from the fact of his father having been a dancing-master. The former derivation seems to me the more plausible. . . . His rule of Winchester College was a long and prosperous one ; and as long as it lasted he was able to carry out his favourite maxim, ' No innovation ! '

T. A. Trollope.

What I Remember, i. 127-31.

Bentley and Son, 1887.

BUT a becheler of holy devynyte come to that cytte [Coventry] and whenn he come to preche by-fore the Kyng, as Maystyr Wylliam Saye Dene of Poulys and Dene of the Kyngys chapylle, hadde desyred and asygnyd, A. B. C. axyd hys name, and his name was Mayster Wylliam Ive, at that tyme beyng at Wynchester in Wycham ys college [a Winchester scholar, 1425]. And A. B. C. sayde that they moste nedys se hys sarmon and hys purposes, that he was avysyd to say by-fore the Kynge the Sonday nexte comynge.   And he fulle goodly toke them hys papyr ; and they seyng and redynge hys papyr, commaundyd to leve owte and put away many troughtys.   But that same Mayster Wylliam Ive sayde but lytylle, but whenn he come to pulpyt he spared not to say the troughthe, and reportyd by-fore the Kyng that A. B. C. made the sarmonys that were sayde fore, and not thoo that prechyd, and that causyd that the men that prechyd hadde but symplle sarmons, for hyr purposse was alle turnyde upsodowne, and that they hadde made love days as Judas made whythe a cosse, with Cryste for they cyste ovyr the mane.   The grete rewarde that he hadde for hys labyr was the rydynge of viii^{xx} myle yn and owte for hys travayle, and alle hys frendys full sory for hym.' [1]

William Ives, Headmaster, 1444-54

Chron. of William Gregory, Skinner (Camden Society), 1425.

' MONODY ON THE DEATH OF DR. WARTON '

. . . THY cheering voice,

O Warton ! bid my silent heart rejoice,

And wak'd to love of Nature : every breeze,

On Itchin's brink, was melody : the trees

Dr. Joseph Warton, Headmaster of Winchester College

[1] Unfortunately this episode is placed in 1458, while College records show that Ive ceased to be Headmaster of Winchester in 1454.

Wav'd in fresh beauty : and the wind and rain
That shook the battlements of Wykeham's fane,
Not less delighted, when with random pace
I trod the cloister'd aisles : and, witness thou,
Catharine, upon whose foss-encircled brow
We met the morning, how I lov'd to trace
The prospect spread around—the rills below,
That shone irriguous in the fuming plain ;
The river's bend, where the dark barge went slow,
And the pale light on yonder time-worn fane.[1]

The Rev. W. L. Bowles.

**A Defence of
Dr. Warton**

SPLEEN gave the word ; th' envenomed arrow sped,
Nor spared the classic Warton's hoary Head.
Where were ye, Muses, who were wont to roam
Near Itchin's stream, or Beaufort's sacred Dome ?
Or ye, who lapp'd in Wykeham school of yore,
Now bloom transplanted on fair Isis' shore,
Why loiter'd ye ? or why still mute the tongue
Of Bards, whose lyre their Warton whilom strung ?

. . . . . .

Thus far, incens'd at Calumny, the Muse,
A nameless satirist, and his foul abuse,
Had dared to censure ; eager to reclaim,
And vindicate her Warton's injured name.—

. . . . . .

Witness ye guardians of this lettered Place,
Whose mind he stored with every Attic grace,
No prouder æra Wykeham's Annals vaunt,
Than when the Muses, to this favourite haunt
By Warton led, forsook th' Aonian springs,
And Itchin flow'd responsive to their strings.

. . . . . .

[1] St. Cross Hospital.

O ! could my Muse thus tune her plaintive lays,
And sing in equal strains her Warton's praise,
Then, when thy well-loved Reynolds' colours fade,
(As fade they must) thy fame should bloom, Blest Shade !
Beyond the Pencil's reach ; for thee the Nine
A wreath with Collins, Lowth and Young should twine,
Immortalise thy name to Wykeham dear,
In lines thyself might not disdain to hear.

On the death of Dr. Warton in 1800.
Quoted in *The Wykehamist*, December 1905.

THE noontide hour is past and toil is o'er,
   No studious cares the vacant mind employ ;
Yet hark, methinks no longer as before
   Yon mead re-echoes with a shout of joy.

On the death of Dr. Warton

What sudden grief has seiz'd the youthful band ?
   Say, Wykeham's sons, why reigns this silence round ?
Why do ye thus in mute attention stand
   And listen to that death-bell's awful sound ?

Ask ye the cause ? 'tis Warton's knell, and lo !
   The fun'ral train appears in black array ;
Down yonder Hill with solemn steps and slow
   The Hearse winds on its melancholy way.

Led by Affliction the sad sight to view,
   The thronging youth suspend their wanton Play,
All crowd around to bid the last adieu,
   Or lost in thoughtful musings steals (*sic*) away.

Yes, holy shade, for thee these tears are shed,
   The sullen death-bell's ling'ring pause between,
For thee o'er all a pious calm is spread
   And hush'd the murmurs of the playful scene.

Oh name to Wykeham's sons for ever dear,
　　Whilst thus for thee these floods of tears we pour,
Thy partial spirit seems to linger here
　　Blessing awhile the scenes it lov'd before.

Within these walls to every duty true
　　'Twas thine to form the duteous mind of youth,
To ope the fame of Glory to their view
　　And point the way to science and to truth.

And lo ! the Plants that grew beneath thy care
　　Now in maturer age majestic stand,
And spread their clust'ring branches to the air
　　And stretch their shadow o'er a smiling land.

Youth may forget his transitory pow'r
　　But manhood feels a deeper sense of woe ;
And sure to them thy name is doubly dear
　　Who to thy care their ripen'd Honours owe.

They heard th' inciting dictates of thy tongue,
　　For thou couldst smooth the way thro' learning's maze.
Oft on thy words in deep attention hung
　　Till emulation kindl'd into praise.

O mark their grief e'en now in tender Hues
　　By memory trac'd thro' their days of youth return,
But, ah, fond mem'ry ev'ry pang renews
　　And points in speechless agony to thine urn.

So strain their tears but thron'd on high,
　　Haply the Seraphs hallow'd Choir among,
Lull'd by soft sounds of sweetest minstrelsy
　　While Wykeham listens and approves thy song.

Oh for a spark of that celestial fire
  With which bright Fancy warm'd thy kindling soul,
When erst the full choros of thy living lyre
  Held all the listn'ing passions in control.

Alas though vain the wish tho' weakest lay
  Which feebly chants a Warton's name,
Yet happy shade there still remains a way
  To raise the lasting monument of fame.

Be our's the virtues thy example taught
  To feel, preserve and practise while we live,
Thus only can we praise thee as we ought,
  The noblest tribute this thy sons can give.

So when Affliction at the close of Eve
  In yonder dim-seen Cloisters shall appear,
No more in fruitless anguish shall we grieve,
  But learn the lessons of true Wisdom there.

There while she sees the sculptur'd bust arise,
  Rais'd by the hands of gratitude and Love,
Virtue shall consecrate her tend'rest sighs,
  And thoughts exalted thy rapt spirit move.

Then Wykeham's sons with ardour more imprest
  Shall breathe one prayer that such their lot may be,
Prais'd by the wise and good to sink to rest,
  And mourn'd by tears such as they shed for thee.

> C. Lipscombe, afterwards Fellow of New College and
> Bishop of Jamaica.
> Add. MS. 29,539, ff. 28B, 29 and 29B.

I DO not know that Gabell was altogether an unpopular man, **Gabell and**
but he never inspired that strong affection that his successor **'Gaffer'**

did. His manner was disagreeable. In short, he was not so completely a gentleman as Williams was. . . . It used to be said, I remember, that of the two masters of Winchester, one snored without sleeping (Gabell), and the other slept without snoring. Gabell was, in truth, always snorting or snoring (so to call it) ; but the accusation against Williams of sleeping was, I think, justified only by his peculiarly placid and quiet manner. He was a remarkably handsome man : and his sobriquet among those of the previous generation rather than among us boys, was ' The Beauty of Holiness '—again with reference to the unruffled repose of his manner. We boys invariably called him ' Gaffer.' Why, I know not.

T. A. Trollope.
What I Remember, i. 125-6.
R. Bentley and Son, 1887.

§ 4. SOME FAMOUS WYKEHAMISTS

Wykeham's Sons

MAY Wykeham's sons who in each art excel,
And rival ancient bards in writing well,
While from their bright example taught they sing
And emulate their thoughts with bolder wing ;
From their own frailties learn the humbler part
Mildly to judge in gentleness of heart.

William Somerville, 1677-1742.
See *The Wykehamist*, June 1886.

Public Schools vindicated

SAY, Muse, by what allurements wast thou won
To guide the pen of thy deluded son ?
How couldst thou bear to hear thy Cowper's verse
Arraign his earliest and his kindest nurse ?
Surely thou still regardest as thine own
Thy Wharton's laurel and thy Busby's throne !

.   .   .   .

'Tis ours to boast that hence an Otway sprung,
A Ken, a Lowth, a Collins, and a Young.

.　　.　　.　　.　　.　　.　　.

Rail on then, Sophists ! vent your feeble hate
Against these nurseries of our good and great,
Arraign the virtue of our Public Schools,
Call them the seats of sinners and of fools ;
If so, I deem it glorious to be one,
And proudly boast that I am Wykeham's son.

' The Reply to Cowper's Tirocinium,' by George Cox, which won
    the Gold Medal for English verse at Winchester College
    in 1827.   Quoted in *The Wykehamist*, June 1870.

THROUGH glades and glooms ! oh sweet, oh sad,   **Collins**
    The path of song, that led through these
Thy feet, that once were free and glad
    To wander under Winton's trees !
Now in soft shades of sleep they tread
By ways and waters of the dead.

There gentlest Otway walks with thee,
    And Browne, rejoicing in the dead :
By solemn-sounding waters ye,
    By arching willow valleys, led,
Think on old memories of her,
Courtly and cloistral Winchester.

So memory's mingled measure flows
    In shadowy dream and twilight trance :
Past death, to dawn of manhood goes
    Thy spirit's unforgetting glance,
Through glades and glooms ! and hails at last
Those loveliest scenes long past, long past !

There dwell thy loving thoughts ! but we,
   Who know not yet thy sacred gloom,
Who love the sunlight on the lea,
   Till death will mourn thy early doom ;
And, dying, hope among the dead
To walk with thee, where poets tread.

L. P. J. (Lionel P. Johnson).
The Wykehamist, December 1888.

Collins at Winchester

THERE is a curious incident of this singular and unfortunate man, which will show what a quick feeling and sensibility he possessed from his earliest days.   The boys on the foundation at Winchester College are lodged in seven chambers.   Collins belonged to the same chamber with William Smith of Chichester, afterwards Treasurer of the Ordnance ; by whom he was observed one morning to be particularly depressed and melancholy. Being pressed to disclose the cause, he at last said it was in consequence of a dream : for this he was laughed at, but desired to tell what it was ; he said he dreamed that he was walking in the fields where there was a lofty tree ; that he climbed it, and when he had nearly reached the top, a great branch upon which he had got failed with him, and let him fall to the ground. This account caused more ridicule ; and he was asked how he could possibly be affected by this common consequence of a school-boy adventure, when he did not pretend, even in imagination and sleep, to have received any hurt, he replied that the Tree was the Tree of Poetry.   The first time that Mr. Smith saw him, after they had left the College, was at an interval of twelve or fourteen years ; and when, in a deplorable state of mind, he had long been under confinement : but no sooner had his old school-fellow on this occasion presented himself, than he exclaimed, ' Smith, do you remember my Dream ? '

The Preface to William Crowe's edition of William
Collins's Poems, 1746.

WHAT becomes of poor dear Collins? I wrote him a letter 'Poor dear
which he never answered. I suppose writing is very troublesome to him. That man is no common loss. The moralists all
talk of the uncertainty of fortune, and the transitoriness of
beauty; but it is yet more dreadful to consider that the powers
of the mind are equally liable to change; that understanding
may make its appearance and depart, that it may blaze and
expire.

Dr. Johnson to Dr. Joseph Warton.
Wooll's Warton, p. 238.

I LEFT Winchester in September 1762. I had been indulged 'A man too
there too much; Dr. Warton erred in the contrary extreme from soon'
Mr. Hale [of Salisbury grammar-school]. I did nearly what I
liked, and as boys always wish to be men, I thought myself a
man too soon.

Diaries and Correspondence of James Harris,
First Earl of Malmesbury, ed. 1844.

FROM thence[1] he [Sydney Smith] was sent, with his youngest Sydney Smith
brother, Courtenay, to the foundation at Winchester [1782];—
a rough apprenticeship to the world for one so young, from which
Courtenay ran away twice, unable to bear it. My father suffered
here many years of misery and positive starvation; there never
was enough provided, even of the coarsest food, for the whole
school, and the little boys were of course left to fare as they
could. Even in old-age, he used to shudder at the recollections
of Winchester, and I have heard him speak with horror of the
misery of the years he spent there: the whole system was
then, my father used to say, one of abuse, neglect, and vice.
It has since, I believe, partaken of the general improvement of
education. However, in spite of hunger and neglect, he rose in
due time to be Captain of the school, and, whilst there, received,
together with his brother Courtenay, a most flattering but

---

[1] A private school at Southampton kept by the Rev. Mr. Marsh.

involuntary compliment from his schoolfellows, who signed a round-robin [to Dr. Warton, then Headmaster], ' refusing to try for the College prizes if the Smiths were allowed to contend for them any more, as they always gained them.' He used to say, ' I believe, whilst a boy at school, I made above ten thousand Latin verses, and no man in his senses would dream in after-life of ever making another. So much for life and time wasted.'

At school he was not only leader in learning, but in mischief, and was discovered inventing a catapult by lamp-light, and commended for his ingenuity by the master, who little dreamt it was intended to capture a neighbouring turkey, whose well-filled crop had long attracted the attention, and awakened the desires, of the hungry urchins. He was fond of telling an incident which happened to him when either at Winchester or Oxford, I am not sure which. A friend who was making a tour, wrote in great distress, asking him to lend him five guineas ; he had but four, which he was conveying himself to the post, much lamenting he had not the sum wanted ; when he suddenly saw shining on the high-road before him another guinea, and no owner being to be found to claim it, he with joy enclosed it in another cover to his friend.

I have heard my father speak of one of the first things that stimulated him in acquiring knowledge. A man of considerable eminence, whose name I cannot recall, found my father reading Virgil under a tree when all his schoolfellows were at play. He took the book out of his hand, looked at it, patted the boy's head, gave him a shilling, and said, ' Clever boy ! clever boy ! that is the way to conquer the world.' This produced a strong impression on the young Sydney. Whilst at Winchester he had been one year Praepositor of the College, and another Praepositor of the Hall. He left Winchester, as Captain, for New College, Oxford. . . .

Memoir of the Rev. Sydney Smith, by his daughter,
Lady Holland.
Longmans, Green and Co., 1855.

THE charm of her mind and manner extended even to her Sydney Smith's Mother correspondence. I heard a singular proof of this the other day from a schoolfellow of my father's, who said that when he or his younger brother Courtenay received one of her letters at Winchester, the schoolboys would often gather round and beg to hear it read aloud.

Memoir of the Rev. Sydney Smith, by his daughter,
Lady Holland, 1855.

IN 1807 he was removed to Winchester, where, having entered Thomas Arnold as a Commoner, and afterwards become a scholar of the College, he remained till 1811. In after-life he always cherished a strong Wykehamist feeling, and, during his head-mastership at Rugby, often recurred to his knowledge there first acquired, of the peculiar constitution of a public school, and to his recollections of the tact in managing boys shown by Dr. Goddard, and the skill in imparting scholarship which distinguished Dr. Gabell ;—both, during his stay there, successively headmasters of Winchester.

He was then, as always, of a shy and retiring disposition, but his manner as a child, and till his entrance at Oxford, was marked by a stiffness and formality the very reverse of the joyousness and simplicity of his later years.

Dean Stanley.
Life of Dr. Arnold, sixth edition, 1846.

HE was from his earliest years exceedingly fond of ballad poetry, Poet Arnold which his Winchester schoolfellows used to learn from his repetition before they had seen it in print ; and his own compositions as a boy all ran in the same direction. A play of this kind in which his schoolfellows were introduced as the *dramatis personæ*, and a long poem of *Simon de Montfort* in imitation of Scott's *Marmion*, procured for him at school, by way of distinction from another boy of the same name, the appellation of Poet Arnold.

Dean Stanley.
Life of Dr. Arnold, sixth edition, 1846.

A diligent Student

AT Winchester he was a diligent student of Russell's *Modern Europe*; Gibbon and Mitford he had read twice over before he left school; and amongst the comments on his reading and the bursts of political enthusiasm on the events of the day in which he indulged in his Winchester letters, it is curious, as connected with his later labours, to read his indignation, when fourteen years old, ' at the numerous boasts which are everywhere to be met with in the Latin writers.'

Dean Stanley.
Life of Dr. Arnold, sixth edition, 1846.

Goddard and Arnold

THE confession made by Arnold when he came to Goddard's study, ' I have come to tell you, sir, that I have found out that I was wrong,' and Goddard's reply, ' Ay, Arnold, I knew you would come,' show the feeling that existed between master and pupil.

Illustrated London News, January 31, 1891.

Dean Hook [Walter Farquhar Hook] at Winchester

IN 1812 . . . the brothers [Walter and Robert] were removed to ' Commoners,' Winchester. Their father had become a Canon of Winchester, and this circumstance probably led to the selection of the school. . . . In October 1813 he [Walter] writes to his brother, who for some cause was absent from school: ' I hate this place more and more every day. I was licked yesterday more severely than ever before. I cannot run or hollow out loud even now without hurting my side, and I am to be licked again to-day for writing this: yet I should not be able to write at another time as I go "at top of hall" and get so much to do. I begin to fear my licking. If I am killed, which I think I shall be, tell Etheridge [the school butler] to send you my books, and hope that I am in heaven happier than all of you; if for my sins I am condemned to hell, pity me, dear Robert, pity me. Let Milton be buried with me, as he has gone through all my hardships with me.'

Writing a year later, he says that though he still hates the place, he is not so rebellious as he used to be, and regards his prison-house from a more philosophical point of view. ' I endeavour to find out the Comforts, if any there be, and not the miseries of this place, for as my dear and beloved bard, the honour of England and of the whole of this terrestial orb says, " the mind is its own place and can make a Heaven of Hell, an Hell of Heaven." '

W. R. W. Stephens.
Life of Walter Farquhar Hook.
R. Bentley and Co., 1878.

IN 1812, the year in which I went to Winchester, my father was a candidate for the representation of the city of London in Parliament, but the old Tory members were returned by a majority of 1000.

William Page Wood, Lord Hatherley, at Winchester

When I entered Winchester, Dr. Gabell was head-master and Mr. Williams the second master, while Dr. Huntingford, Bishop of Hereford, was warden of the College. I and my brother were not on the foundation, but were members of commoners, and, as such, pupils of the head-master. The number of commoners was then limited to 130, and that of the College or foundation boys to 70. We remained at Winchester till May 1818, and I always recognise the inestimable value of the instruction which I there received. Dr. Gabell especially was pre-eminent as a teacher, though defective in his management as a master, owing to his bad habit of mistrusting the boys and leaving nothing to their sense of honour. Dr. Williams, on the other hand, was admirably qualified to win the affection of his pupils by his gentlemanly and confiding treatment of them, though his teaching was not so searching and effective. Dr. Gabell allowed nothing to be slurred over ; not the slightest Greek particle was to be dropped by carelessly allowing the voice to sink ; and the method which he adopted (though it would be tedious to state it here in detail) was such as to render escape from detection impossible on the part of the ignorant and care-

R

less who were not prepared with their lessons.   No boys reached the Universities so thoroughly masters of their books which they affected to know, as the pupils of Dr. Gabell.   It is great praise to him to say that he enabled every boy to gauge himself and to measure his own ignorance.

The Rebellion of 1818   The whole administration, however, of a public school should rest on confidence in the gentlemanly spirit of the boys.   The discipline of the school depends at Winchester upon the head boys called prefects.   These boys should never be required to act as spies, and should themselves be treated with such trust as to make them ashamed to abuse it.   In consequence of a failure on Dr. Gabell's part in these respects, a want of confidence had sprung up between him and the head boys ; and the conduct of one of the tutors which assumed too much, as the boys thought, the character of espionage, led in May 1818 to a rebellion.   At this time having worked my way up from the lower form, and having gained the prize in each form, I was the second prefect in commoners.   I deeply regretted afterwards the pain I must have occasioned to a really kind (though I still think mistaken) master, but at the time I heartily joined in the insurrection. It lasted about twenty-four hours, during which time the boys were masters of the old collegiate buildings, where they had barricaded themselves and withstood a summons by a magistrate attended by the constabulary.   The military were then sent for— a very foolish step, for there had lately been a quarrel between the boys and the men of the regiment about the use of a bathing place.   Dr. Gabell, however, bethought himself of an ingenious scheme.   He said the boys had better all go home.   They marched out of College with this intent, and met the military in the churchyard, who were ordered to charge them, when it must be confessed the boys ignominiously fled, having happily no weapons but bludgeons at hand, and the military being fully armed.   Two who were fortunate enough to be made prisoners dined afterwards at the mess.   The rest of the boys were easily captured afterwards, whilst they were packing up, by the locking

of the outer gates. The head boys were called up *seriatim* before the master and second master, and the first and third prefects were expelled. I was then called up, and I asked what had become of the other two, as a paper had been signed by the first three forms that all would share a common fate. My inquiry was not answered, but I was sent into another room to reflect in order to submission. From the window of this room, however, I saw and conversed with the other two prefects and learned their expulsion, and immediately on my return I stated that I must follow their example. I left the school taking with me my youngest brother,[1] who had signed the paper as well as myself.

The reason why I received such lenient treatment was, that up to that time I had been very regular in my conduct and was somewhat of a favourite with the head-master; and it was supposed that as I was younger than many of the prefects, being only sixteen years old, I had been misled by them. This, however, was not the fact. I had no special, personal grievance, but I had conceived the most intense disgust at the constant want of confidence and the suspicions exhibited by the head-master, of the extent of whose regard for myself, as subsequently expressed in a letter to my father, I was not then aware.

The masters (most erroneously) afterwards attributed my conduct to my ' Radical propensities,' derived, as was supposed, from reading the *Morning Chronicle*. . . . My youngest brother was sent back to Winchester, and I myself was sent shortly afterwards for two years to Geneva.

W. R. W. Stephens.
Memoir of Lord Hatherley, i. 11-14.
Richard Bentley and Son, 1883.

I CAN assure you that it adds no little to any pride that I may feel on that account to know, that whatever share of success has attended me has reflected honour on Winchester. . . . I said

Roundell Palmer, First Earl of Selborne, Coll. 1825

[1] Mr. Western Wood.

just now, before a larger assembly, and I am glad to be able to repeat it before you, that my past connexion with this College has made me love the very stones of the City of Winchester. . . . I love the familiar sight of this quadrangle ; I love your playing-fields, but especially your Hills, and all the life that is associated with them.   To the early influences of the School and the Meads, and, above all, to the Chapel close at hand, I attribute great part of the impulses which have guided me in that career to which you have so kindly and complimentarily alluded. . . .

> The Lord Chancellor (Lord Selborne), replying to
> the Senior Prefect, *Ad Portas*.
> *The Wykehamist*, May 1873.

Anthony
Trollope at
Winchester,
1826-29

WHEN I was twelve there came the vacancy at Winchester College which I was destined to fill.   My two elder brothers had gone there, and the younger had been taken away, being already supposed to have lost his chance of New College.   It had been one of the great ambitions of my father's life that his three sons, who lived to go to Winchester, should all become fellows of New College.   But that suffering man was never destined to have an ambition gratified.   We all lost the prize which he struggled with infinite labour to put within our reach.   My eldest brother all but achieved it, and afterwards went to Oxford, taking three exhibitions from the school, though he lost the great glory of a Wykehamist.   He has since made himself well known to the public as a writer in connection with all Italian subjects.   He is still living as I now write.   But my other brother died early.

While I was at Winchester my father's affairs went from bad to worse.   He gave up his practice at the bar, and, unfortunate that he was, took another farm. . . . He had no knowledge, and, when he took this second farm, no capital.   This was the last step preparatory to his final ruin.

Soon after I had been sent to Winchester, my mother went to America, taking with her my brother Henry and my two sisters,

who were then no more than children. This was, I think, in
1827. . . . Then my father followed them, taking my elder
brother before he went to Oxford. But there was an interval
of some year and a half during which he and I were at Winchester
together.

Over a period of forty years, since I began my manhood at a
desk in the Post Office, I and my brother, Thomas Adolphus,
have been fast friends. There have been hot words between us,
for perfect friendship bears and allows hot words. Few brothers
have had more of brotherhood. But in those schooldays he was,
of all my foes, the worst. In accordance with the practice of
the College, which submits, or did then submit, much of the
tuition of the younger boys from the elder, he was my tutor ;
and in his capacity of teacher and ruler he had studied the
theories of Draco. I remember well how he used to exact
obedience after the manner of that law-giver. Hang a little
boy for stealing apples, he used to say, and other little boys will
not steal apples. The doctrine was already exploded elsewhere,
but he stuck to it with conservative energy. The result was
that, as a part of his daily exercise, he thrashed me with a
big stick. That such thrashings should have been possible at
a school as a continual part of one's daily life, seems to me to
argue a very ill condition of school discipline. . . . After a
while my brother left Winchester and accompanied my father
to America. Then another and a different horror fell to my
fate. My college bills had not been paid, and the school trades-
men who administered to the wants of the boys were told not
to extend their credit to me. Boots, waistcoats, and pocket-
handkerchiefs, which, with some slight superveillance, were at
the command of other scholars, were closed luxuries to me.
My schoolfellows, of course, knew that it was so, and I became a
Pariah. It is the nature of boys to be cruel. I have sometimes
doubted whether among each other they do usually suffer much,
one from the other's cruelty ; but I suffered horribly ! I could
make no stand against it. I had no friend to whom I could pour

out my sorrows. I was big, and awkward, and ugly, and, I have no doubt, skulked about in a most unattractive manner. Of course I was ill-dressed and dirty. But, ah! how well I remember all the agonies of my young heart ; how I considered whether I should always be alone ; whether I could not find my way up to the top of that college tower, and from thence put an end to everything ? And a worse thing came than the stoppage of the supplies from the shopkeepers. Every boy had a shilling a week pocket-money, which we called battels, and which was advanced to us out of the pocket of the second master. On one awful day the second master announced to me that my battels would be stopped. He told me the reason,—the battels for the last half-year had not been repaid ; and he urged his own unwillingness to advance the money. The loss of a shilling a week would not have been much,—even though pocket-money from other sources never reached me,—but that the other boys all knew it ! Every now and again, perhaps three or four times in a half-year, these weekly shillings were given to certain servants of the College, in payment, it may be presumed, for some extra services. And now, when it came to the turn of any servant, he received sixty-nine shillings instead of seventy, and the cause of the defalcation was explained to him. I never saw one of those servants without feeling that I had picked his pocket.

When I had been at Winchester something over three years, my father returned to England and took me away. Whether this was done because of the expense, or because my chance of New College was supposed to have passed away, I do not know. As a fact, I should, I believe, have gained the prize, as there occurred in my year an exceptional number of vacancies. But it would have served me nothing, as there would have been no funds for my maintenance at the University till I should have entered in upon the fruition of the founder's endowment, and my career at Oxford must have been unfortunate.

Anthony Trollope, *An Autobiography*.
William Blackwood and Son, 1883.

AN old Wykehamist, who was at Winchester when Matthew **Matthew** Arnold entered in Short Half 1836, recollects his coming very **Arnold** well, and his being placed junior in Senior Part, Fifth Book, which was considered remarkably high. One of the first things he did was to complain to the Doctor (Moberly), that the work of Senior Part was not sufficiently heavy, and that there was nothing to do between 7.30 and 8 A.M. In consequence of this the Doctor promptly ordered that Senior Part should henceforth learn and say portions of Cicero's Orations during this half-hour ; and a Commoner Tutor was brought into School especially to hear this lesson. . . . Arnold's conduct in causing an extra morning lesson to be introduced was resented by many, who thought that the work of Senior Part was already sufficient.

The Wykehamist, May 1888.

I THINK . . . he [Archbishop Whately] had a prejudice against **Archbishop** public schools in general, and that for some reason or other **Whately and** he disliked Winchester in particular. . . . Whether it may **Wykehamists** have been that any antagonism between Whateley and Shuttleworth caused the former to be prejudiced against Wiccamical things and men, or whether the relationship of the two feelings were *vice versâ*, I cannot say. But I certainly thought and still think that I suffered in his estimation from the fact that I was a Wykehamist.

T. A. Trollope.
What I Remember, i. 196, 201.
R. Bentley and Son, 1887.

WHERE is our friend with his gibes and his sallies ? **E. D. A. M.** Where be the lances lay couched in his eye ? **(Mr. E. D. A.** Is it the Bey or the Shah that he rallies ! **Morsehead)** Who is the butt for his artillery ?

Ay! did you know him? each pucker and dimple,
　　Flashed its mild lightnings on heaven and on earth:
Nothing too recondite, nothing too simple;
　　Boys, men, and angels were food for his mirth.

Jests were the myriad smile of an ocean
　　Ample as Nature and deep as the soul:
'Twas but the surface that quivered with motion;
　　Down in the depths lay the calm and control.

Wit was the mirror, but wisdom lay under,
　　Seaweeds and starfish and treasures unsumm'd,
Hearken awhile, and you caught the sea-thunder,
　　Dolphins sang soft and leviathans humm'd.

Manifold fry swam the sea of his letters,
　　Sword-fish and cuttle-fish, noble and churl,
Fresh as the brine; nothing nasty, no tetters:
　　Dive to the bottom,—you 'd light on a pearl.

Gone is our Socrates! gone the arch-satyr,
　　Loved to put forth the grotesque and the odd:
Blessings on oddities! cases don't matter;
　　Open the box, and there fronts you the god.

How he loved Truth and pursued after Duty,
　　Hated hypocrisy, cant and parade:
Thought the great thoughts, was enamoured of Beauty,
　　E'en as a Paladin worships a maid.

Aeschylus, Dante and Vergil and Homer,
　　He was their prophet; they sang from his lips:
Yet he would welcome each timid new comer,
　　Epic or lyric, new sermons, new quips.

Ay ! and he lifted us ! often we grumbled,
  Stung by a barb that flew straight to its goal :
' Better and better ' he cried, and we stumbled
  Upward and onward, to conquer our soul.

Edmund, we thank you for words deem'd unkindly,
  Standards too high and impossible creeds ;
Youth is lighthearted and reckons so blindly :
  You took our measure, and sowed the right seeds.

Thirty long years did he pose as tormentor,
  True to himself, and to us, till the end,
Wrought, fought and conquered ; our kindliest mentor,
  Poet and critic and angler and friend.

Eyes felt the stress, and head whispered a warning,
  ' Time for a change.'   So, to gladden the slums,
Edmund just gave us the slip, took the morning
  Quietly, guiltless of trumpets and drums.

Do you recall the last verse of his chapter ?
  ' Domum ' and Christmas afire in our veins :—
Chamber Court rang with his name (none were apter)
  Night caught the glow and re-echoed our strains.

What was the farewell he left to his College,
  Standing bareheaded and under the stars ?
Was it a plea for fresh fire or new knowledge,
  Nobler Athene or lordlier Mars ?

Nothing of *self* then ; no jest and no moral,
  Nothing pedantic or brilliant or new ;
Straight from his heart came this one thought before all,
  ' Please give a cheer for the Commoners too ! '

This was his testament : long may it stay with us !
This is *your* Founder, and this is *your* Hall :
Work with us, play with us, sing with us, pray with us ;
Scholars and Commoners, Wykehamists all.

Lines by M. J. Rendall (then Second, now Headmaster of Winchester
College) read in College Hall, March 19, 1904.

§ 5. 'THAT RASCAL TOM'

'That rascal Tom'

. . . I REMEMBER to have heard my father, who was in College
under Dr. Warton, say that Tom Warton, the headmaster's
brother (and the well-known author of the *History of Poetry*)
used frequently to be with the boys ' in chambers ' of an evening ;
that he would often knock off a companion's ' verse task ' for
him, and that the Doctor the next morning would recognise
' that rascal Tom's work.'

T. A. Trollope.
What I Remember, i. 135.
R. Bentley and Son, 1887.

'A Son of the Muses'

IN these Wintonian fields roved another son of the Muses, whose
' shade ' (as he himself might have expressed it), would no doubt
disdain association with that of the author of *Endymion* ; I
mean the Rev. Thomas Warton, Fellow of Trinity College,
Oxford, Professor of Poetry, and Poet Laureate, which famous
and prosperous man of letters came often on a visit to his
brother, the Rev. Dr. Joseph, master of Winchester School,
himself a bard of note.

'Where shall the Muse, that on the sacred shell,
    Of men in arms and arts renown'd,
    The solemn strain delights to swell ;
Oh, where shall Clio choose a race
    Whom Fame with every laurel, every grace,
    Like those of Albion's envied isle has crown'd ? '

Hush, Reverend Shade !—yet for thy diligent annotation,
Tom, of Spenser and of Milton, pass not unkindly remembered.

Strange, that along with intense study of these masters thou
couldst pursue thine own scrannel pipings undismayed.

William Allingham.
Varieties in Prose, ed. by his widow.
Longmans, Green and Co., 1893.

SAY, shall the Muse o'er the fall'n hero's bier
Th' eternal monument of glory raise,
Swell the loud pæan of harmonious praise,
And high Ambition's banner'd trophies rear,
While silent flows the tributary tear
Which to her favourite Son the sorrowing pays.
Unstrung her useless lyre and mute her lays?
But hark! a strain divine now strikes mine ear:
The sacred Bard his independent fame
Shall from his own immortal verse receive.
Soon dies the Warrior's and the Statesman's name,
His aid if no recording Poet give:
But wreaths of endless bloom shall Warton claim
While Wit, while Learning, and while Fancy live.

*On the death
of Thomas
Warton*

Sonnet in *The Wiccamical Chaplet*, ed. George Huddesford, 1804.

§ 6. VARIETIES

Effigiem servi si vis spectare probati,
Quisquis es, haec oculos pascat imago tuos;
Porcinum os quocunque cibo jejunia sedat;
Haec sera, consilium ne fluat, arcta premit;
Dat patientem asinus dominis jurgantibus aurem;
Cervus habet celeres ire, redire, pedes;
Laeva docet multum tot rebus onusta laborem;
Vestis munditiem; dextera aperta fidem;
Accinctus gladio; clypeo munitus; et inde
Vel se, vel dominum, quo tueatur habet.

*'This
emblematic
figure well
survey'*

TRANSLATION

A TRUSTY servant's portrait would you see,
This emblematic figure well survey ;
His porker's snout—not nice in diet shows ;
The padlock 's shut—no secret he 'll disclose ;
Patient the ass, his master's voice will hear ;
Swiftness in errand, the stag's feet declare ;
Loaded his left hand—apt to labour saith ;
His vest his neatness—open hand his faith ;
Girt with his sword ; his shield upon his arm ;
Himself and master he 'll protect from harm.

VISITOR—CICERONE

The Trusty Servant : A Dialogue

VISITOR.   What is this figure painted on the wall ?
Fit subject this for learning's sacred hall !
Is it a learned ass ?

CICERONE.   Oh no, Sir, pray
Observe the snout.

VISITOR.   A pig's.

CICERONE.   That is to say
He hath no longing after dainty food,
But likes enough, even of the coarsest.

VISITOR.   Good.
But wherefore hath a pig's head ass's ears ?

CICERONE. It means that, like an ass, the creature bears
All patiently.

VISITOR.   Indeed ! then cuffs and blows
He takes as favours ?

CICERONE.   Aye.

VISITOR.   Beneath his nose
The padlock shut, chaining his under jaw,
Keeps him from glutting his voracious maw.
Is that its office ?

CICERONE.   No.   It means that he
May be depended on for secrecy.

VISITOR.   Ah, truly !   What a trim garb !

CICERONE.   Which doth mean
That he is orderly, and neat, and clean.

VISITOR.   Good.   And his right hand open ?

CICERONE.   His good faith
Betokens : you may credit all he saith.

VISITOR.   Good, good.   And by the stag's feet what is meant ?

CICERONE. That he runs swiftly when on errands sent.

VISITOR.   Aye, very good.   Why doth his left arm wield
These implements of toil, and bear a shield ?

CICERONE. He is inured to labour, and, with sword
And shield, upon occasion can afford
Protection to his master.

VISITOR.   True—he has
A sword.—Then this odd compound of an ass,
And pig, and stag, and man, is meant to show
What a good servant ought to be ?

CICERONE.   Right so.

VISITOR.   In my mind a strange ornament to grace
A seat of learning !—Yet not strange—the place
Is not unaptly chosen.—Are not we
All servants ?   All have duties—none are free.
He who by study hath the knowledge gained
How best to serve, true wisdom hath obtained.

Christopher Wood.
Reminiscences of Winchester, c. 1860.

WHEN I was at Winchester there were twin brothers who were **The twin**
so exactly alike that if they themselves knew which was which **substitute**
it was more than any one else did.   On one occasion they turned
this likeness to account in a very ingenious manner.   They were
both in the same Part, and both took up [in one lesson at any rate]
the same standing-up.   One of them, who knew his tolerably

well, went to the master and got through successfully ; on
going out he met his brother, who was just going to say his,
in great trepidation, as he was not prepared ; however, a bright
idea struck the more fortunate brother : he changed his neck-
cloth, tousled his hair, put a bit of sticking-plaster on his nose,
went back, and said his lesson a second time on his brother's
account with great *éclat*.

School Life at Winchester College, by the Author of
The Log of the Water-Lily, 1866.

A 'Varying'   I AM tempted to give one instance of such a 'varying.'[1]   It
belonged to an earlier time than mine—the time when *Decus
et tutamen* was adopted as the motto cut on the rim of the five-
shilling pieces.   The author of the 'varying' in question had
been ill with fever, and his head had been shaved, causing him
to wear a wig.   *Decus et tutamen* was the theme given.   In a minute
or two he was ready, stood up, and taking off his wig, said,
' *Aspicite hos crines ! duplicem servantur in usum ! Hi mihi
tutamen nocte* '—putting the wig on wrong side outwards ;
' *Dieque decus*,' reversing it as he spoke the words.   The memory
of this ' varying ' lives—or lived !—at Winchester.

T. A. Trollope.
What I Remember, i. 119.
R. Bentley and Son, 1887.

IN OBITUM ——
SCHOLAE WINTON
ALUMNI

'Immaturâ
morte
peremptus'

Undique dum Britones gaudent, Paeana canentes
   Quod mæret laceras Gallia victa rates,
Nos numeros mutare et flebile condere carmen
   Nos subitò in lacrymas ire coegit amor.

---

[1] Just before going out from morning or evening school at the end of
the day's lesson, the 'informator' would give a theme, and each boy
prefect was expected there and then to compose a couple or two couple
of epigrammatic lines on the spot and give them *vivâ voce*.   These
compositions were called ' varyings.'

Occidit heu puer immaturâ morte peremptus
  Quem Musae ornarunt ingenuusque pudor :
Mœnibus at procul a nostris Morbi ite nefandi !
  Luridaque Autumni filia Febris, abi.
Quin huc pulchra veni, Catherinae [1] in vertice nata
  Et semper nostros ritè beato Salus !

A Wiccamical Chaplet, by George Huddesford, 1804.

THE Wykehamist whose soul retains   πέμπε
Dim memories of his boyhood's days,
Keeps, somewhere backward of his brains,
The ' Pempe-book '—that ancient ' haze ' ;
That surest of all lawful ways
To gull the simple—safe to score on—
Firm-built upon the classic phrase
Of πέμπε πρότερον τὸν μῶρον.

C. D. LOCOCK.
' Ballade of Red Tape ' in *Olympian Echoes*.
London, St. Catherine's Press, 1908.

WHEN at the end of the summer holidays in that year, 1820, **Mother**
I returned to College, again brought down to Winchester by my **Gumbrell**
father in his gig, I confess to having felt for some time a very
desolate little waif. As I, at the time a child barely out of the
nursery, look back upon it, it seems to my recollection that the
strongest sense of being shoved off from the shore without
guidance, help, or protection, arose from never seeing or speaking
to a female human being. To be sure there was at the sick-
house the presiding ' mother '—Gumbrell her name was, usually
pronounced ' Grumble '—but she was not a fascinating representative of the sex. An aged woman once nearly six feet high,
then much bent by rheumatism, rather grim and somewhat
stern, she very conscientiously administered the prescribed

---

[1] Mons Collegio vicinus, ubi ad Dies Festos
  Pubes Wiccamica se lusu indulgent.

' black-dose and calomel pill ' to those under her care at the sick-house. . . . Tea was provided there for those ' continent,' instead of the usual breakfast of bread and butter and beer ; and I remember overhearing Mother Gumbrell, oppressed by an unusual number of inmates, say, ' Talk of Job, indeed ! Job never had to cut crusty loaves into bread and butter ! '

I saw the old woman die ! I was by chance in the sick-house kitchen—in after years, when a prefect—and ' Dicky Gumbrell,' the old woman's husband, who had been butler to Dean Ogle, and who by special and exceptional favour was allowed to live with his wife in the sick-house, was reading to her the story of Joseph and his Brethren, while she was knitting a stocking, and sipping occasionally from a jug of college beer which stood between them, when quite suddenly her hands fell on to her lap and her head on to her bosom, and she was dead ! while poor old Dicky quite unconsciously went on with his reading.

T. A. Trollope.
What I Remember, i. 119-20.
R. Bentley and Son, 1887.

' Damme Hopkins ' THE brother of this chaplain[1] was the manciple of the college, and was known among us as ' Damme Hopkins ' from the following circumstance. His manner was a quaint mixture of pomposity and *bonhomie*, which made a conversation with him a rather favourite amusement with some of us. Now the manciple was a very well-to-do man, and was rather fond of letting it be known that his independent circumstances made the emoluments of the place he held a matter of no importance to him. ' Indeed,' he would say, ' I spoke to the Bishop [the Warden] a few months ago of resigning, but the Bishop says to me, " No, no, Damme, Hopkins, you must keep your place." '

T. A. Trollope.
What I Remember, i. 140.
R. Bentley and Son, 1887.

[1] A ' sporting chaplain,' one of the three College chaplains who were also minor canons of the Cathedral.

'Tis the place and all around it as of old each hungry boy— 'Octo'
Octo, sugared bun, confound it, put me down a bob—La Croix.
Many a morn at your familiar cage I've gazed with longing eyes,
Whilst my olfactory organs caught the whiff of kidney pies.
His ices, though the smallest, are the best
In all the realm produced ; what recreant boy
Shall dare prefer e'en Gunter to La Croix ?

The Wykehamist, June 24, 1910.

During the war Winchester had been one of the depôts of Boiled Beef
French prisoners, and the beef in question [boiled beef] was then
given to them. When there were no more Frenchmen it was
given to twenty-four old women who were appointed to do the
weeding of the college quadrangles. It must be understood that
this arrangement was entirely spontaneous on the part of the
boys, though it would have been quite out of the question for
any individual to say that he for his part would eat his own beef.

T. A. Trollope.
What I Remember, i. 102.
R. Bentley and Son, 1887.

The interesting event of a vacancy having occurred at New 'Speedyman'
College, whether by death, marriage, or the acceptance of a living,
was announced by the arrival of ' Speedyman ' at Winchester
College. ' Speedyman,' in conformity with immemorial usage,
used to bring the news on foot from Oxford to Winchester.
How well I remember the look of the man, as he used to arrive
with all the appearance of having made a breathless journey,
a spare, active-looking fellow, in brown cloth breeches and
gaiters covered with dust. Of course, letters telling the facts
had long outstripped ' Speedyman.' But with the charming
and reverent spirit of conservatism, which in those days ruled
all things at Winchester, ' Speedyman ' made his journey on
foot all the same !

T. A. Trollope.
What I Remember, i. 99.
R. Bentley and Son, 1887.

'THE TIME IS OUT OF JOINT'

The Vagaries of Time

LAST night, while in the silvery west
Jove's planet leaned on Venus' breast,—
While from New Field I heard complain
Sad ghosts of trees untimely slain—
A voice familiar, yet estranged,
Came floating thro' the belfry-bars,
Then over Meads and Flint Court ranged,
Then shivered to the stars.
Sadly it stammered, ' I—I—I 'm
The oldest living Wykehamist !
First but not last upon the list
Of those who don't know time !

On the old lines I stand, and yet,
Though nought I learn, and nought forget,—
All that I murmur, day or night,
Tells of a chaos infinite,
An oracle of meaning strange,
An echo of eternal change.
Long since, I thrilled thro' all my wheels,
When College bells rang courtly peals,
When Charles and Nelly, worthy pair,
Came down to taste the Hampshire air
And show the sad land, sick with strife,
The real gaiety of life.
And I have seen Rebellion red
In College Chambers rear her head !
I saw the young conspiracy
Tear up the flints and bear them high
To be their plot's artillery—
I saw the puzzled redcoats stand
Bewildered at the youthful band,

And more than half inclined to slay
The senseless Don who stirred the fray.
Strange life, strange tricks of young and old
I have beheld, and yet behold—
Strangest, perhaps of all,
Is the new Punch-and-Judy sight,
The queer lie daubed in black and white
Upon the Chapel wall!
Alas, with long experience
There comes as well a weakened sense
Of time and tune ; I mix
And muddle up my chimes and quarters,
And sorely I mislead the porters!
Think not too hardly of me, when
At Ten-Fifteen I stammer Ten,
At the Half-Past proclaim the Hour,
Lisp out a casual Three, at Four,
Or hiccup Five, at Six!

I stand at least (give me my due!)
As to your fathers, so to you,
A type of the Wiccamic mind,
Until some old time dimly true,
Somewhat bewildered at the new,
And always just behind!

Therefore forbear to chide my ways—
Bethink you how my many days
My works corrode and canker—
(This joke is Hood's—a modern bard!)
Tho' my offence is rank, 'tis hard
If *your* offence be rancour!

I do beseech you, young and old,
Bear with me till my tale is tolled!

Bear with me—spare to mock,
O College Prefect, wise and good !
O College Junior, gay of mood !
Your friend,
                    THE COLLEGE CLOCK.'

The Wykehamist, February 1892.

AVE ATQUE VALE

VERSES WRITTEN IN A GROVE AT WINCHESTER COLLEGE

'Farewel'

O DRYAD, whose protection gives to tow'r
These aged elms (with leafy heads around,
Which spread glad refuge from the furious rays
Of Phœbus, darting more malignant fire
In fell conjunction with the raging star
Of Sirius :) farewel, thy grove ! where oft
Th' unwilling muse I woo'd, or gave my soul
To contemplation, nurse of thought, or fed
With greedy pleasure on the muse's charms :
That muse, who studious of her much lov'd sons,
Wharton or *Lowth*, from Hippocrene brings
The stream prolific, and has taught to flow
In *British* numbers, who by nature lent.

. . . .

                              . . . I go
(Where conscious *Isis* rolls her ling'ring waves
With admiration slow) to that fam'd dome
Where he, who gall'd proud Gallia's stubborn neck
Beneath the *British* yoke, drank deep the spring
Of classic-knowledge, and matur'd his soul
To seeds of high renown :—his shady grove
O may some pitying brother Dryad lend !
With secret pleasure there shall mem'ry oft
Retrace thy silvan scenes ; shall paint, in thought,

Fair *Cath'rine's* verdant summit ; or shall plunge,
Eager, amid th' imaginary flood
Of *Itchin's* silver urn ; or pensively
Recall those happier softer hours, which flow
With sorrow'd speed on friendship's balmy wings :
Friendship, glad offspring of the virtuous heart :
Friendship, whose dear remembrance e'er shall glow
Deep in my faithful breast :—to fancy's eye
In green-clad beauty may each summit rise,
Grateful as *Cath'rine's* ; gentle *Isis* flow
Grateful as *Itchin* ; other groves supply
The loss of thine ; divided friendship's wounds
No skill can probe, no soothing med'cine cure.

From a magazine entitled *Miscellaneous Correspondence*, etc.
(ed. Benjamin Martin), vol. i., 1755 and 1756, p. 182.

THE Spring shall visit thee again   On leaving
Itchen ! and yonder aged fane
That casts its shadows on thy breast,
(As if, by many winters beat,
The blooming season it would greet)
With many a straggling wild-flower shall be drest !
But I, amidst the youthful train
That stray at ev'ning by thy side,
No longer shall a guest remain
To mark the Spring's reviving pride.—
I go not unrejoicing ; but who knows,
When I have shar'd, O world, thy common woes,
Returning I may drop some natural fears ;
When these same fields I look around,
And hear from yonder dome the slow bell sound,
And think upon the joys that crown'd my stripling years !

The Rev. W. L. Bowles.
On Leaving Winchester School, 1782.

WOULD I still wore the long black gown,
In cloistral habit vested :
Would that all thoughts and cares I rested,
Dreaming on *Twyford Down* :
　　Glad but to mark,
　　How the clear lark,
Singing, the sunlight breasted !

On *Hills* to lie, some endless hour,
Watching the stream wind slowly
Through verdant *Water Meads*, past holy
Saint Cross, the greyheads' bower :
　　While low *Downs* brood
　　In quietude,
And gentle melancholy.

Here walked, by each fair river path,
Good Brothers of the Angle :
Whose sweet thoughts knew to disentangle
Peace from the days of wrath :
　　Here *Walton* went,
　　Here *Chalkhill* spent
Calm hours, untaught to wrangle.

.　　.　　.　　.　　.　　.　　.

Here, beneath Winton trees, first breathed
A faery lyre enchaunted :
Ah, *Collins* ! at what cost was granted
To thee the laurel, wreathed
　　With faery flowers,
　　At moonlit hours
Plucked in wild woodlands haunted !

Still round the *Cloisters*, airs of Death
Wander, and touch the dreamer :
Music of Death, tired man's redeemer !
Rest thee, lie down ! it saith.
    Who rested here,
    Death's lover were :
Death's friend, not Death's blasphemer.

Thy Browne, who saw the ages pass
In funeral procession ;
Whose eyes explored Death's vast possession ;
Was it thy holy grass,
    And *Chauntry* dim,
    First called on him
To make his soul's *Confession* ?

.   .   .   .

Whose face flashed there ?   What voice was that,
Voice, that comes back and lingers ?
Whose hand touched mine with flying fingers ?
Whose laugh is this, whereat
    Down the dim track
    Old joys come back
And songs of long-lost singers ?

Up *Hills* our years would find the climb,
That grassy climb, grown steeper :
We 'd rest in *Trench* ; and *Trench* was deeper,
We 'd fancy, in our time :
    Then, passing *Maze*,
    To turn and gaze,
Tranced, like a dreaming sleeper !

The mountainous *Cathedral* grey ;
College, so fairly towered ;
And *Wolvesey* ruins ivy-bowered ;
And *West Gate*, far away :
Silent and still,
To gaze our fill,
By memory overpowered !

.   .   .   .   .   .

Lionel Johnson.
'Winchester,' in *Ireland and other Poems*,
Elkin Matthews, 1897.

Passing out

FROM old Wykeham's gates generation after generation pass out—as the gladiatorial line filing before the ivory chair—with the same pathetic legend on their lips : ' *Morituri te salutant !* '

Alma mater ! we who are passing from thy halls, thy home, thy shrine ; we, nourished with thy life, and taught by thy examples, and ripened to thy traditions ; we, just dying to boyhood, salute thee ; to thee we owe a debt, a tear, a noble life.

The Wykehamist, July 1879.

Matri Wiccamicae

I WILL return to thee, dear grey mother,
Set my life throbbing with thine once again,
Burn with delight that regret cannot smother,
Dally and joy with thee, yearn to remain.

Fetters unite us which years will not sunder ;
Woven with laughter and tears is each ring,
Mirroring each myself, wide-eyed with wonder,
Meeting the birth and the glow of my spring.

Thou 'twas who taught me the rapture of living,
Gave me to know and to worship the day,
Mingled the gloom of young griefs in the giving,
Glory of battle with scars of the fray.

Thine was the cup whence I drank to my measure,
   Nectar that cheers and sustains to the end,
Man's highest privilege, perfectest pleasure,
   To give and to welcome the love of a friend.

.   .   .   .   .

The Wykehamist.

CREEPING backward through the valley of Time,   **A Dream of**
   Tracing the tangled skein of lost ways,   **Winchester**
Comes my sad soul, seeking with a rhyme,   **Days**
   To build again a palace of dead days.

Very faint at last comes the echo of voices—
   Friendly voices, once loud in my ears ;
So faint that scarcely my sad soul rejoices,
   But rather sighs, half gladly, half with tears.

Out of the curious by-ways of memory,
   Come many ghosts.   Hither come the pale doubt
That quenched a flame of friendship, once so fiery,
   I had thought only Death could put it out.

A crowd of faces are looking at me ;
   Most of these have I loved, all I have known.
Whose face is that looking at me wistfully ?
   Can that be the boy's-face that was mine own ?

Alfred Douglas.
The Wykehamist, June 1893.

Nos patriae fines, nos dulcia linquimus arva

THESE hoary haunts, in which youth's rosy flower   **'Nos dulcia**
   Budded and bloomed and faded, sanctified   **linquimus**
By countless human lives, vested with power   **arva'**
   That may not be denied ;

The soul's calm harbour, where the curling wave
    Stills to the gentle swell, where the loud roar
Murmurs and sings, which the same waters lave
    That dash upon the shore ;

Downs, meads, and rivers, grown a part of me ;
    Faces, beloved, unloving, which have drawn
My heart to them for an eternity,
    As twilight melts in dawn ;

All these must fade from me.   Forth I must fare
    Into the unknown world ; must leave the coast
And strike to the mid sea, grey, cheerless, bare,
    Where many a bark is lost.

The past is gone ; the past can be no more ;
    The past hath done its work ; the past is fled.
Time may flow on, but time cannot restore
    The life-breath to its dead.

O sunset evenings, O thou peaceful hill,
    O mist on still St. Cross, O glorious fane !
Thou hen among her chickens, ye shall fill
    These eyes, this heart again ;

But peace will not reign with you.   Tho' I gaze
    O'er grassy sea specked with its human foam,
Greeting the grey walls thro' the summer haze,
    They will not be my home.

φροῦδός τις.
The Wykehamist, October 1890.

WINTER is fast receding ;
  The Spring is in the air ;
Herbert is gently leading
  Hock Stapler from his lair.
Whittier's lad is weeding,
  And oh ! that I was there.

The old familiar faces
  Fill each familiar spot,
Gracing with all their graces
  (Or such as they have got)
The same delightful places,—
  But I, alas ! do not !

Soon, with the ' flannelled ' season,
  Cometh the month of May ;
You will have ample reason
  Then to be blithe and gay :
I shall be o'er the seas on
  Voyages far away.

Summer will bring the ' willow ' ;
  (Oh ! may it bring me rhymes !)
Mate and his Mate will pillow
  Their heads beneath the limes.
I shall be o'er the billow—
  Away in foreign climes !

Then when the year is dying,
  Winton will still be fair,
E'en though the leaves be flying,
  E'en though the trees be bare ;
The bard will still be sighing
  ' Oh ! that I might be there ! '

Smoketh the year's last ember,
  Canvas is brown and bare ;
You will enjoy December,
  Sixes will fill the air !
I shall, alack ! remember,
  But I shall not be there.

A. P. Herbert.
'The Wail of an Old Wykehamist,' in
Poor Poems and Rotten Rhymes.
P. and G. Wells, Winchester, 1910.

Ave atque vale

FARE thee well, Winchester, we wander far,
  Thou standest ever the same ;
We rush, swift as a heavenward voyaging star,
  Pass ; and become but a name.

Our bones lie scattered in every place ;
  Where'er, midst our working we fall,
Our lives are merged in the life of the race,
  Our days pass as shades cross a wall.

But thou, mother, passest never away ;
  In starlight, sunshine, storm,
O'er troubles and trials, day after day,
  Towers unshaken thy form.

The Wykehamist, July 1893.

A true good-bye

DEAR WINTON ! thou hast shown the love,
  That circles all thy sons, to me ;
How can I ever hope to prove
  The deepening love I feel for thee ?
O grant it still may flower and live—
  Thy vision fades before my eyes—
Take—it is all I have to give—
  The truest of all true good-byes !

29/7/98.

R. W. Seton Watson.
Scotland For Ever, etc.
Edinburgh : David Douglas, 1898.

OUR latest sunset gilds the dreaming vale,
   To smile farewell the very shadows glow ;
The far hills vanish : dewy slumber steals
   On silent meadows and the Itchen's flow.

Domum Night

K. J. F.
' Domum Night,' in *Poems.*
Wells, 1906.

FRAUGHT with the sadness of a dying day,
   The sun's last gleam is loitering on the Hill,
Warming to gold the Chapel's lichened grey ;
   And here in Meads some few are lingering still,
To part reluctantly and pass away.

**Vale.
Domum
Night,
1907**

Aye pass away, as others passed before,
   Familiar for a season to our eyes ;
Then presently their place knows them no more.
   Now, when our time has come to snap the ties,
'Tis little wonder that our hearts are sore.

Throughout the cloud and sun of six long years,
   The School has been a parcel of our life,
Seen our perplexities and soothed our fears,
   Watched silently above our mimic strife,
Joyed with our joy, and sorrowed with our tears.

At every turn the place grows dearer yet,
   Associations crowding to the mind,
Trifles which none of us will e'er forget
   In after life, with boyhood far behind,
Seen in a golden haze with blind regret.

Darkly as visions seen within a glass,
   Soft as the lilt of some forgotten rhyme,
Those vanished scenes before our memory pass,
   The long cool after-light of Cloister Time,
With shadows lying barred across the grass.

Once more we listen to a sweet refrain,
  The music where the ball and willow clicks;
Once more we crowd round ' Canvases ' and strain
  Our lungs in cheering some victorious Six,
Living the life we shall not live again.

The great School eddies o'er its yearly blanks,
  Filling and wiping out their every trace;
And though we grieve to step from out the ranks,
  Our lines have fallen in a pleasant place;
Let us remember this, and render thanks.

Old heroes stretch their hands from out the past,
  Across the centuries their tones we hear,
Saying, ' Our great traditions hold you fast,'
  Saying, ' Ye children of a later year,
See that ye be not wanting at the last.'

So let us part and step from out the ken
  Of School, and Youth, with all it has to give;
We shall remember—and remembering then
  Endeavour thus to work and thus to live,
That Wykeham's Manners make us also Men.

                    J. L. Crommelin-Brown.
                    Poems and Parodies.
            P. and G. Wells, Winchester, 1908.

Ad Amicos

WHEN veils of mist are laid on Itchen's streams
And phantom sea-gulls flicker in and out;
When Scholars pass in ghostly rows about
Those solemn courts, our citadel of dreams:
If old bones ache and winter's poniard seems
More penetrating than it wont to be,
Your golden platter's brave charáctery
Shall be my sun and warm me with its beams.

Twelve years in College! All the glory lives,
The poor and weak things vanish. You and I
Joint Scholars drank of Hippocrene and fed
On hero-visions for our daily bread.
Hail bright remembrancer! But tell me why
Age still accepts the gold and boyhood gives.

M. J. Rendall.
Lines written in acknowledgment of a gift of a silver dish
after twelve years as 'Second Master' in 'College,'
1899-1912.

A Farewell

Good luck attend you as you go,
 And light whatever path you tread;
May your life ever onward flow,
 To high success and honour led!

Where'er you go, whate'er you do,
 We know you never will forget
Winton's old kinship, strong and true—
 What Wykehamist forgot it yet?

All we, your fellows, have the right
 Your new career to watch and bless;
And, when you 've conquered in the fight,
 Fling wide the floodgates of success.

To every
Wykehamist

July '97.

R. W. Seton Watson.
Scotland For Ever and Other Poems.
Edinburgh: David Douglas, 1898.

INDEX

T

Printed by T. and A. Constable, Printers to His Majesty
at the Edinburgh University Press